THEORY
IN PRACTICE

Chris Argyris
Donald A. Schön

THEORY IN PRACTICE

Increasing Professional Effectiveness

Jossey-Bass Publishers · San Francisco

Published by

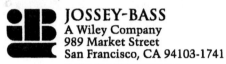

JOSSEY-BASS
A Wiley Company
989 Market Street
San Francisco, CA 94103-1741

www.josseybass.com

Jossey-Bass books and products are available through most bookstores. To contact Jossey-Bass directly, call (888) 378-2537, fax to (800) 605-2665, or visit our website at www.josseybass.com.

Substantial discounts on bulk quantities of Jossey-Bass books are available to corporations, professional associations, and other organizations. For details and discount information, contact the special sales department at Jossey-Bass.

We at Jossey-Bass strive to use the most environmentally sensitive paper stocks available to us. Our publications are printed on acid-free recycled stock whenever possible, and our paper always meets or exceeds minimum GPO and EPA requirements.

Jossey-Bass also publishes its books in a variety of electronic formats. Some content that appears in print may not be available in electronic books.

Library of Congress Catalogue Card Number LC 74-3606
ISBN 0-87589-230-2
ISBN 1-55542-446-5 (paperback)

FIRST EDITION
HB Printing   10
PB Printing   10 9 8 7

A joint publication in
The Jossey-Bass
Higher and Adult Education Series
and
The Jossey-Bass Management Series

JOSSEY-BASS CLASSICS
are works of enduring value that have
shaped thought and practice in their fields.
Practical and authoritative, these books
are timeless resources for professionals.
We are pleased to introduce these
important works to a wider readership
in a high-quality paperback format.

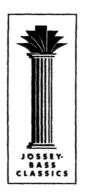

JOSSEY-
BASS
CLASSICS

Contents

Introduction to the
Classic Paperback

In *Theory in Practice,* we began to lay the foundations for understanding and explaining features of human action, especially as
they occur in social systems such as organizations. From the outset,
we were interested in understanding how to create events, not
simply observe them. Our theory was not only about action but
about how to create action. Moreover, we began with a bias, which
we still hold, toward designing and carrying through on actions
that could serve as liberating alternatives to the status quo.
Therefore, a major focus of our work has been and continues to
be developing interventions that produce rare events.

As our thinking evolved, learning became a key construct.
We defined learning in terms of outcomes and processes. We have
never knowingly separated the two in our research, because
effective intervention that produces rare events and eventually
makes them a part of a new status quo (that itself is more learning
oriented) requires both outcomes and processes.

We identified two outcomes of learning: first, creating a
match between intention and effect (where the learner had never
before produced such a match) and second, detecting and cor-

xi

recting a mismatch. In both cases, the criteria for learning include not only the framing of an idea or design but also its implementation. How do you know when you know something—when you can produce what you say you know?

We decomposed the process of learning into discovery (or diagnosis) of a problem, invention of a solution, production of the solution, and monitoring the implementation in order to enhance its effectiveness. (The monitoring may lead to new discoveries.) This process can be observed at individual, group, intergroup, and organizational levels. It is put into effect by human beings, but what they can execute and how are significantly influenced by the context in which they act.

Responses to the Book

Theory in Practice has been widely read by consultants, organizational development practitioners, and educators, especially those interested in continuing education.

For many of its readers, the book stimulated an interest in learning to implement the ideas expressed. But it provoked widespread misunderstandings (to which we may have contributed). For example, many readers have misunderstood model II as "openness" or have interpreted model II as another version of McGregor's Theory Y (McGregor, 1960). Indeed, like McGregor's work, our theory of action perspective, with its emphasis on free and informed choice, valid information, and internal commitment, was a development of ideas first put forward by Kurt Lewin: "democratic group climate," "interpersonal effectiveness," and "research in action" (Lewin and Grabbe, 1945). But McGregor's was a formulation of the human relations approach to interpersonal, group, and organizational action, emphasizing the achievement of consensus among potentially conflicting views and a participatory alternative to conventional authoritarian concepts of management. In contrast, *Theory in Practice* emphasized the inquiry-oriented dimension of Lewin's thinking, with its focus on giving and getting valid information, producing the conditions of internal commitment, and fostering free and informed choice on the part of the actor and those affected by the actions. Drawing on attribution theory, we emphasized the public testing of attributions ordinarily kept private (for example, an attribution in the form, "You appear to agree with me but harbor deep reservations that you are not expressing"). We advanced the idea that patterns of interpersonal action were manifestations of theories of action, usually tacit, that individuals had acquired early in life and continued to hold. We distinguished these theories-in-use from the espoused theories that people are accustomed to offer as explanations or justifications for behavior. We emphasized the *reciprocal* nature of interpersonal action—that is, the idea that the values embedded in theories-in-use are enacted and experienced both by the actor and by those affected by the actor's behavior.

Many of those who read *Theory in Practice* remained blissfully unaware of the gap between their own ordinary patterns of behavior (which fell, almost invariably, well within the pattern we described as model I) and the model-II theory of action they espoused. When people did become aware of the gap, they were often shocked and dismayed. Model II then seemed like pie in the sky, both unrealistic in the normal Machiavellian world of everyday organizational life and too hard to bring about as a rare event in one's own behavior or the behavior of others. For some readers, however, the challenge of achieving the transition from model I to model II seemed attractive, even imperative. Those readers wanted help with implementation. They wanted to know how to get there from here. At the same time, they challenged the formulations we had given in *Theory in Practice,* both of the end-in-view and of the path for getting there.

Our Further Research

In the period between 1974 and 1991, we developed, along four different lines, ideas first presented in *Theory in Practice.* First, we examined the relationship between personal and interpersonal learning and the processes by which organizations might become model-II environments. Second, we focused on the place of interpersonal theories-in-use within the broader systems of understanding and know-how that make up professional knowledge and on the relationship between the theory of action approach to education and what Schön has called "reflective practice" (Schön, 1983, 1987, 1991). Third, we focused on educating organizational researchers, consultants, and managers in the theory of action approach and its use in organizational development and change. Finally, we have concentrated on a kind of action research that we believe is essential to such education.

Organizational Learning. An illustration of the first focus was a study of entrepreneur-owners of business firms who wanted to learn to use model-II action strategies and eventually help their subordinates do the same (Argyris, 1982). The study was especially useful in guiding our attempts to help individuals learn model II and then create organizational analogues (which we called OII Learning Systems).

In the course of this inquiry, we began to develop a clearer understanding of the relationships between theories-in-use and associated patterns of thinking and feeling. As Argyris began to teach the executives in his program how to design and carry out experiments to test their new ideas in a more rigorous way than they had until then, he found that participants felt threatened and tended to react defensively. As he questioned their basic cognitive maps, he challenged their sense of competence and confidence. He continued to work with the executives and was subsequently able to describe the kind of reasoning, especially the causal reasoning, associated with their defensive strategies and feelings and to distinguish it from the "productive" reasoning and feelings associated with model II (Argyris, 1985).

The CEOs in Argyris's study became close to one another. They operated as a support group for at least twelve years after his interventions ended, and most of them continue to do so to this day. Indeed, some of them joined one another's boards of directors. Argyris agreed to their request for help in diffusing their learning throughout their organizations. He soon realized, however, that he did not have access to as many skilled researcher-interventionists as he needed to complete the project and thus would have to limit his research to two organizations.

At the same time that Argyris was carrying out this study, Schön was conducting a series of workshops on the theory of action perspective for directors of research organizations in

Brazil. The two project experiences reinforced what we had begun
to see in the later stages of writing *Theory in Practice*, namely, that
there were significant gaps in concept and practice between the
spheres of personal and interpersonal learning, and between
those and organizational learning. We saw that we lacked a
systematic perspective on organizational learning and that we
needed to do for organizations what we had begun to do for
individuals. Our efforts to build models of organizational theory-
in-use and learning culminated in *Organizational Learning* (Argyris
and Schön, 1978), in which we tried to make explicit the relationship between individual and larger-system variables. We did it
through such concepts as limited-learning systems (in the case of
model I) and "the good dialectic" (in the case of model II). That
is, we showed how human beings armed with model-I theories-in-
use created organizational (or group, or intergroup) learning
systems that were limited largely to single-loop learning. We also
specified that a less limited learning system (in any social unit)
would have the features of the good dialectic. A necessary condition for creating such a system, we thought, would be to help
individuals learn model II. Although model II alone would not be
sufficient to build an organization's capacity for double-loop
learning, it would enable the organization's members to inquire
more effectively into the organization's strategy, structure, information systems, and the like.

    *Education of Interventionist-Researchers, Consultants, and
Other Practitioners in the Theory of Action Approach.* It became
increasingly evident that one of the important limitations on our
ability to help individuals learn model II was our capacity to teach
it to relatively large groups (that is, of 25 to 100 participants)
under conditions where they could not only learn the concepts
but practice the skills required. Awareness of this problem led to
a line of research that integrated teaching, intervention, and
organizational change. In *Reasoning, Learning, and Action*, Argyris
(1982) presented detailed descriptions of how classrooms could
be used to provide experiential as well as conceptual learning.

    That line of inquiry was continued in several different field
research studies. For example, Argyris developed a program for
a large corporation where the managing directors and their

immediate subordinates came together to develop long-range corporate strategy. As the executives learned model II, they examined their group dynamics to improve their double-loop learning about strategy and help create a home organization adept at strategic learning once they went back (Argyris, 1989).

In our two decades of research, the idea of learning, in organizations and indeed in whole societies, has increasingly gained currency. The idea of "the learning organization" has, like excellence and total quality (and earlier, innovation and flexibility), become a banner for reform in the public, private, and nonprofit sectors.

Argyris has worked extensively with consulting firms, which he believed would be increasingly called on to help public and private organizations with their attempts at organizational learning. In studying consulting organizations, he has examined the role of consultants as double-loop learners, the relationships they create with their clients, and defenses against learning within consulting and client organizations (Argyris, 1985).

In the course of helping individuals unfreeze their defensive reasoning and learn to think more rigorously and productively as they evolved toward model II, Argyris found that managerial disciplines such as strategy and accounting were, in effect, theories of action that could be used to help manage organizations; scholars had developed relatively rigorous specifications about how to use them and how to diagnose and correct errors that might arise in the process. As in interpersonal theories of action, a key feature common to such disciplines was their causal reasoning: that is, the reasoning required to implement the theories. Another characteristic common to all these disciplines was that their designers strove to make their causal reasoning as explicit and rigorous as possible.

An interesting dilemma arose whenever the correct (or incorrect) application of the disciplines gave rise to conditions that were embarrassing or threatening to the participants. Under such conditions, the participants activated their model-I skills and hid behind their OI defensive routines. Thus, precisely when strategy (or another consideration) required the implementers to adhere to rigorous thinking, they added a heavy dose of defensive reasoning and, in consistency with model I, projected the blame onto the organization's strategic processes and defensive routines (Argyris, 1990).

When the consultants encountered defensive client reasoning, in turn, they experienced embarrassment or threat and predictably reactivated their model-I causal reasoning processes. Often, this limited the learning potential of client-consultant relationships; the clients blamed the consultants, and vice versa. Organizational development professionals were equally disposed to become defensive. Ironically, those who espoused learning, trust, and interdependent control exhibited the opposite of those virtues when they felt threatened (Argyris, 1989, 1990). This was found to be true for highly regarded professionals *outside* the organization (Argyris, 1991). In these studies, therefore, one could not argue that the gaps between espoused theory and theory-in-use were caused by inadequate training or organizational control by superiors.

Action Research. Another important theme in our research has been the education of *researcher*-interventionists. Our seminars at Harvard and MIT are designed to develop specific research skills: we educate graduate students to conduct research that draws on the data from organizational interventions and at the same time provides information and insights that are immediately useful in such interventions.

Argyris, with his students, wrote about this process in *Action Science* (Argyris, Putnam, and Smith, 1985). In 1990, Argyris and Schön addressed this issue, in a more theoretical vein, in an unpublished paper, "Normal Science and Action Science Compared," and Schön has developed it further in a paper called "Causality and Causal Reasoning in Organizations" (Schön, 1990).

Action science is a type of action research introduced by Kurt Lewin and unfortunately altered by many of those who continued Lewin's research tradition. What Lewin emphasized was the conduct of research usable in the world of practice, which could provide a valid test of features of the theory. Moreover, Lewin hoped, as John Dewey did, that scientists would help to create a better life, a life where human beings had an important say in shaping their own destiny. Both Lewin and Dewey were centrally concerned with democracy, both developed rigorous theories, and both conducted interventions and experiments to test their theories. With their concern for producing "liberating alternatives," they stood in marked contrast to many scholars who advocated such alternatives yet conducted research that reinforced the status quo—that is, the worlds of models I and OI.

At the time of this writing, Argyris is completing a manuscript entitled "Actionable Knowledge," a follow-up to *Action Science*. There is a profound gap, Argyris asserts, between applicable and actionable knowledge. The former tells you what is relevant; the latter tells you how to implement it in the world of everyday practice. A major portion of "Actionable Knowledge" describes an action science study that has lasted five years (and is still in progress). In it, Argyris's primary aim is to diagnose and reduce organizational politics, especially at the highest levels of the organization. His second aim is to help the consultants become more competent at implementing their "technical" knowledge, when doing so is difficult or resisted by the clients. His third aim is to create learning systems within the consulting firm to help make it a continuing double- (and single-) loop learning organization and to help the firm's clients do the same.

Reflective Practice. Theory in Practice is subtitled "Increasing Professional Effectiveness." Schön, in his research and teaching from the mid 1970s to the present, has concentrated on the nature of the knowledge revealed by the work of competent practitioners, the competences associated with the kinds of practice that we tend to identify as distinctively professional, and the shortcomings of established patterns of professional education. In two books (which were initially intended to be one), *The Reflective Practitioner* (1983) and *Educating the Reflective Practitioner* (1987), he questioned the then-prevailing idea of technical rationality— the view that practical knowledge consists in adapting means to preset ends, and that practical knowledge becomes professional when it is based on systematic, preferably scientific knowledge. Schön also challenged the approach to professional education modeled on technical rationality, which Edgar Schein once called the "normative professional curriculum": first teach people the relevant basic science, then the relevant applied science, and finally give them a practicum in applying these sets of knowledge to the everyday problems of practice (Schein, 1973). Schön proposed to turn this model on its head. He argued that the larger part of what we identify as practice knowledge consists in largely tacit knowing-in-action and in the capacity of practitioners to respond to surprise in the midst of action through a process of on-the-spot reflection and experimentation that Schön called reflection-in-action. He distinguished these kinds of knowing from reflection *on* the basis of assumptions derived from everyday practice. A central part of the task of professional education, Schön argued, was to formulate "what we already know," that is, to capture in explicit form the insights, values, and strategies of action that competent practitioners bring to situations they encounter in practice. That cumulative, unformulated understanding, Schön thought, accounted for what practitioners do well and also for the ways in which they tend to get stuck. The challenge for professional education was to effect a new kind of marriage of applied science, on the one hand, and knowing- and reflection-in-action, on the other.

Within this conception of professional knowledge and education, Schön identified a critically important place for the theory of action perspective. Interpersonal theories-in-use help to determine how practitioners hold their technical know-how and how they try to deploy it effectively in their relations with their clients and collaborators. Because model-I theories-in-use are often the source of the impasse for practitioners, reflecting on theories-in-use is a prerequisite for improving professional performance. Moreover, defensiveness tends to inhibit the practitioners' reflection on and transformation of their practical knowledge as a *whole*. The creation of a model-II behavioral world relatively free of defensiveness is critical, therefore, for transforming reflective inquiry into practical knowledge in the contexts of both practice and professional education.

Our Teaching and Our Students' Research

There was something odd about attempting to implement the ideas of *Theory in Practice,* since the book was, in the first instance, an attempt to formulate a theory that would do justice to the intervention practice that Argyris and, to a lesser extent, Schön, had been developing for many years. In an important sense, the implementation had preceded the theory. But *Theory in Practice* also called for an extension of the earlier practice, and its explicit formulation posed the problems of implementation in a new way.

From the early 1970s on, we were approached by many students, practitioners, and teachers who were eager to know more about what our book really meant and wanted help in learning to live out its ideas. We responded through our teaching and consulting, through the research that often grew out of those activities, and through our attempts to help our doctoral students conduct research aimed at testing or extending the boundaries of our ideas.

Our teaching included a large course that Argyris taught at the Harvard Graduate School of Education, and later at the Harvard School of Business Administration, from the early 1970s to the early 1990s, and an advanced seminar in the theory of action perspective that we taught together for several years running in the late 1970s and early 1980s. Together, we also conducted workshops in the theory of action perspective in Norway, in Toronto, and at the University of Texas. Increasingly, our doctoral students and visiting academics with whom we came in contact have developed their own versions of this teaching, for example: Diane Argyris, William Isaacs, Philip McArthur, Robert Putnam, and Diana Smith, in the United States; Wim Overmeer, in France; Claudio Ciborra, in Italy; Ron Smith, in Canada; and Vivian Robinson, in New Zealand.

Over the years, our students have explored in their doctoral research various features of the theory of action approach. Some of them have investigated philosophical issues raised by model II. Joiner (1983), for example, sought the philosophical roots of model II in an idea of collaborative inquiry, which he traced from the ancient Greek philosophers to Kurt Lewin. Others have applied the theory of action approach to problems of personal or organizational development. Gross (1980), for example, formulated and implemented a model of the consultant-client relationship that would facilitate individual and organizational learning. Smith (1987) proposed a typology of approaches to conflict resolution in which she grouped the theory of action approach with those that present interpersonal conflict as an opportunity for personal growth. And Overmeer (1989) analyzed the model-I organizational world of a large building and real estate development firm and showed how it affected strategic learning at the firm. Still other students have concentrated on difficulties encountered in the transition from model I to model II. Sayles (1984) diagnosed the defensive routines of a radical professional organization, which had been created to counter the defensive routines of the profession it represented. Putnam (1990) proposed a new way to understand impediments to learning model II and heuristics for overcoming them. And Isaacs (1991) described and analyzed the dilemmas that arose when model-II ideals were incorporated into a corporate credo.

What Has Held Up, What Has Not?

It is nearly twenty years since *Theory in Practice* was first published. During these nearly two decades, extraordinary in the changes that have occurred on the world scene, a great deal has happened in the fields of study and practice touched by the book. It seems appropriate to explore what parts of the book we feel have remained robust and what parts of it we would now reject or reformulate. Of the many issues we might possibly consider here, we shall limit ourselves to four:

1. *The conceptual framework for describing interpersonal action.* *Theory in Practice* proposed a general framework for describing personal and interpersonal action, which served as a basis for the presentation of models I and II. Of the several elements of that framework, a number still seem to us to be useful: the idea of a theory of action as a unit of description for the knowledge that informs action, the distinction between espoused theory and theory-in-use, the relationship between theory of action and the behavioral world, the dynamics of theory of action and its relationship to single- and double-loop learning.

Without abandoning these older ideas, we have added certain new ones: Argyris's defensive routines and his distinction between defensive and productive reasoning; Schön's knowing-in-action, reflection-in-action, and reflective practice. These additions seem to us to indicate an important incompleteness in our earlier formulations. Nevertheless, we believe that our later ideas are essentially compatible with the earlier ones. Defensive routines, for example, represent a *kind* of theory-in-use. Reflection-in-action is a process through which theories-in-use are instantiated, developed, and on occasion modified.

2. *The generality of Model I.* We have a great deal more data now than we did in 1974. We estimate that we have studied the theories-in-use of well over five thousand individuals (about 50 percent of them women). They included individuals with varying degrees of education and wealth; people who work in private and public organizations or as independent practitioners. Most of them acted consistently with model I and most were skillfully unaware that this was the case.

We have visited many organizations whose leaders told us that they practiced model II and that organizational defensive routines there were notable by their absence. So far, we have found neither claim to be true. Most organizations have powerful defensive routines, even though, to our knowledge, they do not formally reward or teach them.

We diagnose individuals' theories-in-use by asking them to write cases, by observing their responses to our cases, by observing and tape-recording the participants in action, and by listening to tape recordings they have made when we were not present. The fact that we get similar results when we use different diagnostic methods, and in a variety of different contexts, strengthens our belief in the general validity of model I.

Finally, we have found that we can talk explicitly to people about model I and model II without affecting the results of our studies. Indeed, we can expose one group of individuals to analysis of the cases presented by a different group, giving the first group an opportunity to learn from the "mistakes" of the second, and we find that the individuals in question are unable to live out a theory-in-use different from model I.

We should like to state clearly that we are not claiming that most human beings act "the same." On the contrary, our claim is that, although actions may vary widely, the theories-in-use under-lying them do not. For example, individuals "save face" in many different ways, still displaying the same theory-in-use: bypass embarrassment or threat and act as if you were not doing so. In our opinion, this observation has important implications for research and practice. It suggests that as to research, behavior is the penultimate variable to study, the ultimate variable being the theory-in-use through which human beings produce their ac-tions. The main task, we believe, is to identify the conceptual models that form the basis for people's theories-in-use. As to practice, the observation described above suggests that practitio-ners should be helped to focus on their theories-in-use, especially the causal reasoning embedded in them (Argyris, 1990).

3. *Is Model II learnable and teachable?* Our experience to date suggests that most people can learn model II. As with everything else, people learn model II in different ways and at different rates. In general, we believe, those strongly disposed to learn model II possess two important characteristics. First, these individuals are able to listen to feedback about the errors they make as they try to learn model II, so long as that feedback is crafted to produce minimal defensiveness, and they strive to correct their errors once these have been pointed out to them. Secondly, once these individuals have received valid and construc-tive feedback, they tend to "hang in" in order to learn. For example, even if it happens that every new action they try out seems wrong and they feel stuck, they realize that recognizing their stuck-ness is necessary for learning. They are willing to persevere in practicing new actions in order to get them right. They are able to feel vulnerable without feeling weak.

The kind of practice essential to learning model II is not routine repetition but experimentation in crafting action. This in turn requires some competence in the use of abstractions, be-cause the learner must compare his or her actions with abstract concepts such as model II.

It is also our experience that people change values at the level of theory-in-use (as distinct from values that are espoused) as they become more skillful with the new theory-in-use. The test of whether someone holds the new values is whether the person can act consistently with them. Again, the kind of practice that is important to learning consists in experimenting with new action strategies coupled with a new set of values. When model-II action strategies serve model-I values, the result is gimmickry.

Model II is more effectively learned by individuals who are grappling with current difficult problems, especially ones that have been avoided or covered up. A most powerful context for learning model II is one in which individuals identify problems that they believe are central in their lives, which they also predict are unsolvable and undiscussable. In this sense, the requisite learning is most likely to occur when it is most needed.

4. *How much does model II capture of what we believe in?* This question, which we have discussed and debated at length, is one that must strike everyone who takes model II seriously. Clearly, model II touches on values that are central to social life and to the traditions of moral philosophy: freedom of choice, truth and testability, the nature of commitment, the possibilities for and limitations on openness in communication among individuals, the basis for trust and cooperation among human beings, the sources of long-term personal effectiveness. Equally clearly, much that is crucial to human life lies beyond the boundaries of model II: for example, aesthetic appreciation, humor, irony, sexual love, and spirituality. It is not that model II is out of order where such things are in question; indeed, the values of model II are often critically important to our commerce with them. It is rather that model II limits itself to the dimension of human life that has explicitly to do with *inquiry* among persons. Its concerns are with making and testing attributions, increasing the discussability and testability of propositions, creating the conditions for informed choice, helping to increase the likelihood that conflict and competition will yield productive cooperation—all of this, especially, under conditions of embarrassment, threat, and shame that tend normally to subvert inquiry. If there is no aspect of human life exempt from such concerns, neither do they exhaust what is valuable in human life.

References

ARGYRIS, C. *Increasing Leadership Effectiveness.* New York: Wiley-Interscience, 1976.

ARGYRIS, C. *Reasoning, Learning, and Action: Individual and Organizational.* San Francisco: Jossey-Bass, 1982.

ARGYRIS, C. *Strategy, Change and Defensive Routines.* New York: Ballinger, HarperCollins, 1985.

ARGYRIS, C. "Strategy Implementation: An Experience in Learning," *Organizational Dynamics,* Autumn 1989, pp. 5–15.

ARGYRIS, C. *Overcoming Organizational Defenses: Facilitating Organizational Learning.* Needham Heights, Mass.: Allyn & Bacon, 1990.

ARGYRIS, C. "Teaching Smart People How to Learn," *Harvard Business Review,* 1991, *60* (3), 99–109.

ARGYRIS, C., AND SCHÖN, D.A. *Organizational Learning.* Reading, Mass.: Addison-Wesley, 1978.

ARGYRIS, C., AND SCHÖN, D.A. "Normal Science and Action Science Compared." Unpublished paper, Cambridge, Mass. 1990.

ARGYRIS, C., PUTNAM, R., AND SMITH, D. *Action Science: Concepts, Methods, and Skills for Research and Intervention.* San Francisco: Jossey-Bass, 1985.

GROSS, T. F. "Illusions, Crisis, Awareness and Realignment: A Case Study of an Organizational Change Project and a Model of the Consultant-Client Relationship." Unpublished doctoral dissertation, Graduate School of Education, Harvard University, 1980.

ISSAACS, W. "The Perils of Shared Ideals: Self-Defeating Dynamics of Organizational Ideology." Unpublished doctoral dissertation, Lincoln College, Oxford University, 1991.

JOINER, B. "Searching for Collaborative Inquiry: The Evolution of Action Research." Unpublished doctoral dissertation, Graduate School of Education, Harvard University, 1983.

LEWIN, K., AND GRABBE, P. "Conduct, Knowledge and Acceptance of New Values," *The Journal of Social Issues,* 1945, *1* (3).

MCGREGOR, D. *The Human Side of Enterprise.* New York: McGraw Hill, 1960.

OVERMEER, W. "Corporate Inquiry and Strategic Learning: The Role of Surprises and Improvisation in Organizing Major Strategic Changes." Unpublished doctoral dissertation, Massachusetts Institute of Technology, 1989.

PUTNAM, R. W. "Putting Concepts to Use: Re-educating Professionals for Organizational Learning." Unpublished doctoral dissertation, Graduate School of Education, Harvard University, 1990.

SAYLES, M. "Action Skills for Radical Democratic Organizations: A Learning Agenda for the Metroville Artists Organization." Unpublished doctoral dissertation, Graduate School of Education, Harvard University, 1984.

SCHEIN, E. *Professional Education.* New York: McGraw Hill, 1973.

SCHÖN, D. A. *The Reflective Practitioner.* New York: Basic Books, 1983.

SCHÖN, D. A. *Educating the Reflective Practitioner: Toward a New Design for Teaching and Learning in the Professions.* San Francisco: Jossey-Bass, 1987.

SCHÖN, D. A. "Causality and Causal Inference in the Study of Organizations." Paper presented at the Colloquium on the Epistemology of the Social Sciences, University of Southern California, Nov. 1990.

SCHÖN, D. A. (Ed.) *The Reflective Turn.* New York: Teachers College Press, 1991.

SMITH, D. "Stalking Conflict: A Critical Inquiry into Third Party Intervention." Unpublished qualifying paper, Graduate School of Education, Harvard University, 1987.

Preface

In summer 1971, Charles E. Brown began a project of training educational administrators to enter existing schools to begin programs of reform. He asked the two of us to consider how these students might be helped to be effective in the interventions they planned to undertake. What skills would they need? What experiences would help them acquire these skills?

We were intrigued with the task because our previous work had centered on the effective functioning of consultants and on constructing theories that affect practice. As we began to design the program, we met obstacles that were both puzzling and exciting. Our initial commitment to integrating theory with practice and affective with cognitive learning raised fundamental, new questions: for example, we could readily identify skills the administrators would be asked to display—among them, planning, communicating, negotiating, listening, and organizing—but as we proceeded we became progressively less sure about what we meant by the term *skill* and about what prevents people from being skillful.

Early in the process, we began to think of skills as programs for behavior. But what did such skills as listening or negotiating consist of? Clearly, the informational content of these programs was enormous, and even those who were skillful in negotiating or listening were often not able to explain their programs to others.

Conceived in this way, skills did not seem clearly distinguishable from strategies for intervention. In both cases a cognitive program was to be mastered, and in both cases the ability to carry out the program effectively went beyond knowledge of the part of the program that could be readily formulated. We began to use the term *theory of intervention* and finally *theory of action* to replace the terms *skill* and *strategy*.

The administrative trainees, we concluded, needed to learn new theories of action in order to increase their effectiveness in school reform. This formulation counterbalanced the prevailing emphasis in T groups or encounter groups on affective experiences alone, which are often powerful to participants but do not help them state what they have learned, teach it to others, or subject their experience to conscious criticism as they apply it to later experiences.

We thought the trouble people have in learning new theories of action may stem not so much from the inherent difficulty of the new theories as from existing theories people have that already determine practice. We called these operational theories of action *theories-in-use* to distinguish them from the *espoused theories* that are used to describe and justify behavior. We wondered whether the difficulty in learning new theories of action is related to a disposition to protect the old theories-in-use.

We found that most people tend to be unaware of how their attitudes affect their behavior and also unaware of the negative impact of their behavior on others. Their theories-in-use help them remain blind to the actual degree of their ineffectiveness. For example, in many of the cases observed we found that an individual *A* perceives another individual *B* as having a theory-in-use that is incongruent with *B*'s espoused theory. But *A*'s theory-in-use prohibits his calling attention to this incongruity. *A* may withhold this information either out of fear (if *B* has more power) or out of what society has taught him to conceive of as diplomacy and tact. Blindness to incongruity between espoused theory and theory-in-use may be culturally as well as individually caused and maintained. In such cases, reeducation has to begin with an attempt to specify the patterns of existing theories-in-use.

These ideas shaped the questions that have led to the structure of this book. Part One answers the following questions: What are theories of action and theories-in-use? What do they describe? What is their status? How are they related to other kinds of theories? What kinds of knowledge do they represent? For the reader who wants to understand the genesis of our ideas, this part is fundamental.

Part Two deals with these questions: What are the specific theories-in-use that determine our efforts at intervention? How do they vary from person to person and from situation to situation? Do they display relatively constant patterns? If so, how do these patterns influence effectiveness in intervention? For readers particularly concerned with both ineffective and effective interpersonal and professional behavior, this part will be of most interest.

In Part Three, we discuss strategies and environments for learning: How do we learn new theories of action? What are the conditions under which we are most likely to learn to apply the patterns of theories of action that enable us to be effective at intervention? And how can these ideas be related both to professional education and to the diagnosis of prevailing theories of action that now inhibit effective professional practice? For educators concerned with the professional and social effectiveness of their students, this part should prove valuable.

Our tentative answers to these questions apply to broader issues than school reform and the preparation of school administrators. They can help to build effective interaction of every sort and to clarify the fundamental social issues underlying the redesign of professional education. Several important, comprehensive studies have treated the reform of professional education (Cope and Zacharias, 1966; Mayhew, 1970, 1971; Carnegie Commission on Higher Education, 1970; Gorden and Howell, 1959). We do not review these studies in the following pages but want to note here their relationship to our position. There is a remarkable degree of agreement on the major reforms these studies propose.

They include shortening the time required to obtain a degree, making the curriculum more flexible so that students may have more choices and fewer required courses, adding courses in the behavioral and information-computer sciences, and reaffirming the importance of the clinical experience in many professional programs. Little in our theoretical framework or empirical research is directly related to these points. Most of the recommendations of these studies came from examining such factors as the need for the professions, students' demands for relevance, great potential contributions from other fields, or soaring costs of education. Our recommendations for professional education are based on the theory of practice we describe; they neither contradict nor, with the exception of the clinical experience, expand the recommendations of these learned councils. We discuss the general characteristics of effectiveness in any kind of intervention, what constitutes effective professional practice, and what specific measures professional schools can take to increase effectiveness in the areas of student training, curriculum design, clinical practice, and continuing education for practitioners, among others.

The value of our perspective is that it does not base the design of professional education on such factors as the demands of society, the cost of education, and the students' changing demands. Important as these factors may be, they are external to the essential nature of professional education and derive not from a view of effective practice but from a view of the demands to be made on that practice by various special-interest groups.

Several forces in society and education have helped to erode the barriers against thinking systematically about professional practice and against integrating thought and action. The turmoil of the 1960s accelerated the pressure for problem-oriented research, and several intellectual thrusts developed momentum in different fields. For example, the image of human nature began to be reformulated. The Freudian concept of libidinal man, propelled by sexual urges, was slowly modified to view man as also motivated by a sense of competence and a need to be effective. Moreover, we now see that one source of human energy is psychological success with challenging opportunities; thus, effectiveness may be connected with psychological health.

As the concept of human nature became more competence-oriented, it also became more active. Man not only is a result of genetic and environmental factors but also is responsible for the ways he uses his endowments and for the world he creates.

Linking individual human behavior with the state of the world in which it exists made it possible to ask how the environment affects its creators and led to the realization that this effect depends on how people experience the environment and that how they experience the environment depends on how they construct it. Individuals are ultimately responsible for the impact of the environment because they learn from personally constructed experience.

These views emanating from personality and cognitive psychology joined the various existential philosophies, whose concept of man was also that he was responsible for his destiny and that he should strive to be an originator rather than a pawn, active rather than passive, responsible rather than helpless.

Finally, research on the nature of effective organizations began to show that organizations were frequently in decay. The ineffectiveness, costliness, and deteriorating quality of products and services were found to be based on the fact that organizations were designed originally to ignore human nature, to ignore individuals' feelings and most of their abilities, and to exploit them.

New designs that reduced these forces for organizational decay were based on an image of man as responsible, seeking to be unique, and internally committed to organizations, partly because organizations could make work meaningful and because the new designs enhanced the quality of life in organizations.

In this book we hope to contribute to these intellectual forces. Our theory of action can enhance human activity, responsibility, self-actualization, learning, and effectiveness and make it likely that organizations will begin to decrease the movement toward entropy and increase the forces toward learning and health. We present a view of man actively seeking to master himself and his environment in a way that makes organizations effective. If we are to accomplish these objectives, we must become aware of both espoused theories and the tacit theories that govern behavior.

Understanding how we diagnose and construct our experience, take action, and monitor our behavior while simultaneously achieving our goals is crucial to understanding and enhancing effectiveness. If we learn to behave differently and to make these new behaviors stick, we will begin to create a new world. In this book we show how new learning environments can be designed to move toward that world.

Acknowledgments

We are indebted to many colleagues and students who, through their criticism and patience, helped us develop our ideas. We wish to thank especially Lee Bolman, Steven Ehrmann, and William Torbert. We also wish to thank Kathryn Hildebrand and Richard Yoder for editorial and typing assistance.

Cambridge, Massachusetts   CHRIS ARGYRIS
July 1974   DONALD A. SCHÖN

The Authors

CHRIS ARGYRIS is James Bryant Conant Professor of Education and Organizational Behavior at Harvard University. He was awarded his A.B. degree (1947) in psychology from Clark University, his M.A. degree (1949) in economics and psychology from Kansas University, and his Ph.D. degree (1951) in organizational behavior from Cornell University. From 1951 to 1971, he was a faculty member at Yale University, serving as Beach Professor of Administrative Sciences and as chairperson of the Administrative Sciences Department during the latter part of this period.

Argyris's early research focused on the unintended consequences for individuals of formal organizational structures, executive leadership, control systems, and management information systems—and on how individuals adapted to change those consequences *(Personality and Organization,* 1957; *Integrating the Individual and the Organization,* 1964). He then turned his attention to ways of changing organizations, especially the behavior of executives at the upper levels of organization *(Interpersonal Competence and Organizational Effectiveness,* 1962; *Organization and Innovation,* 1965).

This line of inquiry led him to focus on the role of the social scientist as a researcher and interventionist *(Intervention Theory and Method,* 1970; *Inner Contradictions of Rigorous Research,* 1980). He has also worked, with Donald Schön, at developing a theory of individual and organizational learning in which human reasoning—not just behavior—becomes the basis for diagnosis and action (*Theory in Practice,* 1974; *Increasing Leadership Effectiveness,* 1976; *Organizational Learning,* 1978).

Argyris has earned honorary doctorates from the Stockholm School of Economics (1979), the University of Leuven, Belgium (1978), and McGill University (1977).

DONALD A. SCHÖN is Ford Professor of Urban Studies and Education at the Massachusetts Institute of Technology, where he currently serves as head of the Department of Urban Studies and Planning. Schön holds a B.A. degree (1951) in philosophy from Yale University, and M.A. (1952) and Ph.D. (1955) degrees in philosophy from Harvard University. He also attended the Sorbonne and received a certificate from the Conservatoire Nationale, Paris, France.

In his work as a researcher and consultant, Schön has focused on organizational learning and professional effectiveness. For seven years before his appointment to the faculty at M.I.T., Schön served as president of the Organization for Social and Technical Innovation (OSTI), a nonprofit organization which he helped to found. He has served in numerous other administrative and consultative roles with governmental agencies and private industry.

In 1970, Schön was invited to deliver the Reith Lectures, which were broadcast by the British Broadcasting Corporation. In 1984, he was Queens Quest Lecturer at Queens University and was also made an honorary fellow of the Royal Institute of British Architects. Schön's other publications include *The Reflective Practitioner* (1983) and *Organizational Learning: A Theory of Action Perspective* (1978, with C. Argyris). Schön is active in a number of professional organizations and is a member of the American Academy of Arts and Sciences Commission on the Year 2000 and the National Research Council Commission on Sociotechnical Systems.

THEORY
IN PRACTICE

PART I

THEORY

Chapter 1

Theories of Action

Integrating thought with action effectively has plagued philosophers, frustrated social scientists, and eluded professional practitioners for years. It is one of the most prevalent and least understood problems of our age. Universities have shunned it on the ground that effective action was too practical or—the best kiss of death—vocational.

We believe that exciting intellectual problems are related to integrating thought with action. Effective action requires the generation of knowledge that crosses the traditional disciplines of knowledge—with as much competence and rigor as each discipline usually demands. This is a difficult task not only because scholars rarely cross disciplines but also because few scholars are inclined and educated to generate such knowledge. The few hardy souls who plunge into cross-disciplinary waters find that their colleagues view the effort with skepticism.

Indeed, as Havens (1973) shows, scholars in a single profession, psychiatry, in more cases than not fail to understand each other: they protect themselves by forming camps that compete with one another, ignoring the problems of relating theory to practice while defending their necessarily limited views. The old ideal of a working relationship between research and practice has yet to be realized.

Another important obstacle to the integration of thought and action is the current concept of rigorous research. The technology of rigorous research works best when it does not deal with real-time issues—for example, when scholars take years to study a decision that took several hours to make. This technology of rigorous research is based on diagnostic techniques that ignore or cannot cope with properties of effective action under real-time conditions: data may have to be ignored, feedback from the environment may be unavailable, and self-fulfilling prophecies may need to be accepted—they may, indeed, be the essence of action.

All human beings—not only professional practitioners—need to become competent in taking action and simultaneously reflecting on this action to learn from it. The following pages provide a conceptual framework for this task by analyzing the theories of action that determine all deliberate human behavior, how these theories are formed, how they come to change, and in what senses they may be considered adequate or inadequate. We use this framework in later chapters to develop a model—model I—of the theories of action that determine the actual behavior of professional practitioners. We then analyze this model from two points of view: the effectiveness of those who hold it and its influence on their ability to learn about their own behavior. We then propose model II, which is more conducive to both effectiveness and learning. Then we consider the problems of transition from model I to model II.

Theories of professional practice are best understood as special cases of the theories of action that determine all deliberate behavior. And whatever else a theory of action may be, it is first a theory. Its most general properties are properties that all theories share, and the most general criteria that apply to it—such as generality, relevance, consistency, completeness, testability, centrality, and simplicity[1]—are criteria that apply to all theories.

Theories are theories regardless of their origin: there are practical, common-sense theories as well as academic or scientific theories. A theory is not necessarily accepted, good, or true; it is only a set of interconnected propositions that have the same referent —the subject of the theory. Their interconnectedness is reflected in the logic of relationships among propositions: change in propositions at one point in the theory entails changes in propositions elsewhere in it.

Theories are vehicles for explanation, prediction, or control. An explanatory theory explains events by setting forth propositions from which these events may be inferred, a predictive theory sets forth propositions from which inferences about future events may be made, and a theory of control describes the conditions under which events of a certain kind may be made to occur. In each case, the theory has an "if . . . then . . ." form.

Theories constructed to explain, predict, or control human behavior are in many ways like other kinds of theories. But insofar as they are about human action—that is, about human behavior that is correctable and subject to deliberation—they have special features.

We can observe deliberate behavior and try to account for it as though it were the behavior of fish or tides—for example, "If population densities exceed an upper limit, people become more aggressive toward one another." Here the "if . . . then . . ." relationship holds between publicly observable phenomena. But we can also regard deliberate human behavior as the consequence of theories of action held by humans, in which case we explain or predict a person's behavior by attributing to him a theory of action. For example, we may attribute to a counselor a theory about the way to handle disruptive students: "It is necessary first to speak to them in their own language and to make it clear that you understand them, then to state the limits of what you will tolerate from them, and only then to try to find out what's bothering them." All such theories of action have the same form: in situation S, if you want to achieve consequence C, do A.

Of course, theories of action do not hold when they are put into such simple form. They depend on a set of stated or unstated assumptions. In the previous instance, we would have to add, for example, ". . . *if* you can be sincere in speaking the student's own language, *if* he presents himself as hostile to you in the first instance, *if* he shows signs of overstepping bounds." A full list of assumptions would contain all the conditions under which you would expect the action to produce the desired result. Such a list would be very long;

in fact, you could never be sure you had completed it. A full schema for a theory of action, then, would be as follows: in situation S, if you want to achieve consequence C, under assumptions $a_1 \ldots a_n$, do A.

From the subjective view, my theory of action is normative for me; that is, it states what I ought to do if I wish to achieve certain results. It is a theory of control. But someone else may explain my behavior by attributing to me a theory of action that accounts for the deliberate behavior he observes. In this sense, theories of action are also explanatory and predictive. We explain or predict a person's deliberate behavior by attributing theories of action to him.[2] A theory of action is a theory of deliberate human behavior, which is for the agent a theory of control but which, when attributed to the agent, also serves to explain or predict his behavior.

We have defined theory of action in terms of a particular situation, S, and a particular consequence, C, intended in that situation. We need now to relate theories of action to theories of practice. A *practice* is a sequence of actions undertaken by a person to serve others, who are considered clients. Each action in the sequence of actions repeats some aspects of other actions in the sequence, but each action is in some way unique. In medicine, for example, a typical sequence would be a diagnostic work-up, treatment of acute illness, a well-baby visit, chronic care, and consultation.

A theory of practice, then, consists of a set of interrelated theories of action that specify for the situations of the practice the actions that will, under the relevant assumptions, yield intended consequences.[3] Theories of practice usually contain theories of intervention—that is, theories of action aimed at enhancing effectiveness; these may be differentiated according to the roles in which intervention is attempted—for example, consulting and teaching.

The rest of Chapter One discusses theories of action because one cannot understand theories of practice without understanding the theories of action on which they rest.

Theories-in-Use

When someone is asked how he would behave under certain circumstances, the answer he usually gives is his espoused theory of action for that situation. This is the theory of action to which he gives allegiance, and which, upon request, he communicates to others. However, the theory that actually governs his actions is his theory-in-use,[4] which may or may not be compatible with his espoused theory; furthermore, the individual may or may not be aware of the incompatibility of the two theories.

We cannot learn what someone's theory-in-use is simply by asking him. We must construct his theory-in-use from observations of his behavior. In this sense, constructs of theories-in-use are like scientific hypotheses; the constructs may be inaccurate representations of the behavior they claim to describe.

When you know what to do in a given situation in order to achieve an intended consequence, you know what the theory-in-use for that situation is. You know the nature of the consequence to be attained, you know the action appropriate in the situation to attain it, and you know the assumptions contained in the theory.

Theories-in-use, however their assumptions may differ, do all include assumptions about self, others, the situation, and the connections among action, consequence, and situation. In the example of the counselor and the disruptive student, the counselor's theory-in-use may have contained the following assumptions: (1) the counselor can speak the student's language; (2) the student will recognize the sincerity of the counselor as he speaks the student's language and will tend to trust the counselor as a result; (3) the school is a place in which the counselor will be permitted to interact with the student alone and to establish a personal relationship with the student; and (4) the student will be more disposed to alter his behavior if he comes to trust the counselor than if he does not. The counselor's theory-in-use may be said to contain these assumptions, whether or not he can state them, if a change in his beliefs about one or more of them were to lead him to change his view of the actions appropriate in the situation.

If theories of action can be attributed to all people who show deliberate behavior, then the scope of the knowledge exhibited in theories of action is immense. Theories-in-use include knowledge about the behavior of physical objects, the making and use of artifacts, the marketplace, organizations, and every other domain of human activity. In other words, the full set of assumptions about human behavior that function in theories-in-use constitutes a psychology of everyday life. All propositions about the structure and operation of society, about the culture, about the design and construction of artifacts, about the physical world—insofar as they function as assumptions in theories-in-use—constitute a sociology, an anthropology, an engineering science, a physics of everyday life. In this sense, everyone is his own psychologist, sociologist, anthropologist, engineer, and physicist.

The psychology, physics, or sociology of everyday life may differ from contemporary formal psychology, physics, or sociology; the sciences of everyday life may have more in common with the formal psychology of a generation ago, or they may contain the seeds of the sciences of tomorrow. In the course of intellectual history, much formal academic knowledge has emerged through making explicit the informal knowledge of everyday life.

The same is true of the knowledge involved in professional practice. There is a theory-in-use of building design (for architects), a theory-in-use of the diagnosis and treatment of disease (for physicians), and a theory-in-use of the planning of cities (for urban planners). There have been a few attempts to make these theories explicit. Scott (1969) outlines what he calls the practice theories of workers in agencies for the blind. He distinguishes between espoused theories of action and theories-in-use and points out that they tend to be inconsistent. The espoused theories hold that the blind are potentially independent, that agencies for the blind function to help the blind realize that potential. The theories-in-use, however, assume that the blind are basically dependent on the agencies, that it is a function of the agencies to sustain the dependence through continuing service, and that the function of a blind person is to adapt to life in an agency setting.

Clearly, specifying the knowledge contained in our theories-in-use would mean codifying the entire body of informal beliefs relevant to deliberate human behavior.

Levels. Each person has many theories-in-use—one for every kind of situation in which he more or less regularly finds himself. We will call each of these a microtheory, although a person's theories-in-use are not independent atoms of theory. One's microtheories are related to one another through similarities of content and through their logic. As with any complex body of knowledge, a person's theories-in-use may be organized in a variety of ways.

Some theories-in-use have a hierarchical structure, which becomes clear as we consider, for example, how general the counselor we discussed earlier feels his assumptions are. For example, does he feel that by speaking a student's language, the student will trust him more readily, or does he generalize this to mean that all students will trust him more readily if he speaks their language? Or does he generalize even further that anyone will trust him more readily if he speaks their language? How far the counselor generalizes this assumption can be established inductively by observing his behavior in similar situations and noting the range of situations in which he appears to operate on similar assumptions.

To what extent is the assumption part of an organized theory? For example, does the counselor have a theory of the conditions under which trust comes to be established in which this assumption figures as a component? This question too may be tested, roughly as above.

A person often holds different and incompatible theories-in-use for situations that appear to an outside observer to be alike. The school counselor, for example, may behave in one way with boys, in another way with girls, and in still another way with members of a group different from his own, although he may behave consistently with each type of student. In this case, he may be said to have a higher-order theory that governs his use of the different subtheories-in-use according to the type of student involved.

Or, the structure of theories-in-use can be determined by their common assumptions. Such an assumption might be, "People will react less defensively when they are less anxious." The resulting structure will not necessarily be hierarchical.

Tacit knowledge. In what sense do we have or know theories-in-use? What is their status? We can consider this question in terms of existence, inference, and learning.

The problem of existence may be stated as follows. How do we know a person's theories-in-use exist if we cannot state them? Although we argue that theories-in-use are manifested by behavior, sometimes we say that a theory-in-use exists even though the behavior that ought to manifest it does not appear; we say that a person intends to do *A*, but something happens to prevent him from doing it. If, then, we say that he has a theory-in-use that he cannot state and according to which, at least in some instances, he does not behave, in what sense does the theory-in-use exist?

There is the related problem of inference. What are the ground rules for inferring theories-in-use from behavior? If the manifesting behavior does not, in some instances, appear, how can we infer the theories-in-use?

There is the problem of learning. How can we change an existing theory-in-use or learn a new theory-in-use when we cannot state what is to be changed or learned?

These problems are at least as old as Plato's dialogue, the *Meno*. The history of attention to this topic leaves us with three main options.

1. We know only what we can state. If we adopt this view, we lose the distinction between espoused theory and theory-in-use; this view contradicts the general finding that people's behavior is often incompatible with the theories of action they espouse.

2. We know only what is manifested by behavior; theories-in-use are only constructs designed to account for patterns of behavior. This view leaves us unable to account for those situations in which people fail to behave according to their theories-in-use and yet may still properly be said to hold theories-in-use (see von Wright, 1972). A person begins an action according to his theory-in-use, but he cannot complete the action: the inhibiting factor may be external— he stumbles or is immobilized by someone else—or it may be internal—he is blocked by some unconscious wish or fear, he is overcome with emotion, he forgets, or he has a stroke. In addition, his behavior may show a conflict of theories-in-use; he may do nothing in the situation, which might be evidence for the existence of his conflicting theories-in-use.

3. We know more than we can tell and more than our behavior consistently shows. This is implicit knowledge, or tacit knowledge, as Polanyi (1967) calls it. Tacit knowledge is what we display when we recognize one face from thousands without being able to say how we do so, when we demonstrate a skill for which we cannot state an explicit program, or when we experience the intimation of a discovery we cannot put into words. Polanyi's concept offers a

useful perspective on the problems of existence, inference, and learning as they apply to theories-in-use.[5] If we know our theories-in-use tacitly, they exist even when we cannot state them and when we are somehow prevented from behaving according to them. When we formulate our theories-in-use, we are making explicit what we already know tacitly; we can test our explicit knowledge against our tacit knowledge just as the scientist can test his explicit hypothesis against his intimations. When we learn to put an espoused theory of action to use, we reverse the process. Instead of inferring explicit theory from the tacit knowledge our behavior shows, we make explicit theory tacit—that is, we internalize it.

Consider the analogy of grammar and speech. Just as we may be unable to describe the grammatical rules that determine how we speak, or even recognize that we know them, we may be similarly unable to describe or even to recognize our theories-in-use. Our actual speech exhibits rules and differentiations more subtle than proposed grammars can account for. Inquirers are constantly trying to push their theories of grammar toward more perfect approximations of the grammars that actually govern speech. The task is complicated by the instability of actual grammars. This is also true of the relationship between our theories-in-use and the constructed theories designed to make them explicit.

Each person has a grammar that governs his own speech, but these grammars are broadly shared among members of a society. Theories-in-use exhibit a similar resemblance; Chapter Four presents evidence that versions of the same model of theories-in-use result from similar upbringing within a culture. Significantly, philosophers of language now debate the status of knowledge of linguistic universals and principles of grammar that natural speakers of the language exhibit but cannot state.[6]

Inferring explicit theories of action from observed behavior has problems comparable to inferring principles of grammar from observed speech. The task is to devise progressively more adequate constructions of theories-in-use that account for regularities of behavior, deviations due to external or internal inhibitions, and behavioral manifestations of inconsistent theories-in-use. When a person tries to construct his own theories-in-use, his evidence includes his behavior, the intimations of his tacit knowledge, and his ability to construct imaginative experiments that indicate what he would do under various circumstances. The outside observer may also find ways to make use of the agent's intimations and imaginative experiments but must beware of the tendency to confuse espoused theories with theories-in-use. His inquiry will be facilitated by the presumption that the agent has tacit knowledge of his theories-in-use that may be elicited in various ways.

Skills and Theories-in-use

Professionals and professional educators—indeed, practitioners of all sorts—often speak of practicing and learning skills as though these activities were of an entirely different sort than learning a theory or learning to apply a theory. This viewpoint suggests that skill learning and theory learning are different kinds of activities; it suggests further that theory learning may be appropriately undertaken in one kind of place (school) and skill learning in another (work).

Skills are dimensions of the ability to behave effectively in situations of action. *Skill* is a hybrid term that refers both to a property of concrete behavior and to a property of theories of action. Skills of all kinds—diving, writing, consultation—depend on certain features of the actor's concrete behavior. If he consistently fails to behave according to his skills, we do not attribute the skills to him. Skills also can be generalized from one situation to another. We may construct the explicit program represented by a skill just as we may construct the theory-in-use manifested by a practitioner's behavior. However, the programs manifested by skills are enormously complex. The informational content of the program corresponding to the skill of bicycle riding runs to four hundred pages and is still incomplete. The program corresponding to a skill is a theory-in-use of great informational content. Learning a theory of action so as to become competent in professional practice does not consist of learning to recite the theory; the theory of action has not been learned in the most important sense unless it can be put into practice.

Learning to put a theory of action into practice and learning a skill are similar processes, just as making one's theory-in-use explicit is like making explicit the program manifested by a skill.

Hence, considering the process of learning a skill may illuminate the process of learning new theories-in-use.

Let us consider the skill of bicycle riding. Suppose that we put the entire program into a student's hands and that he studies the program so that he can repeat it and can state what the program says to do in various circumstances. This ability to repeat the program does not constitute learning the skill for three reasons.

1. There is an information gap between the program and the concrete performance of riding a bicycle; that is, the program never gives a complete description of the concrete performance. However, it is misleading to say that the problem is merely to fill the gap. From a before-the-fact perspective, filling the gap involves problem-solving. When a medical student learns the symptoms of a range of diseases and begins to apply his knowledge or acquire diagnostic skill, the linking of symptom and disease is not a simple matching process. Often the patient's symptoms seem ambiguous to the student. He must screen his array of symptom/disease concepts, narrowing them to reasonable possibilities. He goes through a series of inferences, observations, and tests, all of which fill the information gap between the diagnostic program he has learned and his recognition of the patient's disease.

2. Riding a bicycle requires smooth, uninterrupted sequences of responses. If we interrupt this flow of activity by attending to the particulars of what we are doing or by looping back through the explicit program, we may fall off the bicycle. This is true not merely because of considerations of timing (the learner must compensate for an imbalance immediately, not a few seconds later) but because these sequences depend for their performance on Gestalt qualities that we lose if we attend to the particulars of the explicit program. Thus, learning to ride requires both learning the program and learning to internalize the program. Then one can give appropriate responses on cue without having to make explicit reference to the program. Knowledge of the program must be made tacit; one cannot replace tacit with explicit knowledge.

3. Some of the performances indicated by the program may require changes in sensory competence, muscular strength, physical dexterity, or feeling, none of which is achieved through learning the program for riding a bicycle. For example the program does not

teach the learner to avoid fear, although it may indicate that there is no reason for it; nevertheless, the learner may feel fear, even to an immobilizing extent.

Practicing a skill may consist of allowing the learner to overcome his fear by progressive familiarization with the performance. The learning situation may be designed so he can perform components of the performance in a relatively risk-free situation (training wheels) and increase the riskiness of his performances as he builds confidence. One can type skills by their learning conditions: those that require special conditions of strength, dexterity, sensory awareness, or feeling and those that do not; those that are readily broken up into components and those that are not; those that may be slowed down and still be performed effectively and those that may not; and so on.

These comments about learning a skill apply also to learning to behave according to a new theory of action. In both processes, it is essential to practice, to develop and draw on tacit knowledge, and to be in a learning situation that permits a reinforcing cycle of feeling and performance to begin.

It does not follow that a new skill can be learned only by first learning its program, or that one can learn a new theory-in-use only by first learning its explicit verbal formulation. On the contrary, much learning takes place through imitation without any verbal intervention. Learning may also take place as one person criticizes the performances of another, telling him what changes he should make without trying to formulate the theory of action corresponding to the peformance. (Indeed, the teacher may not know the explicit theory of action but still be able to detect deviations from correct performance.) The teacher may help the student link components of behavior already in his repertoire, or the teacher may put the student into situations that require a performance much like one he already knows.

What, then, is the advantage of explicitly stating the theories-in-use we already hold? If unstated theories-in-use appear to enable the agent to perform effectively, there may be no advantage. But if the agent is performing ineffectively and does not know why or if others are aware of his ineffectiveness and he is not, explicitly stating his theory-in-use allows conscious criticism. The agent's efforts to defend his tacit theory-in-use may prevent his learning to behave differently; he may not be willing to behave differently until he has examined his theory-in-use explicitly and compared it with alternatives. He may be unable to test his theory-in-use until he has made it explicit. And he may be severely impaired in his efforts to teach his theory-in-use to others until he has made it explicit.

Roles Played by Theories-in-Use

Theories-in-use are means for getting what we want. They specify strategies for resolving conflicts, making a living, closing a deal, organizing a neighborhood—indeed, for every kind of intended consequence.

Theories-in-use are also means for maintaining certain kinds of constancy. Certain governing variables interest us (for example, energy expended, anxiety, time spent with others), and we try to keep the values of these variables within the range acceptable to us. Our theories-in-use specify which variables we are interested in (as opposed to the constants in our environment about which we can do nothing) and thereby set boundaries to action. Within these boundaries, theories-in-use provide the programs by which the variables may be managed.[7]

When we say that we pursue a certain end or get what we want, we focus on a single variable and speak of a certain sequence of action concerning that variable exclusively. However, we act within a field of governing variables, all of which are affected by our behavior, all of which we strive to keep within an acceptable range. Instead of actions being related to ends on a one-to-one basis, any given action may affect many variables; all of them are ends in the sense that all behavior is shaped so as to keep all variables within an acceptable range. At any moment, one variable may be more interesting than others and move to the foreground of our attention, but the other variables affected by the action cannot be ignored; they may be considered constraints on our efforts to manipulate foreground variables. That is, whatever we do to manipulate foreground variables, we cannot allow one of the other variables out of its acceptable range. In this sense, formulating and selecting actions is a design problem analogous to the problems of architectural and engineering design, which require achieving desired values of a range of related variables, not just one variable. The actions we take never have only the intended consequence; in the design of behavior, we are continually engaged in attempting to mitigate the unintended consequences of our actions on background variables.

Some actions do not affect all governing variables, and some governing variables are not relevant to each action. However, certain governing variables (for example, level of anxiety, vitality, or self-esteem) seem to be at stake in virtually every action, constraining the directions that action may take. These variables may suddenly achieve the status of foreground ends if some action of ours has inadvertently taken them out of their acceptable ranges.[8]

A governing variable ranges within its acceptable limits, only occasionally rising above or falling below them. When one begins to focus on a new variable, it may initially be above or below these limits. It takes time to bring the new variable within acceptable limits (consider bringing someone back to health or establishing a relationship of trust). In setting oneself an objective in relation to that variable, one sets some requisite pattern of movement into the acceptable range (the objective function). Furthermore, both old and new variables require maintenance in order to keep them within limits; the design problem must not only be solved but stay solved. Once within acceptable range, the new variable joins the other governing variables that make up a person's field of constancy —the set of governing variables that must all be kept constant within their acceptable ranges.

Theories-in-use maintain a person's field of constancy. They specify the governing variables and their critical relationships to one another—for example, which variables have priority. They specify the acceptable ranges for these variables and the objective functions for new governing variables. They describe the techniques and strategies of design by which objective functions may be achieved and constancies maintained.[9]

Theories-in-use are the means of maintaining specific constancies, but they also come to be valued in their own right for the constancy of the world-picture they provide. The inherent variability of the behavioral world gives us more information than we can handle, so we value a stable world-picture, being predictable, and being able to predict. We work at maintaining the constancy of our theories-in-use.

The two orders of constancy—both of governing variables and of the world picture which theories-in-use provide—generate a special conflict. When our theories-in-use prove ineffective in maintaining the constancy of our governing variables, we may find it necessary to change our theories-in-use. But we try to avoid such change because we wish to keep our theories-in-use constant. Forced to choose between getting what we want and maintaining second-order constancy, we may choose not to get what we want.

Theories-in-Use as Theories of the Artificial

The stars are indifferent to our opinion of them, and the tides are independent of our theories about them. Human behavior, however, is directly influenced by our actions and therefore by our theories of action. The behavioral world is an artifact of our theories-in-use.

Theories of the behavioral world are, in Simon's (1969) phrase,[10] theories of the artificial. Many of the constants of the behavioral world are accidental—in the sense that they are created by human convention and continued by human choice—rather than inherent in the nature of the universe.

Moreover, each person lives in a behavioral world of his own —a world made up of his own behavior in interaction with the behavior of others. Each person's behavioral world is therefore artificial not only in the sense that it consists of artifacts of human convention but in the sense that it is shaped and influenced by one's own action and by one's theories of the behavioral world as they influence action. The relationship between theory-in-use and action is special. Here, the action not only applies and tests the theory but also shapes the behavioral world the theory is about. We are familiar with this phenomenon in its pejorative connotations, as in the example of the teacher whose belief in the stupidity of his students results in the students' behaving stupidly. But the usual conclusions of

such experiments is that one should avoid self-fulfilling prophecies—
as if one could. Every theory-in-use is a self-fulfilling prophecy to
some extent.[11]

We construct the reality of our behavioral worlds through
the same process by which we construct our theories-in-use. Theory-
building is reality-building, not only because our theories-in-use help
to determine what we perceive of the behavioral world but because
our theories-in-use determine our actions, which in turn help to
determine the characteristics of the behavioral world, which in turn
feed into our theories-in-use. Consequently, every theory-in-use is
a way of doing something to others (to one's behavioral world),
which in turn does something to oneself. The second-order constancy
that we seek in our theories-in-use is also the constancy we seek in
our behavioral world.

Accordingly, one must examine theories-in-use not at one
cross-sectional instant in time but in the progressively developing
interaction between theory-in-use and behavioral world. One cannot
judge theories-in-use without also judging the behavioral world
created by the theory. And one cannot set about trying to construct
a better theory-in-use without also trying to construct the behavioral
world that is conducive to the development of that theory-in-use.

Theory-Building as Learning

We have already discussed the similarities between learning
a skill and learning to behave according to a theory-in-use. But, in
addition, the formation or modification of a theory-in-use is itself
a learning process.

We see behavioral learning, in George Kelley's terms, as a
hypothetico-deductive process in which behavioral hypotheses are
formed, tested, and modified. That is, behavioral learning involves
the experience-based modification of some elements of theories-in-
use—governing variables, action strategies, or assumptions.

We can then distinguish two kinds of behavioral learning:
we can learn to adopt new action strategies to achieve our governing variables; and we can learn to change our governing variables.
This distinction is similar to Ashby's (1952) distinction between
single-loop and double-loop learning. Ashby uses the example of a

household thermostat. When the household temperature oscillates around a steady temperature, the system may be said to engage in single-loop learning. When the householder intervenes to change the setting of the thermostat, the learning involved is double-loop. ". . . The message which the householder puts into the system by changing the setting is *about* how the system shall respond to messages of lower order emanating from the thermometer [Bateson, 1958, p. 293]." In the first case, the feedback loop connects the household temperature (as sensed by the thermometer) with the valve controlling the flow of hot air or water. In the second case, the feedback loop connects the household temperature not only with the heating unit but (through the medium of the householder) with the thermostat setting around which the household temperature will oscillate.

In the context of theories-in-use, a person engages in single-loop learning, for example, when he learns new techniques for suppressing conflict. He engages in double-loop learning when he learns to be concerned with the surfacing and resolution of conflict rather than with its suppression.

In single-loop learning, we learn to maintain the field of constancy by learning to design actions that satisfy existing governing variables. In double-loop learning, we learn to change the field of constancy itself.

Double-loop learning does not supercede single-loop learning. Single-loop learning enables us to avoid continuing investment in the highly predictable activities that make up the bulk of our lives; but the theory-builder becomes a prisoner of his programs if he allows them to continue unexamined indefinitely. Double-loop learning changes the governing variables (the "settings") of one's programs and causes ripples of change to fan out over one's whole system of theories-in-use.

Chapter 2

Evaluating Theories
of Action

To consider the interaction of theories-in-use and their behavioral worlds, we must look at their tendencies rather than at their cross-sectional properties at any instant in time. Whether theories-in-use tend to create a behavioral world that constrains or frees the individual depends on answers to the following questions: Are the theories-in-use and espoused theories internally consistent? Are they congruent? Are they testable? Are they effective? Do we value the worlds they create? The relationships among these criteria are expressed in Figure 1.

Internal Consistency

In a very simple sense, *internal consistency* means the absence of self-contradiction. But in the domain of theory of action, its meaning becomes more complex.

The most important kind of consistency lies not between propositions in the theory ("This man is generous," "This man is stingy") but among the governing variables of the theory that are

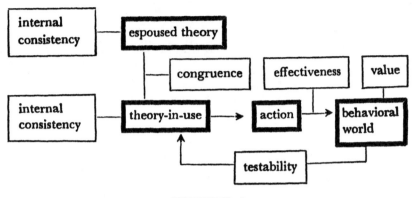

FIGURE 1

related to assumptions about self, others, and the behavioral setting. For example, a theory of action might require two propositions— "Keep people calm" and "Encourage participative government"; if participative government can come about only through heated action, the theory is internally inconsistent, although not logically inconsistent. It is not self-contradictory, as saying a horse is and is not white would be. However, efforts to achieve the governing variables would interfere with óne another.[1]

Each of these variables has a range that is acceptable; within that range, there are levels of preference. As long as calmness does not rise to the point of inertness, we may prefer to have things as calm as possible. As long as participation does not rise to the point of anarchy, we may prefer to have as much of it as possible.

If two or more such variables are internally incompatible in a particular context, one cannot achieve as high a level of preference for both of them taken together as one can for each of them taken separately.[2] If we call such a relationship *incompatibility,* we can reserve the term *internal inconsistency* for the special case in which one variable will fall out of its acceptable range if the other is brought into the acceptable range.

Whether governing variables are incompatible or internally inconsistent depends on a number of factors.

1. Other governing variables—for example, variables related to self-protection, courtesy, or protection of others—may limit the means for achieving some variables.

2. The array of actions envisaged in the theory-in-use may be too narrow. Outside of that array, there may be some means for achieving one variable without dropping the other variable out of its acceptable range.

3. The acceptable range of each variable may be broadened or narrowed so as to make the two variables more or less incompatible.

4. The assumptions in the theory-in-use may be altered so as to make the governing variables more or less incompatible. For example, the assumption "People cannot address the problem of self-government without becoming excited" may be absent from theory-in-use but may be valid in the situation; in this case, the agent would find that he cannot reach acceptable levels of both variables, but he would not understand why.

5. The protagonist may act on his world so as to make it take on characteristics that are either conducive or resistant to the internal consistency of his theory. His behavior may somehow affect people's sense of responsibility in a way that enables participation in self-government without disruption. Or, his behavior may have the opposite effect. Since this behavior is itself a reflection of other aspects of the theory-in-use, theories-in-use may tend to make themselves internally consistent or inconsistent. In the worst case, increasing one's efforts to achieve governing variables decreases one's chance of achieving them; in the best case, increasing one's efforts increases the chance of achieving them.

If two or more governing variables in a theory-in-use are internally inconsistent, then, for given settings of ranges, arrays of strategies, assumptions about the situation, constraining variables, and influences of action on the behavioral world there is no way of falling into the acceptable range for one value without falling out of the acceptable range for the other.

It is important to notice the relationship between internal consistency and constancy. Theory-in-use may be regarded as a program for action designed to keep the values of certain variables constant within acceptable ranges. It is analogous to a computer program for an industrial process that is designed to keep conditions such as temperature and pressure within acceptable limits. The program's internal consistency and the acceptable limits of the variables determine one another. The internal consistency of the theory-in-use conditions the ability of the theory-in-use to achieve the desired constancies; the nature of the desired constancies partly determines the internal consistency of the theory-in-use.

Congruence

Congruence means that one's espoused theory matches his theory-in-use—that is, that one's behavior fits his espoused theory of action. A second (and much-used) meaning of *congruence* is allowing inner feelings to be expressed in actions: when one feels happy, he acts happy.

These two meanings are complementary and show an integration of one's internal (what one who is aware of my feelings and beliefs would perceive) and external (what an outsider who is aware only of my behavior would perceive) state. Lack of congruence between espoused theory and theory-in-use may precipitate search for a modification of either theory since we tend to value both espoused theory (image of self) and congruence (integration of doing and believing).

The caricature of a politician shows him advocating what looks like an espoused theory for the benefit of others, feeling no uneasiness over that theory's incongruence with his theory-in-use. Such an individual probably does not believe in the theory he is advocating although he does have an espoused theory that he believes; incongruence between the latter theory and his theory-in-use may very well cause uneasiness and trigger a change in theory.

The degree of congruence varies over time. One's ability to be himself (to be what he believes and feels) may depend on the kind of behavioral world he creates. A behavioral world of low self-deception, high availability of feelings, and low threat is conducive to congruence; a behavioral world of low self-esteem and high threat is conducive to self-deception and incongruence. If one helps create situations in which others can be congruent, his own congruence is supported.

There is no particular virtue in congruence, alone. An espoused theory that is congruent with an otherwise inadequate theory-in-use is less valuable than an adequate espoused theory that is. incongruent with the inadequate theory-in-use, because then the incongruence can be discovered and provide a stimulus for change. However, given the importance of congruence to a positive sense of self, it is desirable to hold an espoused theory and theory-in-use that tend to become congruent over the long run.

Effectiveness

A theory-in-use is effective when action according to the theory tends to achieve its governing variables. Accordingly, effectiveness depends on: the governing variables held within the theory; the appropriateness of the strategies advanced by the theory; and the accuracy and adequacy of the assumptions of the theory. A strong criterion of effectiveness would require that governing variables stay in the acceptable range once they have been achieved. Some theories-in-use tend to make themselves less effective over time. For example, if an agent tends to become more effective in ways that reduce the effectiveness of others, he may increase the dependence of others on him and make it more and more difficult for himself to be effective. Long-run effectiveness requires achieving governing variables in a way that makes their future achievement increasingly likely. This may require behavior that increases the effectiveness of others.

Long-run effectiveness requires single and double-loop learning. We cannot be effective over the long run unless we can learn new ways of managing existing governing variables when conditions change. In addition, we cannot be effective unless we can learn new governing variables as they become important.

Note that long-run effectiveness does not necessarily mean that action becomes easier. One may respond to increased effectiveness by addressing himself to new governing variables for which he begins by being less effective; progress in effectiveness may be reflected in the sequence of governing variables one tries to achieve.

Testability

Theories of action are theories of control, like the theories involved in engineering, in clinical medicine, or in agricultural technology. They are testable if one can specify the situation, the desired result, and the action through which the result is to be achieved. Testing consists of evaluating whether the action yields its predicted results. If it does, the theory has been confirmed; if it does not, it has been disconfirmed. This tests the effectiveness of the theory.

Special problems regarding testability stem from two related characteristics of theories of action: theories of action are normative (they set norms of behavior) and they are theories of the artificial (they are about a behavioral world that they help to create). There are three basic problems.

1. How can one test theories that prescribe action? How can norms or values be tested?

2. Given that theories-in-use tend to make themselves true in that world, how can they be tested?

3. In a situation of action (particularly in a stressful situation), we are required to display the stance of action—that is, confidence, commitment, decisiveness. But in order to test a theory, one must be tentative, experimental, skeptical. How can we, in the same situations, manifest the stance of action and the experimental stance?

Simple prescriptions ("Don't go near the water!") are not testable because they do not predict results, but if . . . then . . . prescriptions ("If you want to avoid catching a cold, stay away from the water in winter!") are testable. Testing may not be straightforward because assumptions, often hidden, accompany such if . . . then . . . prescriptions. It is assumed here, for example, that you will not expose yourself to other risks of catching cold. Only if we make such assumptions explicit and control for them can we interpret the failure or success of the experiment.[3]

A more challenging problem has to do with the testing of norms or values themselves. Can we test governing variables such as "stay healthy"? In one sense, the answer to this question must be no, because governing variables are not if . . . then . . . propositions and make no predictions. But if one looks at the entire range of variables—the entire field of constancy involved in a theory-in-use —it is meaningful to ask whether, over time, these values will become more or less internally consistent, more or less congruent with the governing variables of espoused theory, and more or less effectively realized. For example, a set of governing variables that includes "stay healthy," "disregard advice," and "seek out dangerous excitement" may turn out to become increasingly incompatible. In this sense, one may test the internal consistency, congruence, and achievability of governing variables. But one may do so only in the context of a theory-in-use in interaction with its behavioral world over time.

The second basic problem of testing theories of action is their self-fulfilling nature. Here are two examples. A teacher believes his students are stupid. He communicates his expectations so that the children behave stupidly. He may then "test" his theory that the children will give stupid answers to his questions by asking them questions and eliciting stupid answers. The longer he interacts with the children, the more his theory will be confirmed. A second example involves a manager who believes his subordinates are passive, dependent, and require authoritarian guidance. He punishes independence by expecting and rewarding dependence with the result that his subordinates do behave passively and dependently toward him. He may test his theory by posing challenges for them and eliciting dependent responses. In both cases, the assumptions turn out to be true; both theories-in-use are self-fulfilling prophecies because the protagonist cannot discover his assumptions to be mistaken or his theory as a whole to be ineffective. The so-called testing brings the behavioral world more nearly into line with the theory, confirming for all concerned the stupidity of the students and the dependence of the subordinates. We call such a theory *self-sealing*.

An outsider may find that the teacher's and the manager's theories-in-use are incompatible with the outsider's perception of the situation. But the outsider operates on a theory-in-use of his own that is different from that of the protagonist. The protagonist himself cannot discover that his theory-in-use is mistaken unless he can envisage an alternative theory and act on it.

The protagonist may find that over the long run his theory becomes less consistent, less congruent, and less effective. This will depend on the stability of conditions under which he operates, the other values that make up his field of constancy, and other factors. As time goes on, the protagonist is less able to get information from others (students or subordinates) that might disconfirm his theory-in-use. Others become less willing to confront, to display conflict, to reveal feelings. In this sense, the protagonist's self-sealing theory becomes progressively less testable over time.[4]

Consider those affected by the protagonist's theory-in-use. The students, for example, may deceive their teacher about their real feelings and beliefs and still remain open to others who reveal that the teacher's assumptions are inaccurate; after all, the students live in many behavioral worlds, not only in the world of the school. But perhaps the students have no behavioral world free of these assumptions. If so, others could not discover real feelings and beliefs different from those that confirm the teacher's theory. Deception of others would have been converted to self-deception. In the behavioral worlds created by such theories-in-use, there would be no way to discover that the teacher's theory is self-sealing. For this, outside events would have to cause the theory-in-use to fail, or someone with a different theory-in-use would have to expose the students to a different behavioral world long enough to recover their awareness of feelings and beliefs different from those expected by the teacher.

The interaction of theory-in-use and behavioral world has a political as well as an experimental dimension. The continued exercise and confirmation of a theory-in-use can be seen as a political process that proceeds from suppressing certain kinds of behavior and information to creating conditions in which others repress both elements. The theory has then made itself true and, by its own lights, effective. Orwell in *1984* and Laing in *The Politics of Experience* both describe such political processes. There need be no conscious construction of theory and reality on the part of a powerful protagonist; one might say that the theory constructs its own reality.

The third basic problem of testing theories of action concerns the stance we should take toward our theories-in-use. One must regard any theory as tentative, subject to error, and likely to be disconfirmed; one must be suspicious of it. However, one's theory-in-use is his only basis for action. To be effective, a person must be able to act according to his theory-in-use clearly and decisively, especially under stress. One must treat his theory-in-use as both a psychological certainty and an intellectual hypothesis.

The apparent paradox is heightened in unstable situations of action where one is overwhelmed by information and unable to develop a grounded theory of what is going on. Here, norms for behavior substitute for knowledge. One need not know precisely what is going on because, independent of such knowledge, norms provide a basis for action.

An interventionist is a man struggling to make his model of man come true. In an unstable and uncertain world that nevertheless demands action, he puts a normative template on reality. All the more paradoxical, then, the demand that theories-in-use be treated as hypotheses.

Hainer (1968) described this existential stance as one of "affirmation without dogmatism." He considers the here and now to be both prior to and more fundamental than one's theory about it, treating theories as perspectives on reality that are also bases for action. Operationally, we are ready to discover that our theory is mistaken and to change it; yet we are reluctant to make such a change since change implies unsteadiness or flightiness that would themselves be a basis for failure. The commitment to focus on the here and now lets us encounter the unpredictable and lets us deal with the next piece of reality when we encounter it, modifying our theory-in-use as events require.

Our ability to take such a stance and to be conscious of taking it (as a part of an ethic for situations of uncertainty) is a model of such behavior for others, reducing their need for here-and-now certainty and allowing them to be freer to test their own theories without giving them up as a basis for action. Their doing so, in turn, further encourages us to do so.

Values for the World Created by Theory

Because theories-in-use are mutually interdependent with their behavioral worlds, it is relevant to ask not only "Is your theory effective?" but also "How do you value the behavioral world created by the theory?"

One cannot and should not clearly separate the questions of knowledge applicable to the construction of the theory and the questions of value applicable to the construction of reality. For, as we have seen, these processes determine one another.

Should a protagonist's theory meet all of the criteria we have described, one can still ask, "How do I value the world he has created?" Even if the theory-in-use is effective for its own values, successfully repressive of all others to the point that testability has no meaning, one may still ask this question.

The manager in our earlier example may become more and more convinced that all of his subordinates are passive and that all initiative in the organization must come from him. But he may also come increasingly to dislike the behavioral world of his organization in which expanding demands on him are accompanied by expanding resentment and distrust.

In short, the criteria so far elaborated provide a basis for judging theories of action, but they do not substitute for the evaluation of the world created by the theory.

It is clear how an outsider, with an independent theory-in-use, could engage in such an evaluation. If the protagonist, himself, is to do so, however, he must begin to make a connection between his own theory-in-use and those features of his behavioral world he most dislikes; otherwise his negative evaluation will have no bearing on this theory. And other governing variables than those contained in his theory-in-use must be alive, or becoming alive, for him; his ability to ask such a question implies that he is able to envisage, even to some small extent, a behavioral world different from the one he has created.

Brief Review

We have so far described a conceptual framework for considering theories of action, their structure and role, their status as tacit knowledge, their interaction with the behavioral worlds in which they function, and the criteria that apply to them.

Theories of action are theories that can be expressed as follows: In situation S, if you intend consequence C, do A, given assumptions $a_1 \ldots a_n$. Theories of action exist as espoused theories and as theories-in-use, which govern actual behavior. Theories-in-use tend to be tacit structures whose relation to action is like the relation of grammar-in-use to speech; they contain assumptions about self, others, and environment—these assumptions constitute a microcosm of science in everyday life.

Theories-in-use are vehicles for achieving and maintaining governing variables within acceptable ranges; the governing variables constitute the field of constancy in which deliberate behavior takes place. Building theories-in-use involves learning about managing variables and learning about changing variables. Theories-in-use are theories of the artificial; they help to create as well as describe the behavioral worlds to which they apply. Hence, theory-construction and reality-construction go together. The constancy of theories-in-use is considered as valuable as the constancy of the behavioral worlds created by those theories.

The concept of theory-building or theory-learning, particularly the kind of learning that requires change in governing variables, involves a paradox. The impetus toward constancy of theories-in-use and behavioral worlds impedes change in the governing variables.

Theory-Building Process and Dilemmas

How, then, do theory-building and learning occur? Some theory-building is a linear increase of building-blocks of experience; new microtheories that extend the application of old governing variables probably develop in this way. However, the kind of theory-building that involves both change in the governing variables and double-loop learning tends to be convulsive, taking the form of infrequent, discontinuous eruptions that are initiated by dilemmas. This pattern of change probably derives from the nature of dilemmas and from the characteristic patterns of response to them,[5] which will be described next.

Dilemmas consist of conflicts of requirements that are considered central and therefore intolerable. The dilemmas that are important to the development of theories-in-use may be organized around several criteria that apply to the relationship between theories-in-use and the behavioral world.

Dilemmas of incongruity arise out of the progressively developing incongruity between espoused theory (on which self-esteem depends) and theory-in-use. For example, a politician who sees himself as believing in participatory democracy is disturbed by the manipulative, rough-shod tactics he uses in his career. Another agent's espoused values of warmth and sensitivity turn out to be incompatible with the pain he finds himself inflicting on others.

In order for such conflicts to become dilemmas, the elements of espoused theory must be central to the protagonist's self-image, and events must emphasize the conflict between espoused theory and theory-in-use in ways that overcome normal attempts to avoid noticing the conflict. A potential dilemma may exist long before it surfaces.

Dilemmas of inconsistency arise when the governing variables of theory-in-use become increasingly incompatible. For example, one person finds it increasingly impossible, in the behavioral world he has helped to create, both to win and to contain the hostility of others when he wins. But the person values both the winning and the repression of hostility. Another person finds it increasingly impossible, in the world of the family he has helped to create, to do his duty regarding his children by punishing them and to maintain their respect. This person needs both to do his duty and to retain the respect of his children for doing his duty regarding them (derived from Laing, 1970).

Dilemmas of effectiveness arise when governing variables, in a theory-in-use/behavioral-world interaction, become less and less achievable over time, finally reaching the point at which they fall outside the acceptable range. For example, a person seeks to keep others calm and controlled by suppressing conflict; the hostility engendered by the suppression reaches an unavoidable boiling point so that no one is calm and controlled. Another person values a strategy of combat because it is familiar, because he knows how to use it, and because its use carries high status with it. But conditions change (others become aware of the strategy) so that the strategy becomes less and less effective.

Dilemmas of value arise when the protagonist comes increasingly—and, finally, intolerably—to dislike the behavioral world his theory-in-use has helped to create. For example, the protagonist values trust within his own group and also values the progress of the group. To achieve this progress, the protagonist is devious and manipulative toward outsiders. Group members, who act as though

they expect people to be generally consistent in their behavior, progressively mistrust the protagonist, and the atmosphere within the
group becomes progressively more manipulative and devious.

   Dilemmas of testability arise when the protagonist, who
values his ability to confirm or disconfirm his assumptions, finds that
he is eventually completely cut off from the possibility of doing so
by the behavioral world he has helped to create. For example, a
manager finds that his subordinates and peers, conditioned by the
mistrust they have come to feel for him and by the punishment they
feel they have received when they "leveled" with him, no longer
give him any valid information at all.

   These kinds of dilemmas are not mutually exclusive; for example, a dilemma of effectiveness may also be a dilemma of testability, depending on the perspective taken. However, all dilemmas
share certain characteristics: there is conflict between some element
of the prevailing theory-in-use and some criterion applicable to the
theory. The protagonist experiences this conflict as a central one—
that is, the values he places on the elements of theory-in-use and the
criterion are central rather than peripheral; in the cycle of interactions between theory-in-use and behavioral world, the conflict gets
progressively worse.

   The dilemmas may be created suddenly, as conditions shift
in the behavioral world, or they may emerge gradually through the
cycles of interaction. In either case, change in the governing variables of theory-in-use tends to be convulsive because of a characteristic pattern of response to dilemmas.

   The responses to emerging dilemmas are not characteristically efforts to effect substantive change in governing variables. We
value the constancy of our theories-in-use and our behavioral
worlds. Hence, theories-in-use tend to be self-maintaining. We tend
to adopt strategies to avoid perceiving that data do not fit, that
behavioral reality is progressively diverging from one's theory of it,
that one's theory is not testing out.

   The repertoire of devices by which we try to protect our
theories-in-use from dilemmas displays great imagination. Some of
the more striking devices follow.

   We try to compartmentalize—to keep our espoused theory

in one place and our theory-in-use in another, never allowing them to meet. One goes on speaking in the language of one theory, acting in the language of another, and maintaining the illusion of congruence through systematic self-deception.

We become selectively inattentive to the data that point to dilemmas; we simply do not notice signs of hostility in others, for example.

The protagonist adopts a political method of suppressing the offensive data; for example, he succeeds in frightening others enough so that they will not reveal their mistrust of him.

The protagonist acts, sometimes violently, to remove the offending elements or himself from the situation. He either gets the trouble-maker fired or—his behavioral world having become unbearable—he moves to California. Or he may resolve to break off relations with his son.

The protagonist acts in subtle ways to make a self-sealing, self-fulfilling prophecy of his threatened theory-in-use—like the manager or teacher in our earlier examples—by using his authority to elicit the desired behavior from others and to cause the rest to be suppressed.

The protagonist introduces change, but only into his espoused theory—leaving his theory-in-use unchanged.

The protagonist introduces marginal change into his theory-in-use, leaving the core untouched.

These devices and others like them, individually or in combination, tend to maintain theory-in-use in the face of the emerging dilemma. Therefore, even if the signs of the dilemma have appeared gradually, the eventual change in governing variables tends to be convulsive. By the time the conflict becomes intolerable, the protagonist tends to have exhausted his stock of defenses; he is well into an explosive situation.

All of these dilemmas are, in a fundamental sense, dilemmas of effectiveness. If the protagonist finds intolerable the inconsistency of his governing variables or his inability to confirm or disconfirm his assumptions, it is because inconsistency and lack of testability also mean inability to achieve minimum realization of governing variables. If incongruity is intolerable, it is because the protagonist finds

that he cannot realize the central governing variables of the espoused
theory on which his self-esteem depends. If there were no need for
effectiveness, there would be no dilemmas.

Hence, the basic dilemma is one of effectiveness and constancy. The protagonist strives to be effective and to keep constant
his theory-in-use and the behavioral world he has created. When,
finally, he cannot do both in spite of his full repertoire of defenses,
he may change the governing variables of his theory-in-use. This
dialectic shapes the theory-building process.

Part Two will show that certain characteristic dilemmas derive from an underlying model of our theories-in-use. By making our
theories-in-use explicit and inferring from them their underlying
model, we can signal and explain these dilemmas. Subsequently, we
will analyze a process of transition from this model to an alternative
one, according to which change in the governing variables may
occur through processes different from those we have so far described.

PART II

ACTION

Part I defined espoused theories and theories-in-use and established the differences between them. Part I also showed that theories-in-use create the behavioral world because people act according to the requirements of the governing variables of their theories-in-use.

Part II will relate specific theories-in-use to effectiveness and learning in human interactions. Our aim is not only to be accurate about the theories-in-use that actually govern human interactions but to describe them so that they can be criticized and changed.

Part II presents a model of the prevailing theories-in-use in our society. Model I consists of a set of governing variables; behavioral actions; and consequences for the behavioral world (at the individual, interpersonal, group, and intergroup levels), for the quality of learning, and for the probable degree of effectiveness. We will describe the diagnostic methods and the sample used to develop the model, which is an abstraction.

Next, we propose an alternative model, model II, that has a different set of governing variables and behavioral strategies that should lead to more effective individual and systemic behavior. Finally, we discuss the transitional process from model I to model II.

Chapter 3

Diagnosing
Theories-in-Use

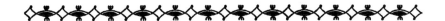

Theories-in-use are complex. If all behavior were to be accounted for, the resulting account would be so complex that it would not help us to understand and guide behavior. Therefore, we need models of theories-in-use—general characterizations of how theory applies to human interactions. Such models would describe the complex range of microtheories-in-use by members of society.

Difficulties

Constructing models of theories-in-use is difficult. Few people think about their theories-in-use. Paradoxically, their theories-in-use prevent them from doing so. Asking people to think about their theories-in-use is not only unusual but contradicts much of what they have learned about understanding and managing behavior. Understandably, people who have done little thinking about constructing their theories-in-use tend to lack the skills necessary to develop them, and the skills they have learned may be dysfunctional in this respect. A central skill for developing theories-in-use is describing directly observable behavior. Few people learn this skill; indeed, we tend to reward children to learn to use abstract concepts to describe their behavior because such concepts are more economical. Such abstract concepts are not always helpful in developing theories-in-use. Constructing theories-in-use requires the diagnostician to minimize his covert attributions about the actor's behavior although this activity—according to some social psychologists—is at the heart of human social life.

Individuals programmed with skills, knowledge, and values dysfunctional to constructing theories-in-use tend to create groups that reinforce their programming; this inhibits the development of group dynamics that facilitate the construction of theories-in-use; it also makes learning difficult because the individuals find themselves locked in not only by their own behavior but also by the group dynamics that these behaviors produce. They are now confronted with what seems like an insurmountable challenge, since the complicated and difficult task of constructing their theories-in-use depends on simultaneously overcoming and altering the dynamics of the group in which they are trying to learn. No wonder that attempts to help individuals construct their theories-in-use evoke reactions ranging from bewilderment ("What *are* you asking us to do?") to dismay ("How will we ever create such a model?") to embarrassment ("I'd feel stupid saying it that way") to fear ("You're asking us to change the basis of our life") and to astonishment ("You mean you're asking us to redesign our culture?").

Method

Constructing models of theories-in-use depends on certain assumptions about the goals of the enterprise for both researchers and participants; about the motivation of the participants; and about conditions that facilitate the task.

A basic assumption is that constructing theories-in-use will help participants become more effective in their interactions with others. Their wish to become more effective is their motivation, which must be strong.

The goals of the process must be to: produce data that help

the individual to learn; help individuals gain insight into the conditions under which their defenses as well as their theories-in-use inhibit and facilitate their growth and the growth of others; provide information from which individuals can design programs for self-improvement, gain help from others, and evaluate their progress; and help individuals learn how to discover their own theories-in-use and generate new ones—that is, learn to generate directly observable data, infer theories-in-use, alter theories-in-use, and test new theories of action.

These goals must be pursued in an atmosphere that allows the individual to reveal his behavior to himself and others with minimal conscious distortion, which would occur if the individual felt defensive; the model-constructing process should be free of questions that could be answered with generalizations drawn from espoused theory and should focus instead on directly observable behavior.

For example, the sentences "*I told* John that he was probably going to be hired," "*I asked* my client to be patient," and "*I tried to get* the group to look at its behavior" do not describe actual behavior but only the speaker's intentions, as the italicized words indicate. Such information is not adequate to generate theories-in-use. We need to know what the individual told John; how the client was asked to be patient; and by what behavior the speaker tried to get the group to look at its behavior. From such information we might infer that John felt he was not going to be hired; that the client felt punished; and that group members felt they were being diverted from important activities.

To study the model-constructing process, we have experimented with role-playing and with group discussions, both tape-recorded and video-taped. However, we have emphasized the use of case studies written by participants according to a common format because these studies are most readily accepted and administered. Our findings from role-playing and group discussions confirm the conclusions drawn from case material.

We asked participants to write case studies that focused on what was actually said, how the participants actually behaved, and how others responded. If the cases participants wanted to describe were large units of behavior, such as a case of long-term intervention, they were asked to select one or two crucial episodes and discuss those in detail; this was to avoid the abstract nature of summaries. For example, a two-hour meeting might be described as "The two sides met and finally agreed on a course of action," or "My role was to be a facilitator." Such abstractions are of little help in constructing a theory-in-use.

To minimize the probability of role-playing in the individual's case study, participants were asked to choose settings in which they were genuinely involved. For example, a discussion about sharing scarce financial resources, choosing a town plan, or developing an underlying social policy would encourage individuals to behave according to their actual interests.

The directions participants were given for preparing their case studies are shown in Figure 2.

Participants were asked to write about a difficult case as well as an easy one. We assumed that a case the individual considered difficult would be one that involved him. We also believed that the difficult case would be important to the participant and would tap his commitment to learn about his behavior and to be reeducated. However, a difficult episode may produce unintended distortion, incompetent behavior, and theories-in-use that are self-sealing. This is why we also asked subjects to describe an easy case; we wanted to see if the theories-in-use differed. Were there more or fewer dilemmas, and were there any differences in the way the dilemmas were treated?

Our study consisted of the following participants: (1) 20 secondary school and university administrators; (2) 60 professionals in the humanities and arts (museum administrators, orchestra managers, drama directors, art professors); (3) 40 business executives; (4) 30 graduate students in education; (5) 15 graduate students in the arts and sciences; and (6) 30 beginning professionals in organizational development (from England). The total population was 195; women represented at least 45 percent of groups 1, 2, and 4, and at least 20 percent of the same groups represented minorities.

Participants find the instructions easy to understand. The most frequent question is about length. We prefer a concise outline to a long essay but leave it up to the individual. The next most frequent question is how will their cases be used? We answer that

FIGURE 2

Please describe a challenging intervention or interaction with one or more individuals that (1) you have already experienced or (2) you expect to experience in the near future.

If you have difficulty with either of these conditions, try a hypothetical case in which you doubt your effectiveness.

Begin the description with a paragraph about the purpose of your intervention, the setting, the people involved, and any other important characteristics.

Next, write a few paragraphs regarding your strategy. What were your objectives, how did you intend to achieve them, and why did you select those goals and strategies?

Next, write a few pages of the dialogue that actually occurred or that you expected to occur. Use the following format.

On this side of the page, write what was going on in your mind while each person in the dialogue (including yourself) is speaking.	On this side of the page, write what each person actually said or what you expected him to say. Continue writing the dialogue until you believe your major points are illustrated. (The dialogue should be at least two pages long.)

Finally, after you reread your case, describe the underlying assumptions that you think you held about effective action.

---

other participants in the study will read them and comment on them, so real names and places should not be used.

An important part of our design for eliciting theories-in-use is group discussion. Taking one case at a time, participants work with a researcher at the task of making explicit the governing variables and the strategies for action that seem to determine the participant's behavior as it is recorded in the case. Then participants try to assess their perception of self and others in the case and what characteristics of the behavioral world are manifested in the case. All participants, including the case-writer, jointly assess the writer's effectiveness in the case situation.

The quality of the group is crucial; it must be a group that helps its members to learn. If some group members have theories-in-use that make learning difficult, doesn't that make the group dynamics less conducive to learning? Many members seem implicitly concerned about this and tend to put on their best behavior. Such behavior is sensed to be forced, which creates a condition of low trust. The group's discussion can degenerate into glib generalities. As this cocktail-party milieu becomes increasingly apparent, some participants begin to confront it, even though effective confrontation may require skills the members have not yet learned.

In such a situation, researchers focused on those dimensions of the group process that seemed to mirror the theories-in-use revealed in the case material and to encourage participants to provide directly observable data, give minimally evaluative feedback, and confront—in themselves and in others—dilemmas of incongruity, inconsistency, and ineffectiveness.

Building a group setting conducive to learning about theories-in-use required work on some of the very dilemmas revealed in the case material. This constituted both a disadvantage (because these dilemmas impede learning) and an opportunity (because the group process itself became a source of additional behavioral data from which theories-in-use could be constructed).

Case Studies

Next, case studies generated by these instructions will illustrate the potential of this approach. We have selected cases that were especially rich in data. The first two case studies were generated by an aware, articulate minister who was concerned about his own and others' growth.

Minister (*difficult case*). The Sunday after President Nixon's decision to invade Cambodia, 50 members of the church met to determine what response they could make. One response was to hold a protest demonstration on the front lawn of the church. That meant seeking the permission of the executive committee, which is responsible for use of the property, or bringing the matter before the congregation for approval. The latter course of action would have required a lapse of several days so members of the congregation could be notified, whereas the executive committee was scheduled to meet the following night. It was decided that a representative group would appear before the executive committee to make an unprecedented request to use the church property for a public protest of U.S. policy in Indochina.

The chairman of the 12-member executive committee is a conservative man who has, in the past, indicated great discomfort when people get upset. He has been told of the unusual request to be made. On entering the meeting room, the chairman found 35 other church members in addition to the executive committee.

This was a pressure setting. It intimidated the chairman, who had not demonstrated flexibility and the capacity to be at ease under pressure in the past.

Chairman: Good evening. I am impressed by the unusual number of our good members who have come here tonight. [The chairman reflects considerable nervousness. After a few opening remarks, he asks the minister to lead the group in prayer.]

The members of the executive committee were assumed to favor the proposal; most people thought it would be passed. To bring the matter before the executive committee rather than to call a special meeting of the congregation made an immediate response to the Cambodian invasions possible, but it left the majority of the church members, particularly the dissenters, with the realization that they had no opportunity to participate in an important decision.

Minister: Lord, these are momentous and agonizing days. Tonight we reflect the anguish that grips our nation and divides its citizens. We need the wisdom of Your spirit as we face hard questions before us. Enable us to be open and compassionate toward one another as we wrestle with these questions in the light of our own faith. Amen.

Chairman: We have a group of visitors with us to make a request. After hearing from them, we may want to go into executive session to consider the matter.

It is clear that I am not neutral regarding the proposal to be made. The institutional church must be responsive to critical current moral issues like this one.

I was convinced that the outcome of the vote would not have been affected whether the executive committee continued in open meeting or in executive session. I did desire full participation by all present, however.

I did not feel that the chairman wanted to hide anything in an executive session but rather that he simply could not cope in the pressure-cooker situation in which he found himself.

I took the position that the chairman's feelings of inadequacy had to be endured by him and that open participation was a goal to be pursued. But, in that room of almost 50 people, no more than two or three would have been able to disagree with the proposal. An overwhelming majority favored

Minister: Mr. Chairman, we all know this is a most unusual situation. Everyone in this room is a member of this church. We might want to consider remaining together throughout the evening as we sort out the ramifications of the request that will be set before us.

Chairman: I brought with me tonight *Robert's Rules of Order,* which makes provision for a committee like this to go into executive session.

Minister: You are quite right in pointing up that provision. I think we need to think through, however, how this congregation can best deal with the situation that is before us, and the implications of the action that will be proposed here tonight. Our by-laws indicate that all meetings of the church are open to all members.

Chairman: I thought we might make a more careful, considered judgment if, after hearing the request, we went into executive session.

Minister: We are faced with a matter that is going to be thoroughly aired by church members in the days ahead no matter what decision is made. If our discussion tonight is open to all who are present, we'll have the advantage of hearing all opinions first-hand rather than second-hand.

the proposal, a heavy imbalance which did not represent the feelings of the entire congregation. The chairman moved that an executive session be held and was defeated; the proposal to use the church lawn for a public demonstration was carried by a vote of 10 to 2.

The immediate objective was achieved, but the price was creating a win/lose situation and making many church members feel that they had not been allowed to share in one of the most momentous decisions that had ever been before the church.

In reading the case, note the following points.

1. The minister did little to alleviate the chairman's discomfort from the pressures of the meeting.

2. The minister's desire to act quickly precluded participation in the decision by other church members. Ironically, President Nixon had used the same strategy of intervention—he had announced his plans for Cambodia in a way that precluded participation in the decision and made resistance difficult. The minister was shocked to realize that he had used the same tactics as President Nixon; however, he defended his tactics by saying there had been so little time. Another participant pointed out that President Nixon had probably used the same excuse. Other participants suggested that the minister should at least have been aware of the dilemma, admitting it to the executive committee.

3. The minister consciously avoided discussing some of his assumptions in order to win. For example, he did not discuss openly the problem of acting quickly versus broader participation.

In a paper the minister wrote after the discussion, he stated: "The comparison to Nixonian tactics hit me very hard; both of us enforcing our will and using our power to accomplish our purposes upon a constituency that contains a significant segment of dissenters.

Both of us are convinced that our aims and actions are right and good; both of us create a closed system that leads to self-fulfilling prophecy. That is not my self-conscious aim, *but that is my action*. I own it—painfully.

"The dilemmas remain. At the personal level, it has been a case of survival for me. I have prided myself on my political acumen (Nixon again), and I have survived. Many of my professional peers have not survived and/or have quit the ministry. Over the years when it has come to the moment of the political votes, I have been quite sure in advance that I would "win," and I have staked my ministry upon the church going in a particular direction—the direction I deemed proper and right.

"This illustrates the dilemmas regarding the nature and task of the church. The church, to be faithful to its own mission, cannot operate by consensus. Historically the church has been apostate, allowing the values and virtues of the culture to supercede the Biblical mandate. Throughout the Old Testament, the prophets are calling Israel to repent and Jesus is vehement in his condemnation of Judaism, as practiced in his day. He draws the line and challenges others to follow.

"Question: how can the church take an advocacy position under my leadership that makes clear its posture regarding the basic moral issues of our time, and still not be manipulative and exercise power in a way that creates a win/lose situation that only corrupts the environment and develops self-fulfilling prophecies?

"Do I trust the membership of the church? Am I willing to be guileless and let it all hang out—allowing the process to be fully and genuinely open-ended? That was a principle I thought I stood for; but what does my behavior say? I have advocated power to the people, but worked like hell to see to it that the people moved in the direction that I thought right and proper. And if I could convince myself that God was on my side, then I would be doubly rewarded —not only winning but being virtuous too. The church has a long history of that, and the results have been uniformly bad.

"I find very compelling that the win/lose syndrome is as significant a moral problem for our society as the specific moral issues (race, war, welfare, and so on) with which I have been concerned. In the geometry of morality, the left and right meet on the far side of the circle, and the people say, 'a plague on both your houses.' I must learn some new behavior—rooted and grounded in a trust of people, with the freedom to make their own decisions, and a process that is genuinely open and not manipulative and self-fulfilling. That is the task."

The following week, the minister wrote another paper as a result of reading and thinking about his theory-in-use as constructed in class. "I am persuaded that my behavior generates a closed system, with nontestable, self-fulfilling results. It is not a self-conscious design, but a result of my doing what comes naturally. That scares me, for it means that my spontaneous behavior produces a system that perpetuates mistrust and diplomacy—and that does not match my self-image of what I want to be and what I want to do.

"I know how to win. I have a decade of data in the Church. . . . I don't have to learn how to be 'successful,' but the gap between what I really want to be and what my present behavior now reveals is enormous.

"On critical moral issues, *I have determined* that the church must act—and I can give all the theological and Biblical reasons—so I have manipulated the environment and people to assure that the church would act, in ways that *I determined* were right. The expectations, the prophecies have been fulfilled. I have won, but what am I now left with? The realization that the win/lose game pollutes the moral environment far more perniciously than all the fine achievements in the name of combatting racism, war, and the scandal of public structures that dehumanizes people. I could scream.

"To the degree that I can recognize my present situation, I think it would be useless to deny and disparage what abilities I have and what things I can do and do well. My need, as I see it, is to become sensitive and self-conscious of the impact of my behavior, and to begin to learn (hopefully) how to behave in ways that are more consistent with my deepest aspirations. It is not a matter of being one thing or another; it means being realistic about all sides of me, and being willing to put into practice behavior that will protect others from my manipulative, controlling, and self-righteous side.

"I don't have to win. I do not believe that I corner the market of wisdom as to what the church ought to do. I am ready to be open and follow the insights of others. I want to function in a way that allows the contributions of others to be exercised—not on trivial issues—but on the gut issues. I am ready to learn something new."

The minister later indicated that he saw a discrepancy between moving the church in the direction he thought was proper and remaining open-minded. He saw that his espoused theory had been participation in decision-making by all church members, but his theory-in-use had been, in the end, to manipulate church members to accede to his views on church policy. He realized that his theory-in-use was a closed system, nontestable and self-fulfilling. These insights enabled him to imagine other patterns of behavior and motivated him to pursue them. He formulated three questions he wanted to focus on: (1) How can I learn to be more open and honest about my views and yet invite others to confront them? (2) How can I develop the skills to advocate my views in a way that encourages others to advocate their views? (3) Can the institutional church be responsive to the basic moral issues of our society? How can I develop the skills to help bring this about without using such immoral techniques as unilateral control and manipulation?

Minister (*easy case*). Twelve church members were at a retreat center for the weekend, with the minister serving as leader. The group had a successful marathon discussion that lasted from Saturday morning until past midnight that night. When the group reconvened on Sunday morning, a sense of accomplishment and good feelings prevailed. However, Ruth, one of the participants, had expressed her detachment both verbally and through body language, although she had said she had come of her own choice rather than to please her husband, who was also a participant. She had been assured that she was free to set her own pace regarding her degree of participation. Today, she was slouched against a wall with a blanket wrapped around her; she said she was very tired and that she was fighting a cold.

> *Minister:* How are people feeling this morning? [A number of immediate affirmative responses follow.]
> *Ruth:* I'm tired.
> *Minister:* You look a bit detached.

On Saturday, Ruth had expressed her conviction that nothing ever changed in a person's life. I took exception to her pessimism. I knew that it was important for Ruth to maintain her own sense of independence and freedom. When the group reconvened Sunday morning, I didn't expect Ruth to break out of her shell.

Ruth: I've got a cold and the kids were sick before we came.

Minister: Are you telling us more than that?

Her "maybe" was her first expression that she had more to share with the group.

Ruth: Maybe.

I felt the need to move very tentatively with her, enabling her to stop at any moment she chose to do so.

Minister: You are free to tell us what we [sic] want. We are here to help, if there is anything that you would like from this group. At the same time, you are free to say nothing. You are Ruth, and that's good enough. Whatever you choose to do, you do for yourself.

The good results others had achieved during the marathon may have been the determining factor for Ruth's tentative reaching out. Her "I'm afraid" was my clue that she might be ready to work.

Ruth: I'm afraid.

She still had to identify that readiness.

Minister: Would you like to try to get at some of that fear with me?

Ruth: Yes.

I asked her to move the physical location of her body in order to reinforce her decision.

Minister: Then why don't you join me out here in the center. [I move out to the center of the group, and Ruth moves away from the wall and joins me inside the circle of people.]

The minister maintains a controlling stance. His interventions tend to reduce Ruth's free choice. For example, when the minister tells Ruth "You look a bit detached," he is attributing feelings to her. His question, "Are you telling us more than that?" exerts pressure for her to reveal her feelings. His next response begins with a Freudian slip—"You are free to tell us what *we* want." Again, he is manipulative; telling a person he is free to do something tends to coerce that person to do what the speaker wishes. When Ruth admitted she was afraid, the minister invited her "to get at the fear" with him, not with the group.

When the minister discussed this case, all but one other participant said they doubted the minister's sincerity in saying, "You are Ruth, and that's good enough." They felt the minister was pushing Ruth to discuss her feelings.

The minister said that he now saw his theories-in-use as protecting himself by (1) speaking in inferred categories ("You are detached."), (2) being blind to his manipulative control, and (3) designing and managing the environment so he was in control.

City planner (difficult case). The university at which another participant, a city planner, was teaching received a grant to study student housing and educational facilities in the inner city. The city planner's research group wanted to develop real prototypes, so they chose an area where major private development was imminent—that is, where change was about to occur. They first contacted the private developers, ABC Corporation, who agreed to give the researchers access to the corporation's technical staff. Just then the project was deferred due to the recession and citizen protest. The research group had committed itself to the study on the assumption that the project was not tentative, but suddenly it was, and the research group was accused of being in league with the developers. A meeting with the community group was held in order to iron out the problem. The city planner offers his impressions:

Appear confident. Assume that the project is to go ahead.	*City planner:* Well, gentlemen, is everyone here who was invited? I see we have a few onlookers. Why don't you come down around the table, too? The reason we're here is to try to explain to you the

involvement of the university in this project.

X is not able to visualize the project. He has always disliked liberals. Emphasize the research aspect and neutrality. But they don't believe in neutrality. Even trying out new solutions in the public interest is a concept that they do not understand.

X: What do you mean, project? It isn't even approved yet.

City planner: I mean our research project . . . [He explains the project]. The fact that ABC Corporation is in the area complicates the problems. . . .

Y: For us, too. Aren't you working for ABC Corporation?

City planner: No. We're here because of our research interest. (Focusses on academic interests and interest to help citizens.) Our only connection with ABC Corporation is that they have given us access to their office and their plans for the area.

Basic mistrust in us; a belief that we're not too smart and may be used. Could be true. Darn it, we're studying an abstraction, as far as they're concerned. Should we try to justify that abstraction or admit that it's a power game and that we inadvertently picked their opponents as one of our allies?

Z: Yes, so they can use you to find out what's going on.

City planner: I don't think so. . . . We can just as well try to solve the problem without ABC Corporation.

They can't understand how we could possibly really mean it about helping them. No trust.

Z: So you're helping them to make the project better. Why don't you help us to try to kill the project? Some of you even live in the area. But, then, you can easily move out.

When the city planner began the meeting, he was aware that the community was hostile to the project. The meeting was called to discuss the issues. Instead of beginning by testing whether the community actually was hostile, the city planner began by taking a positive stance to show confidence that the project will go ahead.

X's first statement questions whether the project is to go ahead. Again, the city planner does not encourage X to say what he feels, and he privately decides that X does not like liberals. The city planner not only ignores the increasingly overt hostility of the community representatives toward the project but responds by focusing on the research group's position of neutrality and rationality.

The community representatives' mistrust becomes even more clear. The city planner is aware of the mistrust; he wonders if there might not be some valid basis for it. Again, he doesn't express any of these ideas because (1) that would mean expressing his feelings, which would (2) lead the city planner to feel he was losing control of the meeting. He helps to smother the community representatives' feelings as well as his own. He makes further attributions about community representatives and does not test them.

In his description of the easy intervention, the city planner manifested similar strategies. He said he "took charge" of another meeting; he made attributions about how to manage, control, and win over the clients; and he suppressed his own negative feelings as well as discouraging the clients from surfacing theirs. To illustrate, we include a few of the comments that he did not share with others: "(1) [Begin the meeting] by establishing credentials, haul in as many names as possible, emphasize that we are not hot-shot consultants. Be positive and persuasive. (2) Businesses like the ones at the meeting are often conservative. They may do something to keep up with a competitor. (3) Flatter the people. Indicate our humbleness but also let them know we're working from a position of strength. (4) They want to keep their information secret but want to find out what others are doing. (5) Tries to brush me off—but I will resist."

Social worker. A social worker is trying to help a client she feels is not really changing his behavior. She writes, "I feel annoyed with him and pretty determined either to cut off our interaction, delve more deeply into his problem, or demonstrate to him that he is in fact not interested in changing at all. The last alternative is fine with me. I dislike wasting my time on futile activity."

We see that the social worker: (1) has already decided the course the next session should take; (2) has attributed characteristics to the client without telling him so he can confirm or deny them; (3) has decided that the responsibility for failure lies with the client and therefore does not explore her possible role in the apparent failure; (4) assumes that she is responsible for the client's behavior; and (5) denies responsibility for her sense of failure. (She states that she dislikes having her time wasted, but a more complete and accurate statement might be, "I dislike being with a client whom I cannot help because I feel that I have been partially responsible for wasting my time.")

Later, the social worker writes, "I knew that I had to be very much on top of the situation so that we would not fall back into our old ways of interacting. I tried to keep my objectives in mind all the time and I tried to push myself to think and evaluate clearly because I knew he did not want to hear what I had to say, and I could slip backward in a weak moment."

This strategy assumes that the social worker is in control and initiates responsibility. However, the social worker's espoused values are to promote client growth and responsibility. Her dilemma is that she is faced with a client whom she feels unable to help unless she violates her espoused values.

Using a different analysis, we might say that although the social worker claims to dislike people who are dependent, passive, and weak, she selects strategies and tactics that reinforce such characteristics. Perhaps she needs clients to exhibit such characteristics so she can accept her predispositions to control others; she may be unaware of this. She may even have selected a theory-in-use that minimizes the probability of being confronted on this issue, by either the client or herself. For example, if she has decided that dependency, passivity, and weakness are the client's fault, if she has to control the client, and if the client senses this theory-in-use, we may hypothesize that: (1) the client will find it difficult to confront the social worker on these possibilities; (2) there is little probability that the social worker and the client will confront and explore these issues; (3) the social worker will not encourage clients to explore behavior that would lead to growth; and (4) the social worker's original diagnosis (that the client was not going to grow) is a self-fulfilling prophecy.

Now let us turn to the case material:

Social worker: You seem to want or expect personal change to be easy.

Client: No, I don't. I expect it to be hard but I know it's for my own benefit. But you must understand I have to work within certain contraints . . . [cut off by social worker].

Social worker: Why? You're working within "certain constraints" now and you're not going anywhere. You're saying you (must) accept these constraints. That doesn't make any sense; you can't change yourself and not expect to challenge your environment.

Client: Why not? I mean, it's me that has to change if I want this to happen. I can't expect the world to change for me.

Social worker: Yes, that's true but as I have told you many times you can make the world change so that you can live more fully in it.

Note that the social worker did not help the client identify the constraints he mentioned. She also focused on how the client can alter his environment by getting a job, even when the client expressed some important fears about himself.

Client: I guess you're right. I know I don't have much self-discipline. That's one of my real faults that I can't do anything about. But now that I see my father coming apart at the seams, I want to change before I get to be like that, too.

Social worker: How much do you want to change? Enough to commit yourself to a job? Enough to risk some arguments with your wife?

Client: Well, I'd like to teach young people something in psychology or religion or history.

Social worker: How do you think you could go about getting what you need to be a teacher for those subjects?

Client: I don't know. I guess I'd have to get a teaching certificate, but that's impossible.

Social worker: Why?

Client: I didn't even finish college.

Social worker: Well, so what? Go back to school.

Client: I'm too old. I'd be laughed at.

Social worker: Now, you know that's not true. People go back to finish up all the time. As I've said before, if you really want to, you can do anything.

Dean of students. John, a dean of students in a small-town college, is black; he has tried to integrate his college more completely and has been blocked by higher officials, who were apparently not interested in living up to their rhetoric on integration. John was in a double bind regarding his job. On the one hand, he wanted to perform his job in a way that would please his superiors. On the other hand, he felt that making integration a reality was in the best interests of the college, which threatened his superiors.

John was asked to meet with the college president and other top officials. "I was determined that these men were to make their decision without any help from me. Yet I was just as determined not to let them off the hook by allowing them to soothe their consciences by repeating over and over that blacks preferred segregation. I was determined to: (1) ask them why this issue was raised in the first place; (2) remind them of the present room-assignment regulation; (3) force them to reach a decision in my presence; and (4) remind them that the college had chosen to integrate and that this meant housing and room assignments, not just classroom situations.

Next, John wrote the following dialogue.

President: John, how do you feel about this whole thing?

Why the hell do you ask me what I think when you know damn well what I think. I am black and we blacks are human, too.

John: Peter, I was told this institution was committed to integration when I was hired.

Then why not try to persuade racists by taking a positive stance? Maybe you're just fooling yourselves about your real feelings about integration.

Dean of men: It is, John, but you must understand the attitudes of the whites who just don't understand the way we do.

At this point I only felt anger and my thoughts were to get the hell out of there before I blew my stack!

John: Well, you asked how I feel; my feelings are that the assignments should not be changed. After all, we can't really predict just what parents' attitudes will be. Many students attended integrated high schools.

President: Yes, but that was not a living situation.

Right! Pass it on to me because you're afraid of what you would do if it were left up to you.

Dean of the college: Maybe we shouldn't change the assignments; if the parents complain, let them talk to John.

What about you guys—the parents haven't complained yet.

Dean of men: I think that's a damn good idea—when they find that John is black, they won't have the nerve to seem so small and narrow-minded.

Why do you keep asking me what I think, man, when in the end it'll be your decision?

President: You know, that may not be such a bad idea. What do you think, John?

I really don't trust you, but I'll string along.

John: I don't mind. After all, it's my responsibility to explain our room-assignment policy. Am I to understand that you will support my decisions and that, whatever decision I make, you will support me against any irate parents?

I know when some rich parent confronts you with this, you won't be able to uphold my decision—which, of course, will be to leave the student in an integrated living situation. I don't know—maybe you will. Haven't you always tried to do what you felt was right?

President: Of course, John. You will have our support and backing all the way. But let's all sleep on this decision and make it final first thing tomorrow morning.

John exercised great emotional control to avoid blowing up. He suppressed important feelings because he thought they would lead to a less manageable meeting. John may have been right—indeed, his superiors might have hoped John would feel this way. The drawback to this strategy is that it permits John's superiors to continue behaving according to espoused theories that are incongruous with theories-in-use; in time, John may find he is not behaving according to his own values, either.

Dean of faculty. Dean Sylvan was asked to tell a professor that she could not return to teaching from a special assignment she had taken on temporarily. The dean writes that his problem was one of salesmanship. The professor had to be helped to see her position more realistically—that is, the way the dean and others viewed it.

I must keep my cool and make every effort to keep the lines of communication open.

Dean Sylvan: Thank you for meeting with me to discuss your request to return to a teaching assignment next year. I was surprised to receive your note because I was unaware of your feelings. I thought things were going well in your new assignment.

How could she help but know? Last year, she tried to get some help in applying for a grant for one of her own projects.

Professor: Things have really not been going well. If I had realized how little knowledge the members of this college had about grants and proposals, I never would have taken this assignment.

Don't go back over the problems that occurred when she was teaching. Be honest, but not to the point of identifying her problems in personal relations. Make her know you appreciate her efforts. How can I persuade her that she has made a contribution?

Dean Sylvan: One of the reasons you were chosen for this assignment was your previous interest and attempt to get others involved in some creative projects. At that time, you indicated you could do more for the college if you had time. You have learned so much as a result of your experiences this year; you undoubtedly know more than anyone else on campus about federal, state, and private funding of experimental projects. It would be a real loss to the college if you didn't pursue this interest for another year. Now that you have submitted four requests for grants, you must feel a real satisfaction knowing that if you hadn't done this work, no one would have.

My God, can she have forgotten so soon?

Professor: It was very difficult work, and I have no way of knowing yet if my efforts have succeeded. When I was teaching, I felt real satisfaction when my students responded to my demands; in their assignments and class discussions, I knew when I was successful as a teacher. The lack of relationships with students really bothers me. I know they enjoyed working with me. They often told me so. Besides, I know more about philosophy than anyone else on campus. My mind is made up. I shall teach next year, as you said I could.

Here we go again. Watch your tone of voice. Do I really sound

Dean Sylvan: I realize how much of yourself has gone into

convincing? I must make her aware that this is not an either/or situation. I blew it.

your work and how important it has been. You are aware of what it means to this college if even one of these proposals is funded. It never could happen without you. Now that so many other departments are interested in studying ways to improve learning in their disciplines, I hope you will talk to department chairmen and encourage them to write proposals. Offer them your help. I know you will accept this special assignment for next year and continue with these projects.

Professor: Are you telling me I can't go back to the classroom?

Don't shut the door. Keep it open.

Dean Sylvan: Don't you think it would be best if you think over what we have discussed? We can meet again in a few days.

Professor: The next time we meet, I'll have my lawyer with me.

Stay calm. Terminate this meeting.

Dean Sylvan: It isn't necessary to have a lawyer. This is something I'm sure we can settle here. Think about it. Will ten o'clock Friday be a good time to meet again?

As he reread his dialogue, Dean Sylvan said that his underlying assumptions must have been (1) he felt he really knew how the other person perceived the situation; (2) he felt he could manipulate the other person; and (3) he felt he was strong enough to divert the individual's awareness of what the real problem was. The dean saw his strategy as being strong, managing others, and winning while keeping the professor calm.

The dean tried to remain calm in order to communicate

without realizing that this creates incongruities that can lead to other difficulties. He wanted to be honest but not to the point of communicating critically relevant information. Furthermore, Dean Sylvan offered insincere flattery; he asked himself, "Do I really sound convincing?" Such insincere flattery not only fails but tends to make the Dean less effective because it makes him suspicious of anyone who flatters him.

Marketing manager. The marketing manager and several other representatives of Company A were asked to inform the president of Company B that two customer representatives assigned to Company B were being promoted and two new ones were being assigned. The marketing manager predicted that this action would upset the president because his firm depended on the two representatives for important technical assistance in installing and using the complicated systems bought from Company A.

The marketing manager's strategy was (1) to review current progress to confirm that things were going well; (2) to announce the new assignments; (3) to correct the president's expected feeling that Company A was not concerned about his company.

Take the initiative and define the job to be done.	*Marketing manager:* I would like to review the purpose of today's meeting.
Oh no! The four of us have triggered off questions in his mind. My strategy of beginning with a review is going to have to be changed. He senses that there are more important reasons, so I'll have to come to the point.	*President:* Yes, what is the objective of today's meeting? Why are four of you here?
	Marketing manager: There are two purposes to today's meeting. One, obviously, is to review the status of our account with you. Second, and the most important reason for the meeting is to review a change that we are making on the account. From time to time,

excellent opportunities come up for our customer representatives. When that occurs, we do not want to block deserving individuals. We obviously cannot control the timing of these opportunities. Well, such an opportunity has appeared for representative I. We are very pleased to advise you that he is being promoted to a new job.

Oh, no! This will really set us back.

President: You can't pull him out when I need him most.

When he hears this, he is going to go through the roof. But I have to tell him and make him understand that he cannot change it.

Marketing manager: Your account has a lot of progress; your people are more than self-sufficient. I assure you, the new representative is very well qualified. [The president is silent and shakes his head.] Well, we can't control when these opportunities occur, and when an individual deserves a promotion, we should promote him. We're also going to promote representative II.

The president is furious.

President: No! No! No! You can't do that. It's totally unacceptable. You know I signed with your company because of the support you promised. I knew I could pick up the phone and someone would help us. Now you're doing this to me! No! No! No!

I've got to use his own argument against him.

Marketing manager: You made the right decision. These changes will give you the opportunity to test our support and commitment to you; let us demonstrate it to you.

President: (Probably feeling that "I can't believe this. I have no

choice and I don't like it. But they
have been excellent in the past.
I'll give them a chance. What else
can I do?) Listen. I hear what
you are saying. I can't believe it.
All right, I'll go along, but I'm
going to make you responsible for
proving your claim.

The marketing manager thought the meeting was potentially
explosive. Indeed, he empathized with the president, but instead of
communicating this empathy or helping the president to express his
feelings, he sought to control him, to prevent any emotional out-
bursts, and to change the president's feelings and attitudes.

The marketing manager's desire to be on the offensive trig-
gered the president's sense of concern. The marketing manager
sensed this and decided to go directly to the point. In doing so, he
emphasized the importance of promoting deserving individuals and
added how pleased he was to announce the change. This did not
deal with the president's feelings and was also not true; the marketing manager was not pleased to advise the president, nor was the
president pleased to hear the news. Such statements lead to low
credibility.

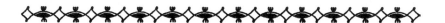

Chapter 4

Model I

Chapter Four will present a model that accounts for the theories-in-use—that is, the general characteristics, the governing variables, the action strategies, and the principal assumptions—exhibited in the case studies described in Chapter Three. First, we will discuss components of the model, then its principal assumptions, and then the consequences of action under the model on the participant's behavioral world.

Gathering Data

Before we describe our methods, it is important to repeat that we tried to relate data collection to the learning needs of our subjects. This requirement meant that data were generated by individuals who were preoccupied with learning about themselves, not with testing our theoretical ideas. Therefore, the case studies and tape recordings consist of much data that are not relevant to the theory. The amount of this nonrelevant information varies with the individual's motivation to learn, with the type of topic, and with the conditions under which the data were collected.

In analyzing the case studies, we used the following methods: We used any comments that provided information about the governing variables, the behavior used, the consequences for the behavioral world, on learning, and on effectiveness. Information about governing variables was primarily inferred from (1) the paragraphs that preceded the dialogue in the case studies, which described strategy and objectives ("My objective was to get Mr. X to agree," "I believe in winning, not losing"), (2) the paragraphs in the left column of the dialogue, which described the person's thoughts ("Play it cool; don't get emotional," "I know where he's going and I've got to prevent him from getting there"), and (3) from the underlying assumptions the individual identified after studying his dialogue ("It's best to stay calm and stick with the facts," "Success is when you get what you wanted").

Information about the behavioral strategies was taken directly from the dialogues. They revealed how the informant perceived his behavior. From that information, we inferred whether the behavior illustrated such actions as (1) unilateral control of the environment ("I felt I had to take charge before this got out of hand, so I said . . ."), (2) unilateral control over the task ("I decided the best way to handle John was to tell him to do . . ."), or (3) unilaterally saving face for the other person ("It was important for me not to upset X . . .").

To determine the consequences on the behavioral world, we relied in part on inferences using behavioral science knowledge. For example, if the individual controlled others' tasks and responses and tried to win, we hypothesized that other people would tend to feel they were being controlled and/or put into a competitive environment. If the individual decided unilaterally and secretly to hide certain key feelings in order to protect the other person, and if we saw from the dialogue that he had difficulty hiding such feelings, we hypothesized that the other person could feel that the individual was behaving defensively. Finally, if the individual tried to control the environment and the task, we hypothesized that the other person probably felt little free choice and internal commitment.

We got additional data when writers identified the consequences of their behavior. Other additional data were inferred from the writer's account of others' responses in the case; however, this second-hand data could have been distorted.

We used four additional ways to obtain more data about consequences and to validate the inferences made about the governing variables and actions of the actor.

1. All respondents, by virtue of being participants in our study, were learners in educational settings, where their cases were discussed. Those who were programmed with model I behavior would be expected to exhibit this behavior in the seminars of this study (which are described in Part III). For example, if A's dialogue indicates he tends to try to control others, he would probably exhibit the same behavior during the seminars.

2. We tape-recorded participants' reactions to each other's cases. A would read B's case and tell B how he (A) would react. We hypothesized that every case that we scored as model I should produce model I reactions in the participants. (None of the students, as the reader will see, were told of our evaluations until they made theirs public.)

3. Another opportunity to obtain further data was when participants were faced with a difficult intervention outside the seminar and asked for help. In such cases, we could observe behavior in a noncontrived setting, and sometimes we were able to include some of the people in the intervention in the seminar.

4. Sometimes we made predictions and tested them in the field. For example, in one seminar, marketing and sales executives met to discuss their most pressing sales problems. The next day, they wrote dialogues of difficult and easy relationships with customers. We analyzed these cases and developed generalizations about them. One of the authors was introduced to the class; his presentation was to give some of his impressions (of what participants later learned to identify as their theories-in-use) and to make some predictions based on information gleaned from the dialogues. Since the dialogues exhibited model I behavior, the predictions were that, over time, salesmen should report increasing misunderstandings and mistrust from customers, as well as increasing difficulty in understanding customers' true complaints. Salesmen would report that customers seem to withhold information. Both customers and salesmen would make more and more private attributions about each other's motives, which would lead salesmen to second-guess the customers' views and arrange customer meetings to deal with these

views (without being certain that their inferences are correct). The sales and marketing executives were astounded at these predictions since they were among the top five problems that had been identified by the group the night before.

Are the dialogues that the particpants write valid—that is, do they represent what actually went on? In one sense, it doesn't matter because the cases are used to diagnose the actor's theory-in-use, not to describe others' behavior accurately. Nevertheless, several reasons lead us to believe that participants do provide accurate information. (1) All of the data were gathered in learning settings. We assume people would not give false pictures of their behavior, which their behavior in class would belie. (2) We assume that people would not go through the psychological trauma of altering their theories-in-use if they did not believe in the validity of their data. (3) At least 60 percent of our population is composed of successful individuals in their professional fields, who are not easily cajoled or impressed by behavioral scientists. (4) Finally, most of our inferences about participants' theories-in-use run counter to their espoused theories. Each individual's data overwhelmingly challenged his competence. It is difficult to see why people would write distorted cases that make them appear incompetent.

Let us turn to model I, which is described in Table 1.

Governing Variables

The first column of Table 1 lists the governing variables—the goals the actor strives to satisfice. We identified four of these. They are:

1. Define goals and try to achieve them. Participants rarely tried to develop with others a mutual definition of purposes; nor did they seem open to being influenced to alter their perception of the task. Illustrative statements were: "Effective action begins with the person responsible defining the purpose"; "A major task for me was to make sure no one deviated from the purpose of the meeting"; and "Strong leadership is leadership that takes hold of the situation without dillydallying."

2. Maximize winning and minimize losing. Participants

felt that once they had decided on their goals, changing them would be a sign of weakness: "I had to prevent X's going on the offensive [to change the purpose of the meeting] while expressing adequate appreciation for his contributions"; "If I can pull this off, my own position will be strengthened"; "Let's face it: life is politics—winning and losing. I strive to win"; "Use whatever means will ensure success, no matter what their merits"; "Cooperate with behavior that achieves goals and temporize with behavior that does not"; "Win—play your cards right."

3. *Minimize generating or expressing negative feelings.* Participants were almost unanimous that generating negative feelings showed ineptness, incompetence, or lack of diplomacy. Permitting or helping others to express their feelings tended to be seen as a poor strategy: "Ask pointed questions but always in a friendly atmosphere"; "Never lose sight of purpose nor diminish the stature of parties involved by upsetting them"; "Withhold negative feelings and always maintain composure"; "Especially at first, it's better to understate than to bully, and better to be gentle than to threaten"; "Convince X that he can give up his job gracefully with a face-saving plan"; "I try to get others to do what I want them to do, even though it may be painful; I set it up so no one is offended"; "Conciliate, be reasonable—at least at the beginning."

4. *Be rational.* Be objective, intellectual, suppress your feelings and do not become emotional: "Be cool. Don't let yourself get emotional"; "Remain as objective as possible"; "Demonstrate sufficient command of the facts"; "People expect policies to have rational explanations, not emotional reasons"; "Be objective and clear, but don't come on too strong"; "Once people know the facts, the job is almost done"; "If others are intelligent and rational, they will change their position, once you show them the facts"; "Hold back your feelings even if it hurts."

Action Strategies

The second column identifies the action strategies that participants adopted. Four strategies were identified.

1. *Design and manage environment unilaterally.* Individuals

Table 1. Model I Theory-in-Use

Governing variables	Action strategies	Consequences for the behavioral world	Consequences for learning	Effectiveness
1. Define goals and try to achieve them.	1. *Design and manage the environment* unilaterally (be persuasive, appeal to larger goals).	1. Actor seen as defensive, inconsistent, incongruent, competitive, controlling, fearful of being vulnerable, manipulative, withholding of feelings, overly concerned about self and others or underconcerned about others.	1. Self-sealing.	
2. Maximize winning and minimize losing.	2. *Own and control the task* (claim ownership of the task, be guardian of definition and execution of task).	2. Defensive interpersonal and group relationship (dependence upon actor, little additivity, little helping others).	2. Single-loop learning.	Decreased effectiveness.

3. Minimize generating or expressing negative feelings.

3. *Unilaterally protect yourself* (speak with inferred categories accompanied by little or no directly observable behavior, be blind to impact on others and to the incongruity between rhetoric and behavior, reduce incongruity by defensive actions such as blaming, stereotyping, suppressing feelings, intellectualizing).

3. Defensive norms (mistrust, lack of risk-taking, conformity, external commitment, emphasis on diplomacy, power-centered competition, and rivalry).

3. Little testing of theories publicly. Much testing of theories privately.

4. Be rational.

4. *Unilaterally protect others from being hurt* (withhold information, create rules to censor information and behavior, hold private meetings).

4. Low freedom of choice, internal commitment, and risk-taking.

tended to plan actions secretly. They attempted to persuade and
cajole others to agree with their definitions of a situation. If they
were organizationally powerful—as the minister or Dean Sylvan
was, for example—they used their power to prevent others from
redesigning the situation. Some new examples follow.

"I decided to strike an authoritarian pose at first, to make
them realize we all knew there was an issue, then let them continue
in a sort of 'supervised haggle.' I knew I had to seem to take the
whole thing completely seriously; if, by indirection, I could lead
them to the point of feeling ridiculous rather than ridiculed, I would
have accomplished my aim."

"I decided to sell them on an idea I knew they did not like,
but I had to get them to agree. I designed the meeting so they
would wind up being on my team."

"I hammered away with our position at every opportunity."

"I had to grab the initiative and keep the ball out of their
hands, or all would be lost. Therefore, my group and I had brain-
stormed ahead of time to come up with all the strategies the other
side might use; I practiced what I would say in order to remain in
control."

2. Own and control task. This is actually a special case of
the preceding strategy, but it is a crucially important one. For
example, the social worker assumed that it was her responsibility to
"get the client off the pot." Dean Sylvan decided that the professor
must be persuaded to remain in her present position; he takes responsibility for convincing her. The minister feels it's up to him to
help Ruth examine her fear. Some new examples follow.

"I knew where he is going and that it wouldn't do any of
us any good if he got there. I decided the best way to stop him
was. . . ."

"I must act quickly so that well-meaning colleagues do not
become further involved and threaten to get the situation completely
out of hand."

"Although they felt our department was becoming independent of the college, my task was to get them to see that the
college was getting a good deal of publicity from our programs."

"I was determined to end the meeting with A and B revers-
ing their decision. My strategy, which I was careful not to reveal,

was to first get A to see the problems he would have with B and then . . . ."

3. Unilaterally protect self. The city planner begins by thinking he should appear confident in contrast to the presumed hostility of the other side to show that the project will go ahead. Dean Sylvan tells the teacher, "there is no need for lawyers." These participants tend to speak in abstractions and without reference to directly observed events. The effect, intended or unintended, is to force others to guess at their meaning. If the others assume that they understand the meanings and act accordingly, the actor can argue (especially if he sees that he is losing) that the others did not understand him. This can be one way for the individual to protect himself. Another problem with this approach is that the other person may misunderstand and attribute invalid motives to the actor, which may go untested because to express them would violate the governing variable that requires minimum expression of feelings. A circular sequence may lead to further misunderstandings. Other examples follow.

"I'm sure you will agree with me that the situation in that department is fraught with difficulties." (The speaker then suggests a remedy, but the difficulties remain unspecified.)

"As you all know, there have been organizational difficulties that we need not discuss at this time. The point is to get beyond them."

4. Unilaterally protect others. Withholding valuable and important information, telling white lies, suppressing feelings, and offering false sympathy are examples of this strategy. The speaker assumes that the other person needs to be protected and that this strategy should be kept secret; neither assumption is tested. Examples follow.

"It was our idea, but give him the credit; it will make him feel good."

"This will appeal to his ego. He loves a good theory session."

"I found X's sophomoric ideas ridiculous, but, for his sake, I could not let my feelings show."

"I must be careful. He is so defensive. I don't want to get him mad."

The strategy, "I disagree with him completely, but I'll be

noncommital as hell," is followed by this overt statement: "Well, I see your point . . . ."

Difficult and Easy Interventions

In both easy and difficult interventions, participants seemed to behave according to the same governing variables and action strategies. Although the actors were more defensive in the difficult cases the theories used were essentially similar. Why, then, did the actors differentiate the episodes as being easy or difficult? Three issues are involved: (1) the participant's degree of effectiveness; (2) how much power and control each person has; and (3) the probability of rejection.

So, whether a case is considered easy or difficult depends on whether the actor: (1) is influential because he and others recognize that he has power (easy case) or is not influential because he and others recognize that he has little power (difficult case); (2) is influential because he and others see him as a competent expert (easy case) or is not influential because he and others do not see him as a competent expert (difficult case); (3) is easily able to define the task in unambiguous, easily accepted terms (easy case) or has difficulty in defining the task in unambiguous, easily accepted terms (difficult case); (4) was faced with a client who was willing to be passive and to accept help (easy case) or was faced with a client who was unwilling to be passive and doubted that he needs help (difficult case); (5) was faced with a client who fears expressing conflict (easy case) or was faced with a client who creates conflict but has difficulty examining it (difficult case); or (6) had few, unimportant fears of rejection (easy case) or had many, and/or strong important fears of rejection (difficult case).

The more difficult the episode, the more the actor would tend to adhere to the behavior outlined by model I.

Consequences for Behavioral World

To the extent that the actor behaves according to any of the four action strategies, he will tend to behave unilaterally toward others and protectively toward himself. If successful, such behavior controls others and prevents one from being influenced by others. But what happens if the individuals one is dealing with resist being controlled and seek to influence the actor? We can predict four consequences. (1) The actors will be defensive. Some, like the social worker and Dean Sylvan, will be authoritarian because they can exercise unilateral control over others. The others will fear their vulnerability and be overly concerned about themselves, as the city planner and the marketing manager were; they will be under-concerned about others. (2) Interpersonal and group relationships will become more defensive than facilitative. Group dynamics become rigid and more a matter of winning/losing than collaboration. (3) Defensiveness in individuals, interpersonal relations, and group behavior will generate norms that support such behavior; norms such as conformity, antagonism, and mistrust will be generated rather than individuality, concern, and trust. (4) There will be little freedom to explore and search for new information and new alternatives, which is understandable, given the first three consequences. Lack of freedom to explore and define goals, to explore new paths to these goals, and to set realistic but challenging levels of aspiration leads to little commitment to group decisions and little risk-taking.

A group of sixty participants, whose individual case studies exhibited model I values and behavior, were asked to discuss the Dean Sylvan case. We predicted that these participants would discuss the case in model I terms. Seminar activities during this session were divided into several phases. First, the participants were asked to advise the instructor, who took the role of Dean Sylvan. Each student asked several questions or made several remarks.

Three observers were selected and publicly instructed to observe the behavior of the faculty member with the purpose of assessing if, when acting as Dean Sylvan, the instructor was making it difficult for the consultants. Of course, the observers were not limited to this task. This task was requested by the instructor in order to make his behavior confrontable and to invite such confrontation by the class.

The role-playing began and 26 participants made their interventions, all of which conformed to model I; they condemned Dean Sylvan, admonished him, coerced him, and offered highly abstract solutions. For example: (1) "You realize, Dean Sylvan, you have not done the professor any good"; (2) "You appear to be more concerned about the institution than about her. Let me give you some examples from your own statements . . ."; (3) "Do you realize that you come across as being more concerned about your own problem than about the professor's?"; (4) "The thing that worried me was your lack of honesty"; and (5) "You have failed, Dean Sylvan, as a Dean and as a human being."

In his role as Dean Sylvan, the instructor tried to respond to these statements in a way that was as supportive as possible: (1) "Yes, I know. That's why I called you in to help me learn how to be more effective"; (2) "You're right, but I was not as aware of that then as I am now"; (3) "Well, it depends upon what you consider my problem. I do know that I was afraid that I would harm the professor"; (4) "That worries me, too. I want to learn to become more honest"; and (5) "Yes, I feel that I want to become more effective."

The supportiveness of Dean Sylvan was confirmed by the three observers. "He tried every way he could to go along with each of you," said one observer. "He sure did, to the point that he was shitty goody," added another. Many of the class members then said that the real Dean Sylvan would probably have been much less cooperative with consultants. The instructor replied that he was trying to be as cooperative as possible so that if the consultants did not perform effectively, they could not blame him for their ineffectiveness.

Some class members then said they would be more effective if the faculty member had played Dean Sylvan's role more defensively. (We would predict people whose behavior is determined by model I to take this position.) The instructor said he was willing to try such behavior. The class sharply disagreed whether that would make any difference in their behavior.

One student asked that the class examine the consultants' solutions: (1) you need to have better communication with your faculty; (2) perhaps an evaluation program would have prevented this problem; (3) you should deal with the professor more sensitively; (4) you are responsible for her development, and I recommend that you arrange a seminar to help the faculty develop themselves; and (5) the first step is for you to meet the professor again and be honest, even if it means hitting her over the head.

These conclusions show the unilateral evaluative and controlling nature of the consultants' interventions and, more important, show the abstract nature of the dialogue. "Being more sensitive," "creating effective evaluation programs," and "developing more effective communications," are all recommendations that Dean Sylvan liked and agreed with, but his problem was how to behave more sensitively, how to create an effective evaluation program, and how to communicate more effectively.

During the next phase of the seminar, participants began to interact much more, agreeing and disagreeing with each other. Again, all the interventions they proposed were evaluative and attributive (with little directly observable data) and competitive. Soon, participants felt frustrated. "We're getting nowhere," said one student. Many agreed but didn't know what to do about it.

One participant suggested that the class was too large; less distance between the consultants and Dean Sylvan would help. The instructor asked if they wanted to test that suggestion, and many students nodded. Five consultants met the instructor at the front of the class and role-played the consulting activities. The results were still the same. The only new data that came forth was the students' awareness of their own competitiveness.

Next, some class members recommended that one or two consultants work with the faculty member. All agreed, and the class was divided into small groups, each to design a more effective intervention that would take place between one or two consultants and the dean. The groups could meet as long as they wished between classes, develop their strategy, select one (or more) consultants, and train them to carry out their strategy.

The results of the smaller group discussions continued to illustrate model I strategies and behavior. For example: (1) "Dean Sylvan needs to be strengthened—he is weak and has to be helped"; (2) "Give Dean Sylvan negative reinforcers by condemning him for his weaknesses and positive reinforcers for taking a harder line"; (3) "How can we convince Dean Sylvan and destroy his confidence in his present view of the professor so it will be easy for the dean to lay it on the line?"; (4) "The dean needs a revolution in his school, and we should help him see it"; (5) "Get Dean Sylvan to level with the professor but do so in a way that doesn't upset her too much"; (6) "Dean Sylvan's conversation has to be strong first, then give in a bit, then get strong, and then give in a bit"; (7) "Dean Sylvan must help the professor save face and save face himself"; (8) "He's got to admit that he has been wrong and get the professor to admit that she has been wrong"; (9) "As I see our assignment, it is to build up the dean's confidence in himself—we've got to build him up emotionally"; (10) "The trouble with the dean is that he has trouble being a tough guy"; (11) "If we encourage Dean Sylvan that way, it may encourage the professor to go back to class, and that would be a defeat"; and (12) "Any way you look at it, Dean Sylvan has to face unpleasantness."

Consequences for Learning

Given the governing variables, the action strategies described, and the consequences on the behavioral world (defensiveness of actor, interpersonal relations, and norms), we hypothesized that there would be little public testing of the theories-in-use. In nearly two-hundred written cases, only two actors tried to test their theories-in-use publicly. We explain this as follows. In order to test one' theory-in-use, one must confront issues such as one's own defensiveness, the defensiveness of others, and the ineffectiveness of the group. Surfacing his own defensiveness may open the actor to confrontation and to an analysis that could, in his view, weaken his position and lead him to fear that he might lose rather than win. Discussing others' defensiveness might lead to embarrassment and anger, resulting in the expression of negative feelings and perhaps rejection of the actor. This would violate the governing variables that require winning, minimizing negative feelings, and minimizing emotionality.

If there is little genuine testing of one's theory-in-use and if one must nevertheless act, then one will act on an untested theory-in-use. Since behaving according to one's theory-in-use will influence the behavioral world, self-sealing processes will probably occur. The following examples suggest how these processes function.

A believes thàt *B* is defensive: if *A* cannot test this and if *A* acts according to his hunch, *B* will probably wonder why *A* is behaving in this way and act cautiously. *A* will sense *B*'s caution and may interpret it as evidence that *B* is defensive.

A believes, without testing his belief, that if he were to surface his feeling that *B* is defensive, his situation with *B* would become less manageable. As a result, *B* need not confront the incongruity between his espoused theory and his theory-in-use. But also as a result, *A*'s behavior is incongruent with his values. The norms for incongruity and withholding are reinforced, which exacerbates *A*'s feelings about *B*.

A believes that he cannot tell *B*—whom he perceives as powerful in relation to himself—what *A* wants. He also believes that he cannot test this assumption because to do so risks eliciting a negative reaction from *B*. He therefore probes cautiously with *B*, asking at first for considerably less than he really wants. *B* perceives *A*'s demand as trivial and responds to it as he thinks appropriate—in a trivial fashion; *B* also does not test his interpretation of what *A* really wants. *A* interprets *B*'s response as evidence of *B*'s inability to respond in a nontrivial way and resolves not to approach *B* on the matter again.

A believes that *B* is incompetent but also believes that he cannot confront *B* about his incompetence because *B* would find that intolerable. Therefore, *A* withholds his feelings about *B*'s incompetence and attempts to remove *B* from the situation in which *A* considers *B* to be incompetent by alleging admiration for *B*'s performance in another setting. *B* doubts *A*'s alleged admiration—although he does not confront *A* with his doubt—and is angered by what he interprets as *A*'s deception. *B* does not test his interpretation of *A*'s deception but instead angrily insists on remaining in the situation in which *A* finds him incompetent. Constrained by his assumption that he cannot confront *B* on his incompetence, *A* now has no way of showing *B* why he should not continue to function in the situation in which *A* finds him incompetent.

The public testing of the assumptions of one's theory-in-use for a situation is essential for developing information that may lead to confirmation or disconfirmation of those assumptions (single-loop learning); it is also essential for developing information that allows others to test their assumptions about the actor and consequently provides the actor with further opportunity to test assumptions again (double-loop learning). Lack of such public testing risks creating self-sealing processes. In the language of Part I, the individual not only helps to create behavioral worlds that are artifacts of his theory-in-use but also cuts himself off from the possibility of disconfirming assumptions in his theory-in-use and thereby cuts himself off from the possibility of helping to create behavioral worlds that disconfirm his starting assumptions about them.

However, public testing of theories-in-use must be accompanied by an openness to change behavior as a function of learning. The actor needs minimally distorted feedback from others. If others provide such feedback—especially if they do so with some risk—and if they experience that the actor is not open to change, they may believe that they have placed themselves in a difficult situation. Their mistrust of the actor will probably increase, but this fact will be suppressed. The result will be the creation of another series of self-sealing processes that again make the actor less likely to receive valid information the next time he tries to test an assumption publicly. As the actor feels himself confirmed in his belief about the ineffectiveness of testing assumptions publicly, he tends to withdraw to private testing, which means a significant increase in the probability of self-sealing processes.

Figure 3 shows four conditions related to public and private testing and openness to change. If the individual is closed to change as a result of valid information from others and tests his hypotheses privately (1), there will tend to be little learning and little behavioral change. If the individual tests his hypotheses privately but is open to change (2), learning will tend to occur to the extent that it does not depend on others knowingly providing valid information. If the individual tests his assumptions publicly, but is closed to change (3), the result will tend to be the mutually defensive self-sealing situation described in the preceding examples. The most effective case for learning is (4): public testing of assumptions and openness to changed behavior as a result. (The differences between public and private testing and an open and closed attitude to change are actually differences in degree rather than the binary choices presented in this discussion for the sake of clarity.)

Testing

Private   Public

	Private	Public
Closed	1	2
Open	3	4

Attitude toward change

FIGURE 3

Under conditions of little public testing of assumptions, low risk-taking, and the resulting high probability of self-sealing processes, we believe there will be little attempt to question the governing variables of model I. The learning behavior according to model I encourages learning that preserves the governing variables of model I and the behavioral world generated by model I; this is single-loop rather than double-loop learning.

Main Assumptions

We have already mentioned some of the main assumptions underlying model I in the discussion of governing variables and action strategies in our case situations; they are summarized next.

It is a win/lose world. Everyone seeks to win and to avoid loss; in my interactions with others, I compete. This assumption is a counterpart to the governing variable, "maximize winning and avoid losing." Participants' remarks show that they hold this assumption; it is also illustrated by the actors' explicit or implicit definition of their interaction as a competitive one.

The question of the truth or falsity of this assumption is a strange one, because, as we have already remarked, the actor can make it true by his behavior. The assumption, coupled with the governing variable, "Win . . . ", and the action strategies designed to implement it, leads to behavior on the actor's part which induces behavior in others of a win-lose, competitive variety—even if the others, confronted with behavior based on a different assumption, might be capable of behaving differently. It is uncertain whether behavior according to model I could create a behavioral world in which this assumption did not hold.

Other people behave according to assumptions of model I. We saw this to be true in the first assumption. We have seen that participants' cases showed that others would be win/lose, controlling, defensive, would withhold critical information, and the like. And, as in the case of the first assumption, we have already described how behavior on these assumptions may induce in others or reinforce in others behavior according to model I.

Rational behavior is most effective. Rational behavior means being objective, intellectual, and unemotional. The cases show that this does not help the actors reach their goals. However, model I tends to prevent people from discovering that kind of behavior is ineffective, and it inhibits exploration of behavior according to different assumptions.

Public testing of assumptions is intolerably risky. We have already adduced evidence that in the cases examined, this assumption tends to be held by participants, and we have given an explanation of the ways in which the governing variables and action strategies of model I tend to reinforce this assumption.

The assumption tends increasingly to be true of the behavioral worlds of model I; that is, the risks of public testing of assumptions tend to increase as the cycles of defensiveness escalate. Whether these risks are at any point "intolerable" depends upon an assessment of the risks involved in failing to test assumptions publicly—and because *these* risks tend not to be anticipated, the calculation of "intolerability" tends not to be made.

This list is illustrative rather than exhaustive of the principal assumptions of model I. It suggests, however, the ways in which model I helps to create (1) a behavioral world in which some of the assumptions hold true, and (2) self-sealing processes in which the actor is cut off from discovering the possibility of a behavioral world in which these assumptions did not hold true.

Long-Term Dynamics

Inferences about the consequences of model I for learning enable us to hypothesize about long-term dynamics of behavioral worlds operating under model I. Feedback from model I behavior tends to increase defensiveness among individuals and to make inter- and intra-group behavior dysfunctional. This often leads to explosions upon failure of the safety-value functions of governing variables ("Minimize the expression of negative feelings by self and others") and action strategies ("Unilaterally protect others"). Model I leads to a kind of hybrid world—a pre-civilized, competitive, hostile, defensive, win/lose world onto which the supposedly civilizing safety valves of repression, containment, and deviousness have been grafted. Such a behavioral world maintains its tenuous equilibrium through Machiavellian safety valves.

However, the safety valves do not remove the difficulties; they only help to suppress them, which requires new defenses that again reinforce the tension in the system. As tension increases, defenses against acknowledging the tension and expressing emotion become stronger. Such defenses act not only to place a lid on the expression of·emotionality but also lead to the suppression of ideas that could surface the existing tension or add to it. But these are the very ideas that require surfacing if the system is to reduce the self-reinforcing feedback and increase the corrective feedback. Ultimately, model I creates a world that will either stagnate—due to the inertia created by the layers of defenses—or will periodically erupt into explosive change.

If the prevailing theories-in-use in our institutions and organizations follow model I, we can see why double-loop learning would tend to occur—if at all—through revolution. This would also clarify why the behavioral worlds created by such revolutions would tend again to become stagnant, self-sealing systems incapable of double-loop learning except through the next revolution.

That most organizations and institutions in our society do follow model I must remain a hypothesis—or, better yet, a perspective that clarifies some of the puzzling features of our behavioral worlds (Argyris, 1964, 1971; Schon, 1971). The theories-in-use shown by the cases in our sample do exhibit model I behavior. To date, the applicability of model I does not seem to be restricted by age, professional status, race, income level, or field of activity; it is as ubiquitous among hard-headed businessmen as among militant revolutionaries, among blacks as among whites, among the discontented young as among the middle-aged.

The degree to which model I holds for individuals may vary.

An actor may be highly oriented toward win/lose competitive dynamics but not manifest them when he is uninvolved in a situation. Similarly, other people may not react toward the actor as model I predicts if they are not highly involved with him or with the issues involved. Time perspective may also influence the applicability of model I. For example, if individuals know they may never see each other again, they may be able to reduce or eliminate some of the defensiveness described by model I. Or, a low evaluation of self-acceptance and autonomy—that is, a need to be submissive and to maintain a low sense of self-acceptance—may mean an individual will not respond to the actor as defensively as model I predicts.

Learning Model I

Given the disadvantages of behaving according to model I, it may seem strange that our sample should have learned such a dysfunctional mode of behavior and stranger still that they should persist in it. If we accept the hypothesis that model I is prevalent in our society, we would raise the same questions about our society. Although there are no well-documented answers to these questions, we do have some suggestions.

Children learn model I from their parents and from significant others because the behavioral worlds of the family, the school, and other social settings conform to model I. Model I is probably learned through a model-I process—through what Kelman (1958) calls compliance and identification, which are based on learning through rewards and penalties rather than through internalization, according to which the individual tries out new behavior and makes it part of his repertoire because it is intrinsically satisfying.

The learning of model I meshes with two social mechanisms that, according to many researchers, are typical of everyday life in our society—attribution and social evaluation. (Argyris 1969.) Attribution means unilaterally assigning intentions to others, without public testing. Social evaluation means that individuals privately compare themselves with others, without open testing. Both processes reinforce and are reinforced by model I.

Once individuals find themselves in organizations, they are

apt to encounter behavioral worlds in which model I again predominates. The assumptions of the special kind of rationality inherent in engineering, technology, and economics (Argyris, 1964), when applied to organizations, suggest that people are taught that if you want to suceed in human relationships and get a task accomplished you should behave according to the following directives. (1) Focus on task-oriented behavior—get the job done; individuals are not rewarded for trying harder but for winning. (2) Focus on behaving rationally and deemphasize and suppress feelings; the more emotions are expressed, the higher the probability for interpersonal difficulties and eventual rejection. (3) Focus on controling others by designing their world; reward and penalize them and expect them to be loyal, which means focusing on values implicit in the first two directives (Argyris, 1962).

Adults programmed with these values tend to create human relationships that emphasize competitiveness, withholding help from others, conformity, covert antagonism, and mistrust while deemphasizing cooperation, helping others, individuality, and trust (Argyris, 1962). Under these conditions, people may learn to give and receive feedback that creates the impression of genuine confirmation or disconfirmation but does not in fact provide it. Interpersonal diplomacy, being civilized, withholding feelings, and suppressing anger and hurt are but a few common examples of what individuals are taught to do to help maintain harmony in interpersonal relationships. Goffman's work (1959) provides examples of how individuals learn interpersonal diplomacy and policy in order to live in a world of pseudo-authenticity.

Adults are probably taught to value attribution and social evaluation just as they are taught the logic of engineering and economics. They teach these values to their children by modeling them and by requiring compliance with them and/or encouraging identification with them. To the extent that adults use model I, they will tend to show low self-esteem, low trust, low openness, and little public testing and learning. With such characteristics, compliance and identification are probably the two major processes for learning model I.

Reasons why people tend to go on using model I have been woven into our argument. Most people are not aware of their theories-in-use and hence are unaware of model I. One consequence of model I is that it rewards suppression of feedback (which people need if they are to modify their behavior) and suppresses the negative consequences of suppression. After years of countless experiences of supposedly having been saved by these defenses and tactics of deception, individuals may internalize them. They teach these defenses to their children and design the world so that it not only reinforces the defenses but considers them attributes of maturity, poise, dignity, and adulthood. Under these conditions, individuals may believe that they value learning, self-acceptance, or being original but be quite unaware of how to behave according to these values.

People who behave according to model I tend to develop group norms to support the model—for example, in the form of organizational structures and policies—and become accustomed to them. Model I conditions cluster and reinforce one another, whether the individual wishes them to or not, and tension, inter-group rivalry, self-sealing attributions, or political lying become viewed as being as natural as apple pie. Once these phenomena become part of the social landscape, individuals see less need for changing them and may even design ways to circumvent or adapt to these processes. Even those who recognise self-sealing behavior on the part of colleagues or friends are quick to discount these behaviors; they say, "If you knew him as I do, you would know that under that ruthless exterior there is a heart of gold."

Chapter 5

Model II

Chapter Five presents a model of theories-in-use that is free of the dysfunctionalities of model I. Participants in our sample and others have led us to assume that there is great demand for a model of theories-in-use that reduces the negative consequences of model I and increases growth, learning, and effectiveness. Research shows that individuals need a sense of competence and try to become more effective in their human interactions (White, 1956).

We also assume that model II will be accepted insofar as it contains governing variables that are highly valued by people in all segments and levels of our society. Model II is an attempt to make operational some governing variables that are broadly espoused, though infrequently realized, in our society.

Although this formulation of model II is a new one, several of its principal assumptions rest on research previously undertaken by Argyris (1970). The authors have tried to learn and to help others learn to behave according to model II in one-to-one, classroom, and organizational settings. Thus, our arguments for the consequences of model II will be based partly on the logic of the model itself, partly on previous research, and partly on our experience of the behavioral worlds we begin to create when we begin to practice model II. Table 2 presents model II.

Governing Variables

The governing variables of model II can be best understood by recalling model I, which consists of competitive, win/lose, rational, and diplomatic behavior that is self-sealing; this last property is the most significant because it prevents the improvement of congruence, consistency, and effectiveness of theories-in-use by preventing learning. Hence, the most significant property of model II is its ability not to be self-sealing, its tendency to permit progressively more effective testing of assumptions and progessively greater learning about one's effectiveness. The central governing variables of model II are presented next.

Maximize valid information. This is the primary governing variable because it justifies the other governing variables and the action strategies are based on it.

People deal with reality by transforming it into perceived, or attributed, meanings. These meanings are the components of the assumptions built into our microtheories-in-use. Each such meaning has a referent in data. The construction of attributions about the physical environment on the basis of directly observable data, both in everyday life and in the laboratory, is a much-discussed process in philosophy of science and in psychology. Such discussions use concepts of sensory data, hypothesis-formation, confirmation and disconfirmation, experiment, or theory-building. Attributed meanings formed about other persons depend on data provided by their behavior. Many of these data, though not all of them, depend on the information-giving choices that others make. Thus, others may choose to reveal behavior from which accurate interpretations may be made or they may suppress such behavior; they may give accurate reports about their feelings, beliefs, assumptions, and states of mind or they may withhold such reports; indeed, as we have seen, they may even falsify them.

Maximizing valid information, then, means that the actor provides others with directly observable data and correct reports so they may make valid attributions about the actor. It also means

Table 2. MODEL II THEORY-IN-USE

Governing variables	Action strategies	Consequences for the behavioral world	Consequences for learning	Consequences for quality of life	Effectiveness
1. Valid information.	1. Design situations or environments where participants can be origins and can experience high personal causation (psychological success, confirmation, essentiality).	1. Actor experienced as minimally defensive (facilitator, collaborator, choice creator).	1. Disconfirmable processes.	1. Quality of life will be more positive than negative (high authenticity and high freedom of choice).	Increased long-run effectiveness.
2. Free and informed choice.	2. Tasks is controlled jointly.	2. Minimally defensive interpersonal relations and group dynamics.	2. Double-loop learning.	2. Effectiveness of problem solving and decision making will be great, especially for difficult problems.	
3. Internal commitment to the choice and constant monitoring of its implementation.	3. Protection of self is a joint enterprise and oriented toward growth (speak in directly observable categories, seek to reduce blindness about own inconsistency and incongruity).	3. Learning-oriented norms (trust, individuality, open confrontation on difficult issues).	3. Public testing of theories.		
	4. Bilateral protection of others.				

creating conditions that will lead others to provide directly observable data and correct reports that will enable one to make valid attributions about them.

Maximize free and informed choice. A choice is informed if it is based on relevant information. The more an individual is aware of the values of the variables relevant to his decision, the more likely he is to make an informed choice. A choice is free to the degree to which the individual making it can: define his own objectives; define how to achieve these objectives; define objectives that are within his capacities; and relate his objectives to central personal needs whose fulfillment does not involve defense mechanisms beyond his control. (The last two items are based on assumptions grounded in research.)

To the extent that an individual cannot control his behavior, it becomes compulsive and repetitive; he behaves predictably and compulsively, although he may not want to. Kubie has shown that this type of response may be the essential aspect of neurotic behavior. Hence, the individual's boundaries to free choice are set by his defense mechanisms, which are beyond his control.

The individual's aspirations must be within his capacities or he will be frustrated, which will lead to regression, which leads to decreased effectiveness, which, in turn, leads to further frustration. As frustration increases, the human being's cognitive and emotive make-up changes to a more primitive state. The greater the change, the more primitive will be the individual's abilities to solve problems, and the less freedom of choice he will have (Barker, Dembo, and Lewin, 1941).

Conversely, the more an individual achieves goals that do not require learning, the more his behavior becomes programmed, repetitive, and routine. The more repetitive one's life is, the more likely the individual is to be primitivized and to have less freedom of choice (Argyris, 1964, 1970).

Hence, freedom of choice depends on meeting minimal conditions of psychological success, as opposed to frustration. The individual's environmental challenges must be sufficient to require more than routine behavior but must not exceed his capacities so that he experiences mainly frustration. Freedom of choice also depends on the individual's ability to direct his activities into zones of experience free of defense mechanisms that are beyond his control.

These conditions are dynamic. An individual may become progressively less able to tolerate frustration, less able therefore to generate nonroutine behavior, and more hemmed in by his own defenses. Or he may become increasingly able to tolerate more frustration, create more opportunities for challenge in his environment, and push back the boundaries of defense mechanisms over which he has no control.

Maximize internal commitment to decisions made. Internal commitment means that the individual feels that he, himself, is responsible for his choices. The individual is committed to an action because it is intrinsically satisfying—not, as in the case of model I, committed because someone is rewarding or penalizing him to be committed.

These three governing variables are interconnected in the following ways. Valid information is essential to informed choice. Freedom of choice depends on one's ability to select objectives that challenge one's capacities within a tolerable range, which again depends on valid information. An individual is more likely to feel internally committed to a freely made decision. Individuals who feel responsible for their decisions will tend to monitor them to see that they are being implemented effectively, will tend to seek feedback to correct errors and to detect unintended consequences, and will therefore tend to obtain valid information.

Free, informed choices and internal commitment increase the likelihood of psychological success, which tends in turn to increase the area of experience in which free choice is possible. Further connections among the governing variables of model II will become apparent as we consider the action strategies.

Action Strategies

Make designing and managing environment bilateral task. Control over any situation must be shared if all participants are to experience free choice in and internal commitment to the situation.

Specifically, situations should be designed so that all participants can experience psychological success. This means that the actor helps others to help themselves define their goals, define the paths to these goals, develop their own realistic levels of aspiration, and relate goals to their central needs. This means also that the actor may invite others to help him in this process. The actor can try to create situations in which he and others can experience a sense of mutual confirmation or disconfirmation—that is, situations in which assumptions can be tested against valid information. In creating such situations, the actor also tends to make himself and others feel essential to the process. Once these three factors are generated, internal commitment to the choice will tend to follow.

Freedom of choice and internal commitment to the choice are both conditions and consequences of the process just described. Free choice and internal commitment are required if an individual is to help others. And if an individual is to help himself by seeking information from others, the others must be free to choose if they are to be of help.

Make protection of self or other a joint operation. In the behavioral world, individuals are interdependent in every encounter. Therefore, unilateral protection of oneself or others cannot occur without influencing all concerned. In the example of Dean Sylvan, his unilateral decision to protect the professor from his perception of her incompetence in teaching deprives her of freedom to respond to that perception. His effort to protect himself from the reaction he anticipates has the same effect. Protecting oneself or others unilaterally should not be an action strategy unless all parties are convinced that more growth-oriented strategies are not possible.

Speak in directly observable categories. Maximizing valid information about oneself and others requires speaking in directly observable categories rather than in inferred categories of attribution and evaluation. It also minimizes others' reliance on the actor, encouraging independent interpretations that do not depend on the actor's interpretations; this is likely to make the actor seem less threatening, which again is likely to lead other people to offer valid information. Discussing directly observable categories and using valid information enables individuals to confront inconsistencies in their theories-in-use and incongruities between theories-in-use and espoused theories. This creates a predisposition toward inquiry and learning.

Consequences for Behavioral World and Learning

If individuals behave according to the governing variables and action strategies of model II, others will tend to see them as minimally defensive and open to learning, as facilitators, collaborators, and people who hold their theories-in-use firmly (because they are internally committed to them) but are equally committed to having them confronted and tested. Defensiveness in interpersonal and group relationships will tend to decrease, and people will tend to help others, have more open discussions, exhibit reciprocity, and feel free to explore different views and express risky ideas. Moreover, group norms will tend away from defensiveness and toward growth and double-loop learning; for example, trust, individuality, power-sharing, and cooperation will tend to become norms, with competition being confronted when it becomes dysfunctional. As these norms are emphasized, authenticity, autonomy, and internal commitment will tend to increase (Argyris, 1962, 1965, 1971a).

In the behavioral world of model II, participants will tend to test publicly the assumptions of their theories-in-use; they will tend to be open to possibilities for change in behavior that may result from that testing. Attributions will tend to be formed openly and on the basis of directly observable data.

Learning cycles are likely to be set in motion. As individuals come to feel more psychological success and more likelihood of mutual confirmation or disconfirmation, they are likely to manifest higher self-awareness and acceptance, which leads to offering valid information, which again leads to feelings of psychological success. As groups manifest higher degrees of openness, experimentation, and emphasis on individuality, individuals in them will feel freer to provide valid information that will tend, in turn, to enhance these group characteristics. As individuals feel higher degrees of freedom of choice, trust, and authenticity, they are more likely to test their assumptions publicly, which is, in turn, likely to enable others to feel higher degrees of freedom of choice, trust, and authenticity—all of which makes everyone more willing to give valid information that enables individuals to test their assumptions. In general, model-II learning tends to facilitate others' learning, which in turn facilitates one's own learning.

The behavioral world of model II tends to lead to both single-loop and double-loop learning—that is, learning that involves change in the governing variables of one's theories-in-use. Bilateral design and management of the environment, for example, makes change in one's initial definition of the task possible.

Theories-in-use based on model II do not tend to be self-sealing. The ability to question and change the values of the governing variables—thereby altering the action strategies and consequences—leads to a behavioral world in which learning and growth are consequences.

We believe these predicted consequences of model II are inherently plausible on the basis of the governing variables and action strategies of the model. They are also based, as we have indicated in some instances, on previous research, which will be discussed in Part III. The description of model II raises the following difficult, related questions, which we will confront in Part III.

Does model II assume that individuals are not to have goals of their own and that they should be willing to compromise their own perceived interests so that a consensual, bilateral definition of tasks can be achieved?

Does model II assume that the world will no longer be competitive and win/lose in nature? Does it assume that all conflicts can be reduced to nonconflicting tasks that may be jointly designed and managed?

What are the limits to the applicability of model II? To what extent is one's ability to behave according to model II limited by inherent psychological properties? For example, defensiveness, personal insecurity, and anxiety cannot be changed through a here-and-now interaction in which someone is trying to behave according to model II. Where does model II leave off and psychotherapy begin? If others in the situation are not prepared to behave according to model II, how can one achieve model II behavior?

Does model II ask us to abandon spontaneity, intuition, and action on feelings we cannot express in rational form?

Methodological Note

Models I and II do not attempt to predict individual variables—that is, the relationship of variable x to variable y. The models predict that people will behave according to a pattern of factors. As Part I showed, any given situation is highly complex and composed of tightly interrelated variables that are subject to many levels of analysis. Rigorous statements like "x is a function of y" have rarely led to increasing the effectiveness of human behavior. Statements of this kind are probably impossible to combine into guideposts for specific behavior. Our task is to identify the pattern of variables the actor needs to manage if he is to be effective in any situation.

Nevertheless, even if behavioral science knowledge could be taught so that an individual could control a situation, such knowledge would help the individual behave only according to model I. Model II teaches individuals to involve relevant others in defining which variables are to be important and what the relationships of the variables are to be.

Traditional research tends to create subject-researcher relationships that are congruent with model I (Argyris, 1968b). Rather than reinforce this type of professional technique, our goal is to develop research methodologies and instruments that are congruent with a model II world. If this could be accomplished, research activities and learning activities would reinforce each other; this, in turn, could offer feedback that increases the probability that subjects would try to give us minimally distorted information.

If research methods and instruments are to approximate Model II, four qualifications must be applied. (1) The research design could not be master-minded and unilaterally controlled by the researchers. Nor could the subjects be requested to cooperate primarily in order to contribute to knowledge about human behavior. (2) The instruments used should produce directly observable data that could be used by the subjects for designing and implementing their learning experiences. Instruments that depend on inferred categories (for example, questionnaires or interviews that do not collect actual examples) would not be used. (3) The hypotheses that researchers develop at any point should be openly stated. The research relationship should be designed so that subjects are strongly motivated to provide valid information; as a result, public statement of the variables and the hypotheses would not tend to cause them to distort the data. In other words, researchers' justifiable concern about contaminating the data would be shared with the subjects. Such involvement would include monitoring the degree to which they may be responding to what they believe the instructors want rather than to what they believe represents their own position (Argyris, 1970). We wanted to design situations in which subjects would be highly involved in the task of producing valid information. (4) We wanted to create a situation in which subjects were so interested in the public and rigorous testing of hypotheses that they would monitor continuously researchers' behavior.

In short, we wanted to design research methods determined by model II variables, which would result in double-loop learning and increasing effectiveness. We decided that we could generate model II research methods in small and large groups that were organized to help individuals change from model-I behavior to model-II behavior.

We reasoned that the transition processes would be difficult for the participants, fraught with tension and frustration. To the extent that they persevered, we would have highly motivated subjects who were willing to try many different learning exercises (each of which could become a mode of testing aspects of the theory) and to repeat them as often as they felt was necessary (giving us unusually lavish opportunities for re-test and replication). This high motivation to learn plus the high emotional cost of learning would induce subjects to develop rigorous tests for evaluating exercises; that they would participate only in exercises that they found, through active testing of the hypotheses, to be necessary.

Our method was to analyze a participant's case studies and assess the degree to which his behavior conformed to model I or model II; the cases overwhelmingly conformed to model I. A few participants described strategies that approximated model II, but their actual scenarios showed behavior congruent with model I.

Next, we publicly predicted how each participant would behave in class; we gave participants tasks in which they controlled the design of the environment—for example, participants became consultants to the role-playing instructors or to each other to help each other learn more effective behavior.

We predicted that all usable behavior would approximate model I (focus on rationality, suppress emotionality, or unilaterally control the environment and task). These predictions were made about several levels of behavior: the actor's behavior toward the instructor; the other's behavior toward the instructor; the instructor's behavior toward the actor (whose case was being discussed) or to the other person; the behavior of the participants toward each other; and the quality of group dynamics (degree of additivity in discussions, defensiveness of norms, degree of double-loop learning).

Participants helped to design any test and were encouraged to confront the validity of tests. Their ideas formed the basis for designing new learning experiences and new tests to evaluate all hypotheses. Researchers and participants were equally interested in these tests, which continued during the time of the study.

More empirical research on the development of model II methods is needed. Seldom are behavioral scientists publicly able to predict subject behavior (behavior that many subjects do not believe they will manifest) and have these predictions confirmed on many different levels of experience, replicated over time and under poorly controlled conditions (our test situations were not designed to encourage either model I or model II behavior, only the most effective behavior). Further research may verify whether the variables we have specified were responsible for creating the change from model I to model II behavior, which will be described in Chapter 6.

Chapter 6

Transition from Model I to Model II

Chapter Six shows the transition activities that may be necessary to change from model-I behavior to model-II behavior. They include, first, producing individual awareness and growth that lead to the development of new behavioral competence; second, individual participants' relationships with the instructors; third, group dynamics of learning are explored; and fourth, the group dynamics are applied to both participants and instructors.

We do not yet fully understand these processes or their interrelationships; the following description of these processes is therefore incomplete and fragmentary. It is differentiated into two categories. First, we describe the instructors designing the learning environment and the instructors' relationships to the participants, because at the outset the instructors are responsible for creating the learning environment. Second, as participants begin to expose their behavior and express the dilemmas implicit in it, we describe the participants' relationships with themselves, others, and the group.

Designing Experimental Environment

The transition processes from model I to model II should be designed according to model II, which is an ideal, something to which we can aspire but rarely expect to reach. It is a model that helps us define overall, intermediate, and short-range learning goals that satisfy the governing variables of valid information, free and informed choice, and internal commitment to the choice.

The basic design characteristics of the learning process will therefore be: (1) free choice to move toward model II based on valid information about the effectiveness of one's behavior; (2) little inconsistency within the espoused theory, within the theory-in-use, or between the espoused theory and the theory-in-use; and (3) a learning environment that produces valid information about each participant's espoused theories, theories-in-use, and any inconsistencies within each theory as well as among them. Valid information makes dilemmas recognizable, which creates tension to resolve them. This tension motivates learning. Note that we assume that individuals strive to behave effectively, and that valid information that they are not accomplishing this objective motivates learning. However, people sometimes say they do not wish to behave effectively; we diagnose this as defensive behavior. The first step with such individuals is to explore and uncover their defensiveness; this should reveal the dilemma and generate motivation toward growth. If it does not, our learning settings will not be helpful.

The instructor's role in the learning environment is a difficult one. Especially during the early phases of learning, participants will probably feel frustrated and uncomfortable and doubt whether they can learn model-II behavior; they may even doubt whether model II is valid. To compound the problem of disbelief and bewilderment, the instructor finds himself expected to feel successful if participants are eventually able to express the feelings and to confront the instructor.

The instructor's goal is to help participants take the first step toward change without a clear idea of what that change will involve and what paths lead to the goal. The instructor does not define goals unilaterally because this would follow model I and therefore

(1) impede the learning of model-II behavior and (2) discredit the usefulness of model-II behavior by example—participants would see that when the instructor is confronted by a difficult situation, he reverts to behavior that he says is ineffective. The instructor must (1) express his commitment to the validity of model-II behavior, (2) design environments for learning this behavior, (3) minimize coercing others toward model-II behavior, yet (4) maintain his commitment to model-II behavior in the face of the participants' sense of failure and frustration.

The instructor's goal may be restated as two paradoxes. The instructor's commitment to having others learn model-II behavior must be strong enough to withstand the difficulties of the instructor's own personal limitations and the participants' sense of failure and confrontation; that is, the instructor cannot express his commitment by coercing participants to learn model-II behavior because then they would not be learning by model-II processes. The second paradox is that the instructor should express his commitment to model II in a way that allows others to confront and reject model II.

Guidelines for Transition

There are no fixed ways to reach this goal since each seminar and each individual's response is different. However, certain guidelines may be helpful. Effective learning (1) is based on personally caused experience, (2) is usually produced by expressing and examining dilemmas, (3) values individuality and expression of conflicts, (4) must be guided by an instructor who has more faith in the participants than they may have in themselves, (5) who recognizes the limits of participants' learning methodologies, (6) whose idea of rationality integrates feelings and ideas and (7) who can encourage spontaneity.

Personally caused experience. The instructor should first create a learning environment in which individuals produce the behavior from which they begin to learn. The behavior should be of two types: behavior that participants feel is congruent with their values yet which produces consequences that they did not expect; and behavior that participants feel exhibits theories-in-use that are incongruent with espoused theories. The instructor should help participants generate free-flowing behavior; he will intervene when he can show that the behavior will tend to be counterproductive to actors' objectives or incongruent with espoused theories. Whenever the instructor intervenes to examine behavior, he should begin by identifying the behavior in directly observable categories (by repeating what the person said or by playing back a tape-recording) and then helping the participant to: (1) look forward—that is, to predict consequences of such behavior on himself and his environment; (2) look backward—that is, examine the governing variables of the behavior; and (3) identify the feedback that keeps the actor resistant toward change.

When the individual begins to design new behaviors, the same three steps are useful for learning about the consequences and effectiveness of the new behaviors. The individual produces the behavior and, with the cooperation of his colleagues, (1) looks forward to predict the behavioral world it would create and the consequences of that world on learning and effectiveness, (2) looks backward to determine which governing variables would apply if the new behavior were internalized into a new theory-in-use, and (3) identifies the feedback from the new model.

These three steps are our definition of experiential learning, which occurs when individuals recognize their theories-in-use and develop, if they wish, additional theories-in-use.

Examining dilemmas. Learning must be based on the discovery or surfacing of dilemmas. In Part I, we identified three types of dilemmas. They were (1) incongruency between espoused theory and theory-in-use; (2) inconsistency among the governing variables and action strategies; and (3) the degree of self-sealing, nonlearning processes that lead to behavioral ineffectiveness. If individuals can be helped to generate directly observable data from which they can infer—or confirm the validity of someone else's inference—that they are behaving incongruently and/or inconsistently and will therefore tend to become ineffective, then we have generated internal commitment for learning.

Why should dilemmas have this effect on people? Our theoretical perspective suggests—and the empirical data confirms—that inconsistency, incongruity, and unpredictability are not considered as valuable as consistency, congruence, and predictability because the former lead to a self-reinforcing cycle of ineffectiveness and non-learning or, at best, some single-loop learning, whereas the latter lead to a self-reinforcing cycle of effectiveness and learning. Individuals aspire to a sense of competence and effectiveness (White, 1956), as their espoused theories of action tell us. But competence and effectiveness are difficult to achieve in a model-I world because there is little valid feedback and much feedback that consists of game-playing and deception. Hence individuals lack (1) specific knowledge of the ways they are ineffective, or (2) knowledge that their action strategies are incongruent with some of their espoused governing variables, or (3) knowledge that their ineffectiveness is a function of their incongruity/inconsistency. Once individuals get valid feedback regarding their ineffectiveness, they aspire to make their theories-in-use consistent with espoused theory. This is how dilemmas lead to new learning.

The design of the learning environment should allow for a balance of dilemmas and their successful resolution so participants experience some psychological success. But psychological success does not depend on such a balance, alone; it results from reaching goals that are challenging and risky. Individuals with model-I behavior will need psychological support to set challenging goals, because they will lack the self-acceptance and inner confidence to withstand the embarrassment of failing while learning. Thus we see the need for a climate of psychological safety that approves of experimentation (Schein and Bennis, 1965). Such a climate does not, however, deny failure and whitewash poor results but examines them to see how they can be eliminated or reduced. The reinforcement that comes initially from others and later from oneself is the knowledge that one has made a genuine attempt and that failure occurred only because one's goals were beyond one's current abilities. Failure to perform beyond one's limits is not the same as failure to perform what one is capable of performing.

What conditions can the instructor create to help assure internal commitment to model II? First, he and group members can reward the individual for his learning and simultaneously encourage him to set realistically challenging (that is, ability-stretching) goals. Second, the instructor can try to help participants through a process of confirmation (Argyris, 1962). The instructor first asks how well an individual feels he has performed and why—that is, he asks for a positive or negative evaluation and the directly verifiable behavior from which the individual made his evaluation. Others are asked whether they agree or disagree with the directly verifiable information and the evaluation. If they agree, the learner experiences a sense of confirmation that he has perceived the world accurately and evaluated his performance in it accurately. His ability to evaluate is strengthened and so is his sense of confidence in this ability, which makes it more likely that he will try his performance again.

If others do not verify the actor's view of reality, they offer theirs and work through the differences until they agree on what actually happened and evaluate the behavior. If their evaluation is different from the actor's, they now have a basis on which to examine the different evaluations. The issues are then discussed until either the actor alters his evaluation, the others alter their evaluation, or all agree that no agreement is possible without further information. The last alternative may also commit all involved to seek further valid information to resolve the problem eventually.

If the individual is never able to achieve the new behavior, he may feel a sense of failure that will be confirmed by others. But if such feelings of failure are based on confirmed knowledge that the individual did his best, the probability that the individual will reject himself is minimized. This, in turn, may tend to help the individual accept his own limits or try to design new, more realistic ways to continue his learning.

It is important that participants learn to distinguish between dilemmas that produce single-loop learning and dilemmas that produce double-loop learning because only the latter lead toward model-II behavior and increased effectiveness. Recall the minister's dilemma of satisfying his parishioners, who wanted the church to take action on Cambodia, and yet not losing the commitment of the executive committee, especially its chairman. This conception of the dilemma is congruent with the governing variables of model I: (1) maximize winning and minimize losing; (2) save face (others' and your own); (3) suppress negative feelings, and (4) strive to be rational. The consequences of such dilemmas are also congruent with model I. The minister saw himself as winning or losing. In a model-I world, one often hears, "You can't win them all," or "Win a few, lose a few." Such attitudes do not lead to learning new behaviors. Indeed, these comments indicate that the actor expects to repeat such incidents.

One of the important things the minister learned was the discrepancy between his espoused theory and his theory-in-use. Once aware of this discrepancy, he could see that his behavior led to unwanted consequences at the interpersonal and personal level. (The chairman and many of the parishioners became angry at the minister's tactics, and the minister felt he had represented only part of his congregation.)

We will call dilemmas of the first type model-I dilemmas and dilemmas of the second type dilemmas of transition from model I to model II or transitional dilemmas. The consequences of recasting the model-I dilemma into a transitional dilemma produced new options for the concerned minister. If he could learn to behave according to model II, he would be able to state his own feeling about the need to act quickly without giving up his commitment to full congregational participation in the decision.

Another facet of this case has recurred in many other cases. The minister identified the cause of his model-I dilemma as the discrepancy between the espoused theory of the church on certain moral issues and its theory-in-use. The blame was shifted to the next larger organizational system. Such blame may be valid, but it serves to reduce the individual's awareness of his own role in the situation. Institutions can change to model-II behavior only when the individuals who belong to them change to model-II behavior.

Valuing individuality and conflict. Does model II assume that individuals are not to have goals of their own and that all behavior should be guided by bilateral consensus?

This is an important concern, especially if the world tends to be model-I oriented. Under these conditions, bilateral relationships and being concerned for the other are understandably seen as reducing the probabilities of winning and of being in control.

However, the governing variables of model II are not the opposite of model I. The model-II governing variables focus on generating valid information, free choice, and internal commitment. These variables may be satisfied if bilateral relationships are created and consensus among the relevant actors is valued. However, model-II instructs the individual to value free choice and internal commitment to the choice. If the individual permits interpersonal or group processes to determine his choices, then he is neither choosing freely nor developing internal commitment to the choices.

Model II encourages the individual to maximize his uniqueness. If, in doing so, he should arrive at goals that differ from those developed by others, he will have done so under conditions of openness, trust, and risk-taking. The individual would therefore feel free to discuss his differences openly with the group. Moreover, if the individual is in a subordinate power position, and if he feels he had adequate opportunity to dissuade the group and that the group publicly confronted and tested all differences, then the individual will probably be motivated to work toward the group goal but still be motivated to generate new information that may change the group's decision. This means one can be externally committed to a decision and internally committed to the decision-making processes that produced the decision yet simultaneously monitor the consequences of the decision thoroughly to seek new, valid information to reconfront the decision without being considered disloyal. In the model-II world, conflicts do not disappear—indeed, the illusion of conflict disappearing is more typical of the model-I world, in which conflicts are settled by power plays based on sanctions, charisma, or loyalty.

Competitiveness that creates win/lose dynamics is reduced in the model-II world because other people are viewed as resources with whom to generate valid and effective problem-solving processes, not competitors. Competition becomes individual competition against one's previous accomplishments.

This should not be interpreted as an argument that all conflicts can be resolved in a model-II world. Individuals who engage in model-II processes may discover that they are internally committed to goals that conflict and that they are unable to invent means of resolving the conflict. In such a case, the individuals will agree to enter into an enclave of model I. However, the means by which they do so will then tend to support model-II behavior thereafter.

We are not arguing that model II guarantees the resolution of all interpersonal conflicts but that model II leaves people free to discover that the goals to which they are committed are not in conflict and that the conflict is not self-fulfilling.

Instructors' faith in participants. At first, participants will experience dilemmas, ineffective behaviors, and failures; they may naturally begin to feel discouraged and helpless, which may lead them to push the instructor for resolutions to their dilemmas. Instructors will find it difficult to withhold the answers being requested and to maintain their role of helping participants design their own solutions. Yet, if participants are discouraged, instructors will see it as a positive sign if these feelings are based on a sense of confirmed incompetence. Instructors must help participants experience sadness without guilt and discouragement without surrender. This is difficult for people who behave according to model I, since guilt and incompetence are related under model I. If we define guilt as anger aimed toward oneself, we can predict guilt to occur in the following cases: if an individual evaluates himself as effective when he suppresses emotions, guilt may arise when he becomes emotional; if he feels he is effective when he saves face (for himself or for someone else), guilt may arise when he fails to save face; if he feels he is effective when he suppresses negative feelings in himself or others, guilt may arise when these negative feelings are expressed. In short, the model-I governing variables and action strategies will make incompetence or lack of control lead to guilt feelings.

The individual following model-II behavior is less likely to feel guilty because he strives to learn from incompetent or ineffective behaviors and is rewarded by others for doing so. He replaces guilt (anger toward oneself) with disappointment or impatience. He tries to evaluate how long it will take him to become more effective as a diagnostic first step. After all, exploring or mapping out one's degree of incompetence is as necessary as making a map of a prison from which one wants to escape.

Limits of learning methodologies   Our learning environments are limited by the competence, motivation, and capacities of both instructors and participants. Our approach makes certain requirements of both groups and succeeds only insofar as both groups meet these requirements.

First, instructors should be able to exhibit model-II behavior under conditions of mild to moderate stress; that is, their theories-in-use must be consistent with their espoused theories. To the extent that their theories-in-use are consonant with model II, participants will be exposed to model-II behavior. At first, participants will observe, question, and confront the instructor's behavior. Later, they may begin to experiment with model-II behavior. They may go through a transition period in which they openly acknowledge that they are trying to mimic the instructor's behavior. Such a statement may be an attempt to make the instructor responsible, thereby making it safe for the participant to experiment with new behavior. The instructor might discuss these possibilities after several such attempts have been made, pointing out the limitations for internalization if behavior is performed without full responsibility for risks.

Modeling behavior is not easy, and some people are better at it than others. Instructors should be as realistic as possible about their competence, admitting both their limitations and the effect these limitations may have on participants' learning.

Minimum standards of instructors' competence have yet to be determined, but we can suggest some guidelines. The instructor should (1) not take up more time for learning about his own behavior than any other participant would; (2) his response to participants' defensive behavior should not be compulsive; (3) he should be able to provide accurate cognitive maps of models I and II; and (4) he should be able to design noncoercive learning environments. Instructors should have internalized model II to the point that they are unconflictedly committed to it and to testing the model publicly and raising questions that challenge its foundations (double-loop learning).

Intense commitment and the excitement of confrontation and confirmation or disconfirmation helps instructors remain effective, especially during the difficult phases when most participants are questioning model II and the instructor's commitment to it. Note that the model, itself, asks for enthusiastic exploration of the possibility that parts of the model may be incorrect and ineffective or that we are not behaving according to the model.

This stance at first appears especially bewildering to participants and may be attacked as being arrogant. Although it is a firm stance—which depends on the individual's confidence in his openness to confrontation—model I is actually the more arrogant model because it requires the individual to win, manipulate, control, and hide these strategies from others.

This does not mean that there will not be episodes in which the instructor may also become unintentionally controlling. Instructors are human beings and, especially under great stress such as attack from many class members with minimum support from others, may behave defensively.

Highly competitive participants who fear failure may feel guilty early in the seminar. Given their low sense of self-esteem (usually associated with extreme fear of failure and competitiveness), the guilt may become intolerable. One strategy that would be consistent with model I would be to seek out any limit in model II and condemn the entire model on the basis of that limitation. For example, some people have insisted model II is useless because racists do not respond to or value the factors in the model. Others may condemn model II because openness is not possible with people who are neurotic and psychologically brittle. We acknowledge the latter case as a limit of our perspective. We would never recommend openness toward others that would harm others. We have repeatedly stated that such actions as openness are, in model II, designed bilaterally, not unilaterally.

Some participants have insisted that model II is invalid in the real world because it does not apply to these cases. In one session, students became angry and hostile, calling the instructor incompetent, foolish, impractical, and stupid and warned other students not to cooperate with him. After several hours of such attack, the instructor became angry and defensive. The aggressive students immediately pointed out that the instructor had not behaved according to model II and therefore had failed. The instructor admitted his defensiveness and added that he had felt it necessary to protect himself. With the exception of one student, the polarization and hostility dramatically and immediately decreased. It seemed that once the students could get the instructor to fail, they could accept the prospect of their own future failures more easily.

Sometimes instructors feel they need to control the group in order to assist learning. This is the paradox described earlier as inherent in the instructor's goals. That is, the instructor must not express his commitment to model II in a way that coerces others to accept model II because then their acceptance would be based on model-I behavior. Another way to put the paradox is: the instructor cannot ask the participant's permission to let him control the participant because the participant has little or no awareness of model II and its advantages. Moreover, the participant cannot have such awareness unless he can enter the environment that the instructor wants to create for him.

Under these conditions, the instructor should make the paradox explicit, then create the learning environment and behave so that others are encouraged to confront or reject the environment.

Finally, there are limits posed by the participants. For example, some individuals cannot diagnose their behavior because they have such strong defense mechanisms against failure that the diagnostic process may be too painful. These difficulties must be respected and the individuals be helped to leave the seminar if it should become too painful. Leaving the seminar would be in everyone's best interests when a participant displays these signs: (1) inability to produce directly observable behavior (through cases or role-playing); (2) compulsive negative evaluation of incompetent behavior (especially during the early phases), guilt feelings, and a predisposition to punishing oneself or others; (3) denial of the validity and usefulness of the diagnostic phases to an extent that he (a) prevents others from further exploration, (b) compulsively berates others for small but genuine progress, and (c) consistently reacts to nonachievement with great guilt or anger.

Integrating ideas and feelings. We regard conventional separation of ideas, feelings, and behavior as inappropriate. Ideas tend to be feeling-laden, feelings have both cognitive and behavioral correlates, and behavior is based on both rational ideas and feelings. Model-I worlds tend to hide these connections, while model-II worlds tend to acknowledge them.

In a model-I world, feelings tend to be suppressed and ideas tend to be revered. Maturity is defined as controlling emotions and being cool, rational, and level-headed. Under these conditions, feelings tend to become separated from ideas, and the feeling components of ideas tend to be suppressed. Ideas are considered objective and associated with effectiveness, while feelings are considered objective and associated with ineffectiveness.

The kinds of feelings experienced and the conditions of their expression are different in models I and II. In model I, feelings tend to burst out when an individual becomes defensive. This tends to support norms for suppressing expression of feelings because feelings are associated with ineffectiveness; this reinforces the model-I assumption that behavior tends to become ineffective as people express their emotions.

The governing variables of a model-II world value all relevant human activity, whether ideas or feelings. Feelings are not suppressed and their expression is not to be considered a necessary cause of ineffectiveness or an indication of immaturity; feelings are not separated from ideas and are considered valid information in the quest for behavior aimed at exploring, reducing inconsistency, and predicting events correctly.

Spontaneity. Although model II values efficiency and competence, it does not reject spontaneity. However, spontaneity does not occur independently; it is an interpersonal phenomenon. *A*'s spontaneity may inhibit *B*'s spontaneity. Spontaneity may be effective or ineffective; it is ineffective if it harms oneself and/or others, becoming self-sealing and reinforcing iow self-esteem and distorted interaction and communication.

In a model-II world, spontaneity that inhibits the generation of valid information, free choice, trust, and double-loop learning is reduced. If the person does behave spontaneously and that behavior inhibits others, then the actor: (1) admits the dysfunctionality before the behavior ("I know this isn't helping anyone, but I'm going to blow up."), (2) admits the dysfunctionality after the behavior ("Okay, now that I've blown my top and I've gotten it off my chest, let's get back to work."), or (3) is open to learning that his behavior had dysfunctional consequences even though he did not see it that way.

To put it another way, model II allows people to express positive and negative feelings in a way that minimizes harming others and creating guilt in the actor if he realizes later that his behavior was dysfunctional.

People in a model-II world are angry, amused, tender, and puzzled at life. What is decreased is the kind of spontaneity that results from expression of pent-up feelings. Such spontaneity is not being yourself but your suppressed self. In a model-II world, as feelings gain an equal status with reason and individuals become more aware of feelings and consciously use them more effectively, an undistorted, truly spontaneous expression of feelings will result.

Model II assumes that all behavior (emotional and intellectual) can be understood according to some theory-in-use. Freud's early writings, for example, describe the economy of human defenses; all defensive behavior, no matter how apparently irrational, makes sense if we understand what motivates it. Freud saw the therapist's task as making sense of apparently irrational behavior. Therapy could be facilitated if the patient could be helped to see that the behavior that seemed irrational, disordered, nonunderstandable was indeed ordered, sensible, and understandable.

The fear that bringing feelings or spontaneity under control of the actors will lead to decreased spontaneity is a predictable model-I fear because control is unilateral. We suggest the development of a model-II world where rationality (the valuing of consistency that leads to competence; the valuing of inconsistency that leads to learning; and both that lead to increased effectiveness) is seen as having both intellectual and emotional components; where understanding the economy of action is valued; and where spontaneity is valued to the extent that it does not inhibit one's own and others' effectiveness.

Chapter 7

Learning Model-II Behavior

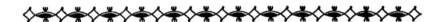

The discussion of guidelines in Chapter Six assumed that the instructor's role is known and accepted by participants, but neither of these assumptions is necessarily valid. Most participants view the instructor's role as helping them to learn. Some participants agree that the instructor knows more than they do, are willing to listen to his views, are willing to see how congruent his theory-in-use and espoused theory are, and then choose how much they will learn from the instructor.

   Other participants—especially graduate students and those who have participated in experiential learning, such as T groups and encounter groups—have difficulty viewing the instructor as someone who is more competent than they are, someone who is more aware of his theory-in-use, someone who behaves congruently, and someone who is initially probably more knowledgeable than they are. Indeed, as we shall see, if the instructor is able to model these competences, some of these students tend to feel intimidated. When the feelings of intimidation are acknowledged, we see that

110

they occur precisely because students realize the instructor's competence. The students' initial skepticism may serve to block the possibility that they have not learned to accept and use dependence for learning.

Instructor's Role in Designing Initial Environment

Whatever the participants' attitudes are, the instructor's initial task is to demonstrate his competence in building consistent and effective espoused theories and theories-in-use and behaving according to them. The instructor must also show that, although he is committed to his own approach to learning, he is equally committed to further learning. Since learning comes from becoming aware of one's own inconsistencies, the instructor views the participants as a potential resource that will become an actual resource only as participants confront him. Effective confrontation of this sort will help the instructor to learn but will also be an example of the effectiveness of model-II behavior.

The first step is to arrange a situation for exposing behavior. The exposure may need to follow specified dimensions because, at the outset, participants will behave according to model I and will produce group dynamics congruent with model I, which are not appropriate conditions for learning. The instructor should expose his espoused theory (model II), offering it as something to be considered as a potential ideal state to strive toward. The instructor should clarify that his goal is for himself and the participants to design environments that produce learning of model-II concepts and behavior and encourage continual confrontation of model-II concepts. In other words, the instructor publicly acknowledges his microtheories of human action, he asks for public testing of his theories, and he simultaneously reveals his biases and intentions regarding the seminar. His message is that the seminar is designed to help participants become more competent in diagnosing their behavior and restructuring it according to their theories-in-use, meanwhile encouraging confrontation of their theories-in-use.

This learning strategy assumes that most participants are not effective sources for learning about model-II behavior. We do not question the genuineness of their motivation, only their competence.

A further assumption is that participants need the instructor more than the instructor needs the participants, especially at first. These assumptions should be tested publicly to see if they are confirmed by directly observable data.

Each participant's assumptions should also be tested. Some participants, especially those with T group or encounter group experience, may value interpersonal closeness more than behavioral effectiveness. Or, a participant may assume he can learn more from fellow participants than from the instructor. Such assumptions should be publicly tested to determine if they are based on valid information. To make such an assumption before one knows the others, however, is not based on valid information nor has it been tested. Why should one hold such an assumption? One answer is that in T groups and encounter groups, the assumption is designed to generate interpersonal closeness. If I value you, you will value me, and we may thereby increase the sense of closeness and decrease the probability of rejection. Such closeness, based on no directly observable data or on public testing of its existence, results from an interpersonal game common in the model-I world, which is a game of controlling others (and, since others do the same, being controlled by them).

For example, one participant said, "I know that I will learn as much from you as I can learn from the instructor." The instructor chose to confront her by exploring openly why she expected to learn from others before she knew whether they could teach her anything. Surfacing this issue also prevented others from accepting her attitude as a norm before the attitude was first tested. Here is their conversation.

Instructor: How do you know you can learn from the other participants?
Participant A: What do you mean?
Instructor: Have you tried to learn from them yet?
A: I feel that I have.
Instructor: I know you do, but, at this point, perhaps you can learn more from me than the others.
A: In your field?
Instructor: Yes.

A: Well, your comments have been good.

Instructor: Why not experiment? How else can you begin to find out who can help you? Indeed, it may turn out that I am more helpful than the class.

A: Now, wait a minute. I'm scared of your competence. I have trouble responding.

Instructor: Is it my behavior that causes you to have trouble responding?

A: I just feel I can learn from others.

Instructor: How would you go about testing the validity of that view?

A: I think I resent your saying that you're the most important one here.

Instructor: I think I am saying that I may be the most important one here for you at this time.

B: You are to me.

C: Me too.

D: Now, wait a minute. . . .

A discussion followed that confirmed that the instructor's ideas and evaluations were more important to most participants than other participants' ideas and evaluations.

Dealing with Participant Dependence

At the beginning of the seminar, the instructor may present model I and model II, which diagnose why individuals and human systems (such as groups and organizations) have the difficulties they do and how to overcome these difficulties. These two models make the diagnostic and action biases of the instructor explicit. They also offer participants an early opportunity to confront these biases. Such a confrontation, in turn, provides experiential evidence of how well the instructor knows his material, how open he is to public confrontation, how willing he is to test publicly hypotheses implicit in his models, and how congruently he behaves according to his action model. The more effectively the instructor performs these activities, the more dependency he may create. Participants may be convinced that the instructor is competent and that they can learn more from him than from other group members; this may be important for modeling effective action.

However, during the first stages of the seminar when each participant is striving to diagnose his theory-in-use, fellow participants can be an important resource. Although each person may be unaware of his own theory-in-use, he may be more aware of others' theories-in-use. Participants may be more willing to listen to fellow participants who are in the same boat, than to the instructor, whose competence may cause feelings of ambivalence and hostility.

In other words, the instructor can help participants design and manage the direction of their seminar by stating the direction he would like it to take and stating that his idea is based on competence and effectiveness in this area. The instructor is then subject to being evaluated. Participants confront their dependence on the instructor by asking "Can we move in the direction described by the instructor?" If they find they cannot, which tends to be the case, there is pressure to question and confront the model. If instructors do not specify their position on these issues, the question of whether the seminar's goals can be met still exists yet cannot be dealt with openly.

The difference between our approach and a less structured one is that the issues of uncertainty, anxiety over personal competence, direction, and failure, may be confronted as participants respond to the instructor's structure. In the less structured approach, the same issues exist but cannot be addressed at such an early stage. Moreover, even if they were, participants' theories-in-use, of which they are unaware, would require them to have a polite, and diplomatic debate in which some people win and some lose and in which the governing variables are not confrontable.

Generating and Surfacing Dilemmas

As a next step in the seminar, a case study can be presented for group discussion. We recommend a case study generated in another group (appropriately disguised and used with the permission of the writer) for two reasons. First, we want to reduce participants' hesitation in discussing the case, which may result because (1) most people do not want to hurt others, (2) they avoid confronting others so others will not confront them, and (3) many participants are trying less to diagnose their behavior than to show others, especially the instructor, how effective they are and how well they compete with their peers. (Their behavior is being informed by model-I governing variables.)

Second, if group members are presented with a case that is not written by one of them, and if it is true that they will feel freer to analyze it, then the behavior that they manifest while analyzing will tend to be a valid specimen, produced under conditions of minimal threat. This is important because the behavior of analyzing the case forms an important foundation for later learning.

The agenda of the seminar group, therefore, is to read a case study that describes a difficult intervention. They are asked to act as consultants to the case's actor to help him manage the intervention more effectively. The instructor takes the role of the actor and behaves in as supportive a way as possible to the class consultants. Several volunteers act as observers to report progress during the diagnostic discussion.

One group discussed Dean Sylvan's case. Recall that Dean Sylvan met with a professor in order to get the professor to agree to remain in an administrative position rather than return to teaching. Dean Sylvan was unable to get the professor to agree; indeed, the professor became even more upset than she had been.

The instructor (role-playing Dr. Sylvan) began the case by telling the class that he needed help from them on the following issues: "Please help me to see how I can communicate to the professor that she cannot return to class in such a way that she will hear our reasons for this action accurately and she will be able to confront the reasons for the action without taking legal action."

The instructor then suggested that each participant who wished could make several short interventions and then let someone else do so. The role-playing lasted about one-half hour. Next, the instructor asked participants to evaluate his role-playing of Dean Sylvan. For example, how difficult was Dean Sylvan? Was he more difficult than the Dean Sylvan in the case? The unanimous vote (of those who did not participate as consultants) was that the faculty member role-played Dean Sylvan in a less defensive, less emotional way than they had expected. Some felt that Dean Sylvan was much too patient. Remember that it is important to explain that Dean Sylvan was role-played to be as cooperative as possible so participants could not blame their ineffective behavior on any apparent recalcitrance of Dean Sylvan.

Then the group was asked to discuss the interaction. The participants acting as consultants felt Dean Sylvan (referring always to the instructor's role-playing) was blocking progress, not listening to them, projecting, displacing, and behaving rigidly. The instructor then asked the two observers (who had been asked to observe the interaction, not participate as consultants) to give their views. They reported that Dean Sylvan had been flexible, listened attentively, tried to use the advice, and was patient. They accused the consultants of being punishing, attributive, controlling, demanding, and rigid. An analysis of the tape-recording confirmed the observers' views. Thirty-five interventions were made of varying lengths, of which twenty-seven were audible. All twenty-seven illustrated model-I behavior, as the following quotes show. "When you gave the professor the special assignment a year ago, what reason did you give her to take that assignment?" "So you are satisfied that the professor's complaints are justified? ["Yes," says Dean Sylvan.] Well, I think you're going to have to square with her. You can't beat around the bush." "Why did you wait a year to speak with her?" "Why did you want to hurt this person? That's the kind of feeling I had throughout. The professor is quite strong and can handle this. You're projecting some of your fears onto her. I'm getting a feeling that whenever you confront the professor, you, yourself, seem to be under great stress and anxiety and that you have really never talked with her about the problem. You are actually manipulating her." "What do you really think of the professor?" "Do you feel the professor's stomping-out behavior is rational?" "You seem to make nice answers to our questions and you stop things. I wonder what you think of the points made so far?"

After a short break, during which participants discussed the differences between the observers' and consultants' views, the group listened to the tape-recording of the role-playing. The consensus was that each person could easily see how others were behaving ineffectively but had considerable difficulty seeing his own incompetence; those who were able to see their own incompetence were shocked.

Group members unanimously agreed that part of their ineffectiveness was due to too little time for each participant to express his strategy fully. They suggested that a smaller group of consultants, each allowed more time to speak, would be more effective. The instructor agreed to try this approach in the next session. When he asked someone to volunteer to let his case study be discussed the next session, no one volunteered; the instructor assigned the task to someone and added that he hoped that, as time passed by, the reasons why participants didn't take more responsibility and initiative for designing and scheduling their own learning would be surfaced and worked through.

During the next session, the individual whose case was discussed became the client. He was asked to define what kind of help he was seeking. Three consultants were appointed by the class, and the rest of the class acted as observers. Again, the members behaved according to model I. An analysis of the tape recording suggested that (1) some consultants, who believed the important task was to define the initial contract completely, tried to do so only to find (a) the client was not ready to do so, (b) they had too little time, and (c) their strategy was not supported by the other consultants. (2) Some consultants thought their task as to decide what the client did wrong and then to test their diagnoses covertly (lest the client understand and distort his replies). However, the client sensed the interventions and began to wonder what the consultants had in mind. He, too, hid this concern and his responses were considered indirect, confused, and defensive. (3) When the consultants felt confident—which for some was at the outset of their diagnosis and for others later on—they tried to sell their diagnoses to the client. As the client described it, "I felt I had to buy their diagnosis," and "Everything they said clearly confirmed, in their eyes, their diagnosis." Clients did not surface these feelings during the role-playing. Again, consultants sought unilateral control, and both client and consultant repressed feelings and fears about each other. Also, participants were beginning to realize that they behaved according to model I rather than model II, which created group dynamics that inhibited learning. For example, they decided that the consultants competed with each other, cancelled out each other's effectiveness, and that other participants behaved in the same way when they told consultants about their ineffectiveness. These conclusions led one participant to say that this confirmed the idea that increased personal effectiveness depends on the behavioral world created in the seminar. The group agreed and decided that during the discussion of the next case there would be one consultant with a helper. This model did not produce significantly different results.

The class began to realize how hard it was for them to accept that a key factor in their ineffectiveness was each individual's adherence to a model-I theory-in-use. They struggled valiantly to blame their ineffectiveness on external phenomena, only to find that they were partly responsible for causing the external phenomena. They began to learn that their personal effectiveness and the group's effectiveness are intimately related; one is not more internal and the other more external than the other.

Participants may understandably doubt the practicality of model-II behavior. The six most frequently asked questions and our answers are listed next.

In the real world, is it possible to have as much time as model II seems to require to solve the problem? Problem-solving may take so much time only because the skills are still new to individuals. In the real world, much time is wasted in meetings, political rivalries, and fights because the proper issues are not discussed. If there really is not enough time, under circumstances of trust, this will be quickly recognized.

Will other people cooperate? Probably not at the beginning. They will probably be as frustrated and resistant as the group members are now being.

Is it right to suppress conflict? Model II suggests that we do the opposite. We are surfacing conflict. Haven't our group sessions become dissatisfying whenever conflict was suppressed?

Isn't conflict useful? All kinds of behavior are, including conflict, are useful if they can be discussed and thus publicly tested. This provides the basis for learning.

Arent's you really asking for a change in the entire world? After all, aren't most organizations administered according to model-I values, structures, and controls? Yes, they are, which is why we don't expect behavior change to take less than a year.

Will behavioral changes last if organizational structures and managerial controls are not redesigned to be congruent with model-II values? Yes, organizational structures and controls need to be redesigned, but such redesign should be based on participants' ideas and implemented by people who are capable of behaving according to model II. The theory-in-use must match the new organizational structures and controls; otherwise, an enormous sense of inconsistency and lack of credibility will result.

Some participants may attack the instructor's behavior or motives in ways that are not supported by the other members. These attacks may persist and inhibit all members' learning. Some members (still in the competitive framework) may secretly wonder how the instructor will cope with being clobbered. Such attacks cannot be ignored. The instructor may respond to these attacks just as he would respond to other inquiries. Thus, if he is accused of being defensive or manipulative, he asks for the directly observable data ("What did I do or say?") that led to the attribution. There may be disagreement on what actually occurred. A tape-recorder would be useful in such a case. Once the data are agreed upon, if the instructor and others conclude that the instructor was, indeed, defensive or manipulative, then he should acknowledge what he has learned and value it just as any other member would.

However, if no such agreement occurs and the attack continues, the instructor may first determine if others in the group are interested in taking responsibility for protecting the group's learning time. If no one else is willing to do so, the instructor, himself, may confront the individual with the rationale that he (the educator) is not a masochist who enjoys being punished, nor, as one member of the group, is he going to sanction the attacks.

Another type of attack is for a participant to cite extreme cases. Thus, openness may be considered threatening and dangerous because honest feedback could harm someone. The instructor may respond that (1) openness means that A says what he believes in such a way that B can do the same. (2) If A has evidence that B could be harmed by A's minimally evaluative and attributive feedback, then it would not make sense to give B such feedback. How-

ever, one could also question *B*'s psychological health. (3) Why
should a principle about openness that applies to thousands of different situations be rejected because it fails in an extreme case?

Confronting Instructor and Peers

As this lesson begins to be seen as valid and conclusive,
participants' dependence on the instructor and the value of his
model begins to increase, as does participants' hostility toward the
instructor. Hostility is difficult for participants to express. They
tend to equate expression of hostility with incompetence and therefore a loss in the win/lose dynamics of model I, but some participants do needle the instructor. For example, "Aren't we letting this
minimally attributive stuff get in our way? Can't we be ourselves?
If you feel like attributing—hell, attribute." Or, "I know this is going to be an evaluative comment, but, hell, I don't know how else
to say it [turning to the faculty member], even if you think it's
bad."

Moreover, participants depended on the instructor, who
seemed to be competent, somewhat assured, and therefore intimidating. This idea seemed easy to surface, especially if participants
considered intimidation the instructor's fault. For example, one episode began with a participant who said he was finding the learning
experience challenging and intimidating. When asked for an example of each feeling, he altered his comment, saying instead that he
meant the instructor was intimidating.

Instructor: What do I do that makes me intimidating?
Participant A: I'm not sure. You seem to be way ahead of
us. I don't know; I'm not sure.
B: I know what's intimidating to me. I'm very much aware
that I'm in a subordinate relationship to you, and this affects my
ability to convey my views to you. I think that one of the barriers
to effective communication can be the anxiety the subordinate feels.
Also, I'm very much aware of your being an authority on the subject. I have to prove to myself that I can present my position and
not be intimidated by your status.

C: May I add something to that? Last week, I felt over-whelmed by the whole class and couldn't respond because things were going too fast.

D: Yes, me too. [To instructor] You, especially, went so fast, that I was unable to formulate a question.

E: I have similar kinds of worries with other faculty members.

A: I felt better last week when you talked with me after class. I realized that I was comfortable in areas that I have some knowledge about.

Instructor: How do others feel? Any other views?

F: There is a gap of competence between you and us. With your years of study, you are prepared and competent, so there is this inferiority situation that can affect our behavior.

C: I should add that, in most situations and here particularly, I very much want people to have a high opinion of me. When I say something and get tongue-tied, will you have a lower opinion of me? Do I trust you enough so that, if I am open, your opinion of me won't go down?

G: I think it's also true that we're worried about the impact we may have on other students in this course.

H: I feel a little distrustful. I don't know if distrustful is the correct word, but I always feel that I'm going down in your book.

E: Yes, I fear that you're making attributions about us and aren't sharing them.

The instructor responded to participants *E* and *C*'s comments first. He said that if he made attributions, he would surface them, provide the directly observable data for them, and then ask the individual to confirm or disconfirm them. He also said he felt little need to make attributions, but when he did make some, he felt compelled to share them and the data on which they were based in order to test them. The instructor added that people who make attributions and refuse to test them are probably saying as much about their own defenses as they are about the other person. Finally, the instructor asked if anyone was implying that he should somehow cover up, play down, or deny his expertise in order not to intimidate the group.[1] Most participants said that they wanted the instructor to behave as competently and knowledgeably as possible. The following dialogue then took place.

Instructor: Let me test something. Are some of you saying that it is somewhat intimidating to be with a person who seems to have thought through what he is talking about?

Participant B: Yes, I've felt that tonight. I've been anxious about my ineffectiveness ever since your lecture showed that you had some criteria to assess effectiveness. I feel a competence gap and yet I'm realizing that one of my first tasks is to accept the gap and work on reducing it.

Instructor: And perhaps I can help to design learning situations to help you and others.

H: I don't feel anxious or intimidated. I guess my view is that the instructor knows more than I know or may even want to know. I want to learn as much as I can from him and others.

I: Me, too. Can we get back to learning more about the theory?

D: I just want to say that I found this discussion valuable. It is an example of generating valid information in a class. Hell, I'm in several psychology courses, but this is the first one in which I'm talking about my own theory.

Instructor: Before we turn to other subjects, I want to test my understanding. You're saying that I should continue to behave as I have; if my behavior gets in someone's way, you will help me to see it. You are now assigning the feelings of intimidation more to yourselves than to me. [Several people nodded affirmatively.] I found this discussion helpful. I wanted to reduce any intimidating effect I had, but I didn't believe it was fair to assign all the causes of intimidation to me.

Instructors may ask for feedback in order to grow, but their already achieved level of effectiveness may seem painfully high to participants; so, focusing on the instructor's learning will not facilitate the group's progress.

Participants also hesitate to reveal their feelings about each other. However, as they begin to realize that others' behavior is partly caused by their own, they conclude that they must begin to level with each other. People begin to ask each other if they are being really open with each other; as these questions are raised, the instructor can assist by providing directly observable data, as the following examples will show.

Participant *D* complained that she was silent in the group because the "level of noise in this group gets very high. I find people being arrogant and hostile, and I can't think under those conditions." *E* and *F*, also quiet members, agreed that some group members were arrogant, hostile, controling, and authoritarian. The group members in question apologized and asked the group to help them reduce this behavior. The instructor immediately played back the preceding events on the tape-recorder. Group members realized that *D, E,* and *F* had made their accusation with the same behavior that they were criticizing, yet this had not been confronted.

Participant *F* seemed oblivious to how dependent he was on the instructor and other members. When he was not present, other participants had described him as appearing to fear taking initiative. In the next session, *F* said the instructor was not helping him to express himself to the group. The instructor felt irritated, partly because *F* had accused him of this several times before. He responded to *F,* "What do you want me to do—hold your hand? Stand on your own two feet!" In the silence that followed, several members seemed stunned by the instructor's behavior. The subject of the discussion was changed. After ten minutes, the instructor asked perimssion to control the group and cut off the discussion. The members agreed. The instructor asked *F* how he felt about what the instructor had said. "Terrible," was his reply. "How about others?" asked the instructor. Their responses included surprise, shock, and anger.

"How did I prevent you from saying this to me at the time?" asked the instructor. "How will I be an effective group member if such behavior is permitted to go by?"

Someone asked the instructor whether his response had been sincere or role-playing. He answered that he had been genuinely angry at *F.* Another member pointed out that the instructor's response had not been helpful. Someone else suggested that the instructor must have been suppressing his feelings about F for a long time. The instructor agreed and suggested that this was what he meant by needing the group to grow. But why had he not surfaced this issue before, asked a few members? "For the same reason that we haven't done so," retorted several others. Again, the group discussed how open and effective they were. "We have got to go beyond strapping on a gun each time we come to the sessions," they concluded.

G wanted to discuss an example of the instructor violating model II by being manipulative. G had made a special effort to attend a past session because his case was to be discussed. To his surprise, when he arrived the group suggested the instructor review model I to help the group understand what had been happening and why. The instructor asked G if he would mind postponing the discussion of his case. He replied, "I made a special effort to be here tonight to discuss my case, but if the group wants to hear about model I, I'll gladly agree." The trouble was, G continued, he had not really agreed with the change and became angry at the instructor for manipulating the group, although he had not said so. Indeed, he added, he had become even angrier at himself when he realized that he had permitted the faculty member to get away with it. The instructor asked for other reactions to the incident. Several people agreed with G. One individual said that although the instructor had behaved in a controlling manner at times, he had identified it as such and had asked the group's permission. Another person noted that the instructor had spent quite a long time pressing G, who had said he really was happy to postpone his case. G and several others denied this. The tape-recording of that session was played; it confirmed that the instructor had indeed supported G, insisting that the lecture be postponed if it upset G—who, it turned out, had participated in the decision the week before to ask the instructor to review model I.

These incidents helped the group explore their feelings toward the instructor, including their tendency to distort relationships with power figures, more openly. The instructor admitted that, although he was intellectually aware that such experiences were inevitable, they still made him impatient and angry. He, too, needed to be understood independent of his power position.

Diagnostic Strategies

The next stage of the group process consists of individuals taking the initiative to experiment with new diagnostic strategies. They strive to learn how to diagnose behavior more effectively. A new diagnostic behavior occurred when the class accepted the instructor's recommendation to try to build a model of the problem implicit in a case before they decided who would act as consultants. G's case was to be discussed. (G's case involved his job as mediator between a medical center and the community it served. Specifically, it concerned a discussion he had had with clients who had complained about the medical services they had received. G sympathized with the clients' complaint and thought it was justified, but he risked losing his job if he didn't defend the medical center, although he thought its personnel were too conservative and rigid. G became impatient during the discussion he described because he felt he had to defend both sides.) G was asked to specify the kind of help he was seeking; he replied that he wanted to gain more insight into, and eventually reduce, his impatience with clients.

The group began the discussion with a conscious attempt to develop a diagnosis based on directly observable data and a clear connection between the data and the diagnosis. The instructor wrote the factors on the board and asked for the directly observable data from which the factor was inferred. Soon, everyone presented his inferences with either data from the case or a request for other participants to confirming or disconfirming his inference.

As the instructor wrote the inferences on the blackboard, he organized them according to models I and II, as Table 3 shows. The first column in Table 3 describes G's actions and focuses on the dilemmas (as inferred by the class from G's case study) that his behavior manifested. The second column contains inferences about the consequences of the dilemmas on G. The third column focuses on the consequences for G's ability to learn under these conditions.

We can predict that G or anyone else functioning under

Table 3. DIAGNOSIS OF WHY G IS SO IMPATIENT WITH CLIENTS

Dilemmas in G's actions	*Consequences of dilemmas for G*	*Consequences for G's predisposition to learn and behave effectively*	
1. He conceives of himself as a mediator yet behaves as an adversary or advocate.	1. The situation is nearly impossible, yet G aspires to win.	1. G suppresses consequences from awareness in order to win.	Ineffectiveness (including impatience toward others and self).
2. He speaks of participants' control yet unilaterally controls the meeting.	2. The level of aspiration for the meeting was unrealistically high.	2. Tensions exist and probably increase over time.	
3. He has great commitment to the community and great commitment to the medical center.	3. G fears losing his job if he does not defend the medical center, yet he also fears failing the community.	3. G is unable to test publicly important hypotheses about the community and medical center representatives.	
4. He diagnoses the physicians as rigid yet behaves as rigidly as they do.		4. There is little learning in this situation.	
		5. Group and intergroup relations are defensive.	
		6. G is personally defensive.	

these conditions would not be effective; his impatience with others would include impatience with himself; which would reinforce the consequences and make it increasingly unlikely that *G* would become aware of the dilemmas in his own behavior. His energies were focused on suppressing the consequences and trying to win without losing the respect of either side.

Once the diagnosis was completed, *G* said he found it extremely helpful. He began to make sense out of an important pattern that he found he had repeated in previous jobs.

The group explored further why *G* should have found the diagnosis helpful. Our inferences about the process were as follows. The diagnosis and the chart (Table 3) had helped him understand the experience better; that is, he was able to relate various factors from different levels of experience and see how they made his impatience an inevitable consequence. It became clearer that he, himself had caused his impatience, yet he could now accept his personal causality with minimum guilt because the dozen other participants, whom he had come to respect, agreed unanimously that they would behave impatiently under these conditions.

The diagnosis also helped *G* think about how he could manage his impatience more effectively. For example, in a similar situation, he could tell his clients that he would probably show strong desires to help and to win. These desires might at times make him appear unhelpful, and if that should happen, he would appreciate it if they would tell him; he would then do his best to correct his behavior. *G* could also design a new consulting relationship with the client in which the factors that produced the dilemmas could be reduced. *G* could also reduce his level of aspiration with less guilt and anxiety, especially if this would help him be more effective with the clients.

This case clarifies some differences between therapy and seminars like those we have been describing, which are called effectiveness education. Therapy helps the individual discover the historical causes of his high desire to win, his fear of interpersonal rejection, the defenses that helped him to be blind to his dilemmas, and other factors. In therapy, this case could have been an excellent catalyst for *G* to begin exploring the pattern of his personality structure. Such an exploration would be necessary and more fruitful than effectiveness education if *G* were unable to listen to the diagnosis without becoming unproductively anxious, if *G* were unable to understand Table 3 as a basis for learning and altering his behavior, if *G* were unable to see his own part in causing his impatience, and if *G* were unable to see that impatience was a manifestation of a broader set of issues than personality. In short, therapy might be necessary if *G* were so closed to learning that he could not learn from an environment beginning to approximate model II.

New Action Strategies

The next stage of the group process may be reached earlier by some than by others. It may be indicated by such statements as "I realize this may be attributive but let me try . . . ," "Let me pull an Argyris . . . ," or "I wonder what Schön would do. . . ." Every attempt to try new behavior is reinforced by the instructor. If the participant credits the instructor with his idea, the instructor accepts the credit but then surfaces the problem of mimicking the instructor—it permits experimentation without responsibility, which can either reduce the sense of failure if the experiment fails or reduce others' possible mistrust if they realize that the actor is experimenting with new behavior that reflects the instructor's model. The latter reason is realistic and functional. The former may be realistic, but it is functional only in the model-I win/lose framework.

Another indication of this stage in the transitional process is when someone designs a new intervention based on his understanding of model II. For example, during the first several group sessions, discussions of case studies always began with the client specifying the kind of help he wanted. One day, a participant who was acting as client said he wanted to change the format: in accordance with model II, he wanted to evaluate his own behavior and then see to what extent his evaluation would be confirmed or disconfirmed by the rest of the group. He also said he didn't want to inhibit anyone from "Letting me have it." Someone asked if that meant he distrusted the group members to be fully honest with him. He admitted that was true and that he felt that way because he had withheld valid information from others. This honest admission led others to be equally open about also withholding information. The episode therefore led not only to more learning by the individual but also to a more effective group. Beginning with one's own evaluation and asking for confirmation or disconfirmation became a norm for several sessions.

One day another member said she would like to try something different. She had taken the next step of rewriting her case study before class and said she wanted to read sections of it to obtain the group's reactions. She had analyzed her case in terms of model-I variables (attributions, evaluations) and rewritten it as she would now have preferred to react in the case. She admitted that the new dialogue, if more effective, did not indicate that she was able to behave more effectively under real-time conditions. She acknowledged that she had spent all evening rewording her dialogue, and that it had been a difficult process. She realized more clearly why the key to her new dialogue was developing new governing variables and new behavior. For example, she would consider dialogue the instructor might use but reject it unless she was certain she could defend it. She said, "Only when I felt I could be firm about the dialogue, only when I took full responsibility for it, and only when I felt I would be glad to have it challenged did I include it. This is why I'm reading it. Actually, I had time to rewrite only about half my case." She was beginning to show unconflicted commitment and simultaneously high openness to inquiry, and she was learning how difficult it was to develop.

Tape-recordings of past sessions could also be used at this stage. Participants could listen to them and recreate the case studies to show more effective interaction.

Once individuals begin to accept model-II values, they can be divided into smaller groups. This allows more active experimenting and practicing with new behavior under the watchful eye of peers who are now more internally committed than formerly to the assumption described at the beginning of the chapter. Although this description of progress from one stage of the transitional process to another may suggest that the events flow in a smooth and orderly way, this is not the case.

For example, there is the case of A, who decided to experiment with new behavior. He began the session by saying "I would like to try something different. I would like to give you my diagnosis of my case and then see if you agree or disagree with it. Also, I'd like to solicit your help in an area that concerns me. I want to make my espoused theory and theory-in-use more similar. I can see that they are different but I do not see why they are different."

The instructor then repeated the charge made to the group by A and asked A if that was a correct playback. A said that it was. A and the instructor asked the participants for their reactions. Those who spoke (about three-fourths of the group) agreed with A. A began by saying, among other things, "From the very start, certain behaviors of mine made certain attributions that made it unlikely for [the other person] to behave in ways other than what I attributed to him [A gave examples here].

"So, I see I helped to make several self-fulfilling prophecies because I did not trust the person. I really started out with, 'this guy can't be trusted with my feelings.' Moreover, I didn't surface any of my feelings that I was being cheated and felt that I was very worried about what he would do.

"I now know that I'll never really know what might have happened if I started by trusting him. For example, I could have started by expressing a few of my feelings. I could have told him, for example, that I was aware that there may be factors impinging on him; that I realized that he was under pressure; that I was worried what would happen to my case.

"I would have been able to see from how he responded to these comments whether this guy could be trusted. If the signs were positive, I could go on and perhaps I could listen to his views more clearly. If not, then I could go to the manipulative pressure strategy that I used in the case but I could use it with less guilt.

"As I see it now, my theory-in-use was: if you do not trust someone, (1) don't test the theory and (2) pressure him with everything you have until he agrees. My espoused theory has always been to be participative, helpful, and all that stuff."

The class discussion that followed seemed forced, full of long moments of silence, and almost no additiveness. This was in contrast to the three previous sessions in which the discussion had been animated and additive. In the previous sessions, however, the structure had been for the members to develop their own analysis of the case and for the individual to be a silent observer (as in G's case). This was the first time that the group had been faced with a client who decided to take the initiative of analyzing his case and asking the group to confirm or disconfirm his diagnosis.

After thirty minutes of the forced discussion, B asked if A would mind if the class returned to its previous model of operating. B asked A if he would now withdraw and let the consultants make their own diagnosis. A said he would, and several people sighed with relief. Apparently this strategy made sense to many members. It did not to the faculty member. Indeed, it seemed as if the direction was not only a reversal but a regression to more primitive client-consultant relationships. He waited for the proper moment to raise the issue. This occurred when the class members who were speaking were describing A in such terms as "being weak," "unclear," and "manifesting inconsistent positions." Yet the faculty member experienced A as taking initiative, being clear about his diagnosis, and including the fact that he had been inconsistent.

The faculty member intervened to present his diagnosis of the group process (lack of additiveness) and to test its validity. The group members agreed that the discussion had been forced, that many comments were unclear, and that there were contributions that were inconsistent (all qualities that A had been told that he was manifesting).

The instructor said, "You (B) asked for the switch and there seemed to me to be a great sigh of relief. Yet the discussion, as several of you pointed out, did not improve. What is happening?"

One member wondered if some members were not threatened by A's approach. It was straightforward; it asked for confirmation or disconfirmation; it therefore placed the consultants on the line. Another member agreed and said that what made her even more anxious was that model II had been described and she now felt that she had to perform effectively according to model II. Three others agreed. When asked what in the individual or group dynamics had led them to feel that they must perform perfectly in the session immediately after hearing about model II, the members said that it was mostly related to their need to feel competent in their relationship with the instructor. They viewed him as grading them continuously and they wanted to get high grades. But another member asked, "If we believe what he has told us, he suggests that it will

take years before we become effective." "And," added still another
member, "if we are going to be worried about grades, then we
should be trying to experiment with model-II behavior because he
will grade us on our attempt to practice and test the new behavior."

A member then stated that *A*, by his strategy, had been controlling the group, and he did not like this. *A* agreed and asked if
others felt that way. Two replied affirmatively. The others said nothing. The faculty member said that he did not agree. He felt that *A*
had taken the initiative and the responsibility to structure his session
with his consultants; that he asked for confirmation; and that these
actions indicated movement toward model II. This comment surfaced the view from two members who had been silent that they too
had experienced *A* as being proactive in a constructive manner. Six
other members said that they had not experienced *A* as behaving
proactively. The tape was played back and, after careful discussion,
the six then agreed that they had not heard *A* accurately. The members then asked why there was distortion. After a lengthy discussion,
they concluded that throughout the entire semester and throughout
this session, they had experienced *A* as weak, timid, and somewhat
feminine. It was difficult for them to express these feelings toward
A; indeed, as two pointed out, feelings of weakness in any male
made them terribly uncomfortable. It is interesting to note that the
two members, other than the faculty member, whose perceptions
of *A* were not distorted were women. This led to an insightful discussion on male-female issues and many feelings were discussed. At
the end of the episode, some asked if one reason feelings about *A*
were difficult to surface might be that the class has been so focused
on cognitive skills. Some members agreed, and others did not, pointing out that people had feelings but were not expressing them. The
instructor suggested that an emphasis on the cognitive could drive
out, in some people, the emotive; he said that raising the issue can
help us keep that in mind. The ultimate skill includes being aware
of both dimensions. Two members then said that their problem now
was less one of being unaware of their feelings and more one of feeling incompetent to express their feelings effectively.

The instructor asked if the group would be willing to try the
entire case over again. They agreed, and *A* repeated his initial state-

ment. This time, *R* began to act as a consultant by consciously and openly trying to use model II.

R (embarrassed): Well, let's see, according to model II, I would say that I have trouble in confirming or disconfirming your diagnosis without several examples giving me some directly observable data.

A: Okay, let me give you a few.

R (again somewhat embarrassed, but less so than earlier): Then, let's see. Again according to model II, isn't there an inconsistency between saying [so and so] and saying [so and so]?

A responded that he found this comment helpful and this led to another member surfacing an inconsistency in the consultant's behavior toward *A*. This, in turn, led *A* to explore some feelings about the consultants, which gave them more insight into their own effectiveness. Members said:

C: This has been one of our most productive meetings.

D: I agree, but think that it is largely because the instructor raised the issues he did. Remember, we began the session certain that the early ineffectiveness was *A*'s fault.

A: I found this meeting very helpful to me.

F: I think the presence of the instructor is helpful. We're still heavily dependent on him and that is an issue we must work on.

H: I saw this session as a quantum jump.

Dependence is also a key issue. Although group members come to feel closer to each other in the course of the group meetings, the instructor must emphasize that competence of participants' behavior, not closeness, is the goal. Since the instructor symbolizes competence, the group depends on him for support and guidance. One member said she needed the instructor's support to try model-II behavior. This was an appropriate time for the instructor to offer further support but also to ask all members to consider their role in supporting each other. The participants agreed, and one suggested that the group divide into smaller units to experiment with model-II behavior without the instructor. Such a session was planned for the next week.

Summary

The transition process from model I to model II is summarized in Figure 4. The processes of learning are based on individuals becoming aware of the governing variables, action strategies, consequences for the behavioral world, learning, and effectiveness of their espoused theories and theories-in-use. As awareness of these variables occurs, individuals can search for inconsistencies in each variable or among them.

Once the inconsistencies are surfaced, validated, and their role in producing ineffective behavior specified, the individual chooses whether he is willing to reduce the consequent ineffectiveness. If he is, he can then begin to explore altering the governing variables, developing new action strategies, and exploring their consequences for the behavioral world, learning, and effectiveness.

The next step is to test the learning. The first mode of testing can be tentative. Participants can ask themselves what would happen if they decided to alter their behavior in accordance with the new models? This discussion is primarily cognitive. It is a nonbehavioral test of one's own and others' espoused theories.

The next step is to test publicly the new insights against actual behavior. This requires experimenting with new behavior. The individual may imitate the behavior of the instructor or his peers, or he may generate his own behavior and seek to have it confirmed or disconfirmed. Much of the new behavior requires the development of a new set of governing variables or personal values. Consequently, new behavior is not learned without questioning old values and creating new ones.

As the individual publicly tests his new concepts by behaving according to their behavioral imperatives, as he receives confirmation that others experience them the way he intends, and as he perceives that they lead to increased effectiveness, the individual will seek to internalize and be responsible for the new behavior.

Internalizing and being responsible for behavior so it may be used in the noncontrived world requires the individual to possess the

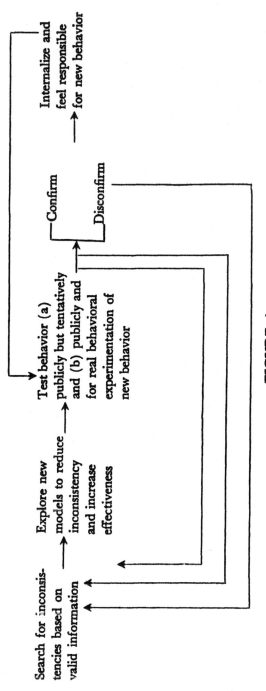

FIGURE 4

necessary skills. Such skills are too complex to remember and retrieve. Therefore, the models help the individual identify the behavior required and then behave effectively under even moderate stress. These models may take the form of simplified programs that provide rules for effective behavior.

Model II enables the individual to deal effectively with his peers, subordinates, and supervisors. Whichever level of behavior he chooses to explore, the same model of learning may be used.[2]

PART III

PRACTICE

This book began by exploring theories of action, incongruities between espoused theories and theories-in-use, the inconsistencies within each set of theories, and, finally, the meaning of effectiveness and the conditions for learning to enhance effectiveness. Next, we illustrated these concepts by presenting case studies that reveal people's espoused theories and their theories-in-use. Finally, we described possible designs of learning environments that would help people change from model-I to model-II behavior. We focused on the individual and interpersonal levels, although we also discussed group dynamics in the seminars; however, our theory of theories of action —with its components of espoused theory, theory-in-use, model I, model II, and concepts of effectiveness—may be used to understand the nature and learning processes of social units larger than one individual.

In Part Three, we indicate how this theory can be used to clarify the present crises of professional education and to redesign professional education so it responds to the dilemmas that many professionals experience. We will discuss professional practice, professional institutions, and professional learning environments.

Chapter 8

Issues in
Professional Education

Today's professional education is paradoxical in several ways. Certain professions—law, medicine, nursing, clinical psychology, urban planning—are attracting students as never before; although waiting lists at these professional schools are long, some observers predict shortages of professionals in these fields. At the same time, discontent is becoming highly visible, not only among students (who may bring to professional schools in the early 1970s the same discontent that created the student revolution in the middle and late 1960s) but also among young professional practitioners, deans of professional schools, and increasingly, faculty. This discontent is expressed among students through manifestos, confrontations, and strikes; young professionals express discontent by creating so-called counter-professions, which oppose established concepts of professional practice and professional identity; professionals express their discontent in publications that analyze the crises and needs for reform in particular professions—the recent work of the Carnegie Commission on Higher Education (1970) is perhaps the most extensive example, and exposés, with titles like *The Making of a Surgeon* and *The Making of a Psychiatrist,* show the seamy side professional practice and education.

Although issues and attitudes differ from one profession to another, this general discontent is characteristic of the oldest professions (medicine, law, the ministry) and of relative newcomers (engineering, business management, education administration, urban planning). Those who are disturbed about the profession itself are also disturbed about the education of professionals. There seem to be five central issues.

Reasons for-Discontent

Whom does the profession serve?   Although the professions are meant to meet society's vital needs, critics say these needs are unmet and that in spite of vast increases in funds to professions, service to those who need help most has declined (Gross and Osterman, 1972). Many students and young professionals want to serve the disadvantaged rather than the established few, but they do not see future professional roles that will allow them to carry out what they regard as the social responsibility of the profession.

A young professor of law describes his students as uneasy and frustrated because they feel dissociated from the community. The dean of a school of architecture and planning says that students want to work on social problems—the problems in or around buildings—not the buildings themselves. The architect's academic skill does not help him carry out his broad social function. Also, students object that the architectural profession serves mainly special-interest groups; students wish to serve the dispossessed, and in their unsupervised field work in school, they do so. When they see that post-graduate institutional arrangements do not allow them to provide their services in any socially responsible way, they are frustrated and depressed and do not want to graduate.

The same sentiments are heard in medicine.

> In one month recently, the interns and residents on the house staff of a big-city municipal teaching hospital were organizing to protest the abysmal treatment of

> low-income patients . . . and to help patients assert
> their own rights. At the same time, other young physi-
> cians and students were working in new health centers,
> free clinics, pregnancy counseling services, welfare rights
> offices, and other community programs in a hundred dif-
> ferent locations across the nation. . . . And these new
> physicians and physicians-in-training regard their time on
> the picket line or in the community as a legitimate part
> of their careers as doctors. . . . Even in the generation
> a few years older, . . . substantial numbers of physicians
> were trying to learn something about the economics of
> medical care, trying to organize group practices for whole
> neighborhoods or areas, trying to bring new kinds of
> medical care services into being . . . (Geiger, 1972, pp.
> 96–97).

These concerns create dilemmas for the student or young professional who cannot see any established professional role that makes sense to him, for the professor who finds himself condemned for failing to make his professional competence available to the disenfranchised, and for the head of a professional office, who says he does not know how he could finance an organization for services to the dispossessed, which is what the young people want.

The advocacy movement, which emerged in the mid-1960s as a response to dilemmas like these, urged (according to its various formulations) the professional to devote himself to the disadvantaged client, speak for him, teach him to be an effective consumer of professional services, or strengthen his ability to pursue his own interests in relation to established institutions. The advocacy movement has spread to professions as diverse as medicine, architecture, social work, planning, and psychiatry, but it has thrived primarily in law—its native field, from which the term and the concept were largely derived—and has led to frustration in most other fields. Clients were less interested in being served by young professionals, less willing to be spoken for, less ready to organize, and the routes to effective advocacy were less clear than the new advocates had believed.

Are professionals competent? It is not surprising that professional schools are criticized because they fail to help students become competent in practice for the disadvantaged. It is surprising to find professional schools criticized because they do not prepare students to be competent practitioners in any sense, yet two lines of argument maintain this is true. The first argues that professional schools, for reasons peculiar to the various professions, do not help students acquire the skills essential to competence in practice in the real world.

In law, for example, one prestigious law school is said to compartmentalize the field of law and then to ". . . get the best people in each field to teach, assuming that hearing what the best practitioners have to say will be the best legal education." Criminal-law courses prepare one for ". . . courtroom battles regarding the first, third, and fourth amendments, in an adversary process, whereas the actual process of practicing criminal law involves working and negotiating in a bureaucracy that processes people, like other bureaucracies." Similarly, "Students are taught rules about contracts and torts, but they find that the practice of law does not consist of applying rules but of negotiating settlements with other lawyers." Law school does not attempt to teach how to cope with a bureaucracy or how to negotiate a settlement. At best, proponents of this view claim, the subject matter taught in law school provides graduate lawyers with a sense of common professional identity and a sense of having jumped the same hurdles, thereby acquiring a shared language that enables legal adversaries to recognize one another as members of a common culture distinct from the cultures of laymen.

In architecture, reform-minded deans inveigh against the concept of architectural mystique. The traditional architectural studio fails because, as one dean puts it, "Teachers practice architecture rather than educating students in architectural practice. They leave intact the hidden magic of the professional design process." Another says, "The traditional studio doesn't address the problem of simulating the client/architect relationship at all. It keeps it under the rug." A third dean says, "We don't suceed in helping our students understand that there are various knowledge bases on which they might move. . . . It's as though they were being trained to be little Rudolphs or little Wrights, totally self-reliant, valuing their own preferences and their own opinions to the exclusion of outside opinion and to the exclusion of methodology that could could be conceptually or publicly applied." Still another says, "Every job of architecture is high risk, going to last a hundred years, *public high risk*—and this helps to explain the need for the mystique." The student is expected to acquire competence mysteriously on his own, or by association with extraordinary practitioners.

Critics of education in both architecture and law agree that the student becomes a competent professional in the office after graduation rather than in school. Depending on the critic, this is taken as cause for alarm or the natural order of events.

The contention that professional schools do not produce competent practitioners is supported by a second argument, which is based on the premise that professional roles are now undergoing radical change. The professional skills of yesterday and today will not be adequate in the future, yet professional schools are preoccupied with the old to the exclusion of emerging competences. For example, Schein (1972), argues that the professions need innovators to improve practice and to clarify the professional's role in society. Such innovators would study who the legitimate client is, who should initiate contact, the nature of the contract between client and professional, the boundaries of the profession, among other issues. Friedman (1973) says the professions need "successful planners"—people who show skill in managing interpersonal relationships in a way that develops self-knowledge, capacity to learn, capacity for empathy, and ability to live with conflict. Gottesfield (1972) argues that professionals must operate in an open, less hierarchical clinical team that includes clients as participating members of the treatment team. Perrucci and Gerstle (1969) stress the increasing scale and complexity of engineering projects, which demand from the engineer increasing management competence and understanding of the human consequences of such enterprises.

Brooks (1967) offers perhaps the best statement of the dilemma of the professional today.

> Both ends of the gap [the professional] is expecting to bridge with his profession are changing so rapidly —both the body of knowledge that he must use and the expectations of the society that he must serve. Both these changes have their origin in the same common factor— technological change. Technology has created a race be-

> tween opportunities and expectations. . . . The four
> professions . . . must bear the brunt of responsibility
> for generating and managing this change. This places on
> the professional a requirement for adaptability and ver-
> satility that is unprecedented (1967, p. 1).

Brooks argues that each of the professions is undergoing a radical
redefinition of its task and of its nature as a profession. He implies
that it is impossible to predict the nature of the changes in professional tasks over the next twenty years.

Does cumulative learning influence practitioners? The scientific community considers itself a community of inquiry. Ever since
the formation of the Royal Society in seventeenth-century England,
scientists have valued communicating their theories, experimental
methods, and results for two reasons: so others could test them and
so others could benefit from them. In contrast to this public, explicit,
and cumulative approach, the community of professionals has
tended to view learning about effective practice as a process that is
private, tacit, and ephemeral. The professional practitioner tends
not to communicate to his peers—perhaps not even to himself, in
explicit terms—what he learns about his practice. It is uncommon
for professionals to test their theories or to benefit from whatever
degree of testing does occur; that is, professionals often function
without considering what they have learned from previous situations.

This characterization is more true for some professions than
others. Over the last century, some aspects of medicine have developed many of the characteristics attributed to the scientific community regarding its inquiry into both basic theory and applied
theories of the diagnosis and treatment of disease. However, this is
not true for certain aspects of medical practice—for·example, learning about the process of making effective clinical judgments or
learning about doctor/patient relationships. Similarly, the scientific
community has been far more public, explicit, and cumulative in
developing scientific theory than in learning about the practice of
scientific research.

Architecture has little tradition of scholarship and therefore
of public, explicit, cumulative learning.

Since buildings are discrete and discontinuous, the building in a sense is only a set of consequences of a theory of some kind; unfortunately, neither in the literature nor in the consumption of architecture do architects spend much time with the theories that underlie these buildings. The same mystique that prevents architectural students from being prepared for competent practice also stands in the way of learning among architectural professionals.

Law has a public, explicit, cumulatively developed body of legal theory, but there is no counterpart for theories of legal practice. The development of competence tends to take place outside the professional school. Indeed, in law as in many other professions, the split between scholars and practitioners has precluded the development of a community for learning about competent practice.

Is reform possible? There are three main dilemmas inherent in the idea of professional reform. First, the profession cannot be counted on to reform itself since it is too much the prisoner of its own world, which may include its own pecuniary interests. But the professional school is hardly the place to initiate reform since it tends to be divorced from the real world of professional practice. Second, if the professional schools could begin to turn out a completely new kind of professional, how would that person fare in a professional establishment made up of professionals of the old type? Third, professional education must be reformed in order to produce the new professionals capable of initiating professional reform; but where are the professionals who will reform professional education? And where is the theory and the competence for the practice of reform?

Can self-actualization occur? Researchers in legal education have found that students consider self-actualization during working hours as important as it is during nonworking hours. For example, young lawyers see their work as meaningless and want more of their total personality involved in their work. They reject the traditional dissociation among lawyers between their private lives and their professional lives. Although researchers have found that lawyers in their thirties may not be as concerned with this issue, many of the mature professionals they interviewed shared the student's view.

Schein finds that:

> From the perspective of the student, many professionals as individuals and many professional associa-

tions have not sufficiently reexamined their role in society, are not delivering a high-quality service to the
right client, and are not responsive to the desire of young
professionals to work on relevant social problems. . . .
In many professions, the early years of practice are perceived as stultifying, unchallenging, and more like an
initiation rite than an educationally useful apprenticeship (1972, p. 53).

Historical Origins

The central issues of today's discontent in the professions
have their roots in the history of the professions. Clearly, what we
now call the professions have their origins in religion. Palmer points
out that:

> *Religious professional* is a redundancy. A profes-
> sional, as I understand it, is supposed to profess, to testify,
> to bear witness to some sort of faith or confidence or
> point of view. Traditionally, at least, it was only because
> he did so that he merited being called *professional*. I
> would argue that in the traditional view, a professional
> was religious by definition—at least in the weaker sense
> of the word *religious* (1973, p. 2).

Each of the professions seems to have been bound up in its
origins with a faith professed—that is, with values to be achieved
through the activities of the profession. Thus, medicine professed
health, law professed justice, education professed truth, the ministry
professed salvation. At some point in their histories, the professions
seem to have transformed their faith into ideology. This ideology is
a central component of what we call the paradigm of the professions, whose other elements include: an ethic that is binding on the
practitioner and is typified by the Hippocratic oath; a set of arts or
techniques that make up the profession's skills; a guild, or brotherhood of initiates, entitled to practice the special arts of the profession; a special relationship to laymen that accords the professional
deference, authority, and trust; an institutional setting, such as the
temple, the hospital, or the court, within which professional activ-

ities occur; and a world-view or theory that sets forth the concepts of the world in which the professional practices and the ways professional activities are thought to lead to the better world envisioned in the ideology. These elements have been part of the professional paradigm throughout the history of the professions; they have evolved in relation to one another, with some elements more prominent than others during different periods, as we can see by examining the development of professions in the western world from medieval times to the present.

First, the priest was the prototypical professional, practicing within the framework of the church, vested with religious authority, an initiate functioning within a sacred brotherhood and combining, in an undifferentiated way, the functions of judge, healer, teacher, and minister.

Second, the professions secularized and differentiated. Medicine, education, and law disengaged themselves from the church and from its theological world-views, from the sacred brotherhood of initiates to form the secular guild, and from the sacred professional ethic to form the secular ethic. The professions differentiated themselves from the priesthood and from each other, developed secular institutions for practice of the new professions, and proliferated. The roles of some artisans and tradesmen (such as architects and engineers) were also elevated to professional status.

Third, the professions liberalized and rationalized. They became open to a wider range of participants. A cumulative written body of professional knowledge was built up, professional learning was systematized, and the professions were associated with the universities. Professional ideologies were transformed into secular ideals of progress. The concept of the professional as guardian of the secular values of society emerged, as did the idea of professional accountability to society at large rather than to the professional guild alone. The multiple professional, like Thomas Jefferson or Benjamin Rush, appeared.

The fourth stage of professional development was the rise of technique, which was accompanied by proliferation of specialization (such as bridge-building engineers) and proliferation of discrete bodies of professional expertise and technique (such as stress analysis in engineering) as bases for professional specialties. Technique dominated the professional paradigm, which paralleled the rise of industrial technology. Institutions suitable for the practice of professional techniques were created—the hospital, the laboratory, the industrial firm. The professional came to be seen, by himself and others, primarily as a technician who applied his professional knowledge, which was the basis of his authority.

The sequence and timing of these stages differs for the various professions although all begin with the Middle Ages and experienced the rise of technique in the nineteenth and early twentieth centuries.[1]

This pattern of the historical development clarifies one criticism of contemporary professions—that technique dominates the professions just as it dominates our society. Palmer argues that,

> Professionals generally have abdicated their traditional function. My definition of professional—as one who professes a faith—is anathema to the engineer, the chemist, the business manager, the academic. They see themselves not as bearers of a faith or proclaimers of a confidence, but as practitioners of technique . . . pure, empirical, pragmatic, marketable technique . . . [that] admits of no need of faith (1973, pp. 2–3).

His criticism of the professions rests on this:

> What these modern professionals fail to understand, of course, is the ambiguity, the tragedy, the demonic quality of the technique itself! They fail to perceive, for instance, that unadulterated technique is largely responsible for the war in Southeast Asia. . . . Technique points to the politicization of reason. Technique consists of those rational modes by which some men try to conquer others. Technique results not in debates and journals but in propaganda, in elite political policies, in war, in institutional racism, and in pervasive forms of public manipulation. Technique is the mode by which both the liberal optimists and the realistic pessimists are trying to have their way . . . (Palmer, 1973, p. 3).

Palmer echoes the more comprehensive criticism of Ellul

(1965), who portrayed the emergence of the concept of technique in our society, its rise to dominance, and its nefarious effects.

Model I and Paradigms of Professions

The dominance of technique is inseparable from what we have characterized as model I. Together, these two ideas clarify the five main issues causing the crisis of the professions.

Professionals create artifacts that are shaped by both the requirements of a task environment, in Simon's terms (1969), and by materials whose properties constrain the creator's ability to respond to requirements. The lawyer's case, the doctor's diagnosis and treatment, the architect's design, the engineer's project, the planner's strategy are all artifacts in this sense.

Such a perspective suggests two kinds of technique: first-order techniques are the arts and skills that comprise professional practice; second-order techniques are the techniques needed to create the institutional settings in which first-order techniques can function.

A profession, then, not only has a practice but also a theory of action in which that practice can become a reproducable, valid technique. This means that the job of professional education consists not only in teaching technique but in teaching the methods by which behavioral worlds in which techniques can work can be created.

The engineer creates controlled environments—such as laboratories or wind-tunnels—to test his designs. These environments have standardized conditions that are uniform from site to site and can be quantitatively measured and varied. The actual environments in which the engineer's designs are to be carried out must also display properties of standardization, uniformity, and susceptibility to quantitative measurement and control. Indeed, the history of the industrial uses of research and development reveals a crucially important middle stage, in which industrial firms seek to convert their production environments to suitable engineering environments in order to make engineering technique applicable to production.

For the physician, the medical hospital, medical laboratory, and physician's office are the artificial environments created to permit predictable application of medical techniques of diagnosis and treatment. These environments are designed to permit measurement of variables considered important in theories of diagnosis and treatment, to permit controlled treatment of patients (for example, to control patient exposure to bacteria), and to subject the patient to conditions in which standardized treatments may be given, insofar as possible, with predictable results. These environments also impose controlled and predictable behavior on patients.

For the lawyer, the courts and related institutions provide an artificial environment of this kind. In the court environment, presentations or arguments are structured according to a routine that is generally understood by all professionals, and arguments are constrained by rules applicable to the type of case involved. The adversary relationships institutionalized in the courts provide the framework within which the lawyer can apply his knowledge of the law. Within this framework, events are highly, though not entirely, predictable; within limits, standard techniques produce standard results.

Similarly, the urban planner's institutional settings set the conditions within which planning practice is conducted. Within these settings, participants are constrained to behave in certain ways that tend to increase the predictability of the uses of planning techniques.

The architect's office and studio, the teacher's classroom, and the psychologist's clinic and laboratory represent similar structured environments.

The professional's knowledge of these structured environments, his certification to practice in them, his ability to understand the language spoken in them and to negotiate in them constitute a great part of his technical expertise and authority in relation to laymen. Part of the fascination of the story of the early days of psychoanalysis consists in the ways early practitioners, notably Freud, introduced standardized conditions (for example, the cultural isolation of the psychiatric session, its uniform duration, the structure of expectations of patients' and analyst's behavior) that would make apparently chaotic events conducive to the predictable application of techniques.

From this point of view, descriptions of the structure of

industrial firms and business organizations take on a new meaning. Veblen, in *The Theory of the Business Enterprise,* describes the industrial firm taking' on the properties of the machines that functioned within it—the division of labor, the standardization of task and job, the quantitative measurement of output, and susceptibility to measurement and control. These characteristics made the business enterprise into an artificial environment in which the techniques of management engineering could be applied—for example, by Taylor and his followers. Argyris (1970) has described the ways these properties of industrial organization were combined with centralization of information and control and coupled with the concepts of economic rationality to create an environment that lends itself to the application of management techniques. The rationalized organization is also the engineered organization; it corresponds to the concept of manager as engineer.

In each profession, second-order technique has created an artificial environment that includes: formal, structured interactions among professionals and among professionals and clients; rules governing the procedures to be followed by professionals and clients; sharp role differentiation, spelling out what is expected of professional and client; the breakdown of activities into component parts that are standardized, uniform, and measurable; and the control of environment so that variables can be altered in limited and sequential ways. The applied theory of the profession spells out, for the range of professional situations, the outputs that can be expected after certain first-order techniques are applied. The second-order techniques create a behavioral world in which first-order techniques may be made to work predictably; in this sense, second-order techniques make self-fulfilling prophecies of the applied theories of the professions. These second-order techniques tend to be used to achieve a self-reinforcing system that maintains second-order constancy—that is, a system in which the world-view and the behavioral world of the professions hold steady.

With the rise of technique in the nineteenth century, the professions have tended to refine and develop the technical aspects of their paradigms and to concentrate on the development of second-order techniques to create the artificial environments in which their techniques will work predictably. The engineering paradigm has become an important model; the other professions have tried to create similar artificial environments characterized by standardized and measurable components, control through the measurement of output, and capability for controlled variation.

These artificial environments tend to contain the underlying properties of model I: they are designed to enable the professional to realize objectives as he sees them, control the task, render the behavior of others predictable, and thereby control it. These environments are conducive to rationality in the sense of using reason to achieve professionally formulated objectives or manipulating the environment to achieve quantitatively measured outputs. Control over others to accomplish the task as the professional sees it is the goal.

Similarly, in the dominant twentieth-century model of the well-managed organization, the manager tries to achieve the task as he sees it by controlling his employees' behavior. He does this by making the work so simple that anybody can do it, and therefore anybody can be controlled; he creates a power structure and an information structure that gives the person at the lowest level little information and the shortest time perspective permissible, while people at the upper levels receive more information, more power, and a longer time perspective.

These artificial environments become model-I institutions since they are designed to permit the predictable exercise of professional techniques based on model I. Moreover, they encourage or even coerce model-I behavior on the part of all participants, making any other behavior difficult or impossible. Yet, these artificial model-I environments interfere with the achievement of each profession's ideological goals. The controlling environment of the law courts interferes with justice; the controlling environment of industry interferes with the rational solving of human problems or the meeting of human needs through technology; the controlling environment of the hospital and the perspective it encourages interferes with health. Such words as "plaintiff," "defendant," "consumer," "personnel," "subject," and "patient" describe people in terms of the artificial environments created by the professions, As the real world of a profession turns into the artificial, model-I world of second-order techniques, the espoused theory or ideology of the profession tends to become merely ornamental. We may now return to the dilemmas of professional education discussed earlier in this chapter.

Clientele. Professional services are regarded as goods; receiving them depends on ability to pay for them, which only the relatively affluent can do. Also, the professions have evolved around the institutions that make their techniques work because they are designed to control the behavior of others. It is not surprising, then, that professional resources would be co-opted by those who seek to control others, or that people drawn to control the behavior of others would seek roles in the professions, or that people who enter professions structured in this way would find themselves engaged in systems that control the behavior of others.

Competence. The ineffectiveness of professional schools in this regard must be attributed to the differences between academic education and the realities of professional practice. Brooks (1967) describes the dilemmas created by the tendency of professional schools to require a background in basic sciences in order to make themselves academically respectable. However, Brooks' main point —the rapid rate of change that makes professional techniques taught today obsolete tomorrow—is one that professionals might not discover in a model-I world, at least not soon enough. Professionals who behave according to model I may not be able to engage in the double-loop learning required to change their paradigms. In a self-sealing world, professionals may find it difficult or impossible to recognize the limits to their ability to predict new professional role demands.

Cumulative learning. Model-I behavior means theory-making and theory-testing that is private, not public, single-loop learning, and competitiveness rather than collaboration. We would also expect the self-reinforcing second-order environment to tend to remain constant rather than to be subject to cumulative development through public learning.

Reform. Professional techniques are in a self-reinforcing relationship with the institutions that have evolved to make those techniques work and to constrain behavior to suit them—they are reinforced by and reinforce these institutions. According to Ellul (1965), technique corrupts and becomes an instrument of control over others, whatever the original intention of the technique may have been. Hence, the professions betray the original values of their paradigms (health, truth, justice) as technique becomes progressively more central to them. That pattern, pointed out by Illich and others, according to which the provider of services defines as client needs whatever his techniques enable him to provide, may be recognized as a professional version of the self-sealing processes of model I. A corollary of that pattern is the professional's inability to discover that clients may not need what the professional can provide; this means professionals will interpret any client dissatisfaction as resistance.

Self-actualization. Self-actualization is incompatible with the tendency of model-I worlds to lead a low sense of effectiveness, self-worth, vitality, and learning. Model I is not conducive to cumulative personal development but instead tends to enable one to make use of only the more primitive aspects of the self. Students and young professionals seem to be asking for a new professional paradigm that differs from the old in the following ways.

Old	*New*
Receive clients. Prove competence, not intent to help (because the client comes to you).	Seek clients. Prove not only competence but the intent to help.
View the problem narrowly and use the technique prescribed. Be effective in your application of technique.	View the problem broadly and seek new organization and technique to deal with it.
Criteria for success are set by the profession.	Criteria for success are changing; it is important to be influenceable by both clients and other professionals.
Tacit knowledge is important in a great professional, who can organize the diagnosis and propose an elegant solution.	Criteria for solution and a diagnosis depend on information and knowledge gathered from all participants. Solution will be satisfying.

Old	*New*
Rejection on interpersonal grounds rarely occurs; minimal attention to interpersonal adequacy is enough.	Rejection is possible on interpersonal grounds even though your technique is sound.
Application of techniques, even if painful, is for the clients own good.	Application of technique means control over others, which seems to impede self-actualization both for practitioner and client. One must submit to being controlled by others in order to control others.
Clients are supposed to be passive, open, and cooperative; the professional is supposed to be firm and fair.	Clients are becoming more educated and more willing to accept control over their lives; they are also becoming more disposed to influencing the professional, being more aggressive, and participating in more in the processes of diagnosis and treatment.
The professional wants autonomy in his work in order to carry out his techniques. This may lead to conflict with the organizations in which he functions. Becoming a cosmopolitan may be a way of dealing with the tension between organization and professional.	The professional wants freedom of choice and internal commitment; he wants the same for his clients. He expects to be challenged by clients and by the organization on criteria that go beyond the criteria of the profession itself.

Chapter 9

Implications for Professional Competence and Practice

Chapter Eight identified five central issues for professional practice and education: who professionals serve, whether professional schools prepare competent practitioners, whether professionals benefit from cumulative learning, whether reform is possible, and whether self-actualization is possible in professional practice. We saw that current conditions are understandable consequences of (1) technique emerging as the dominant feature of professions and (2) institutional settings designed to assure the predictable working of technique. These first- and second-order techniques are aimed at producing predictable behavior and hence controlling others' behavior so the professional can achieve his task, as he sees it, by exercising rationality and unilaterally designing and controlling the situation. Model-I theory-in-use underlies these techniques and creates a model-I behavioral world.

Before we consider how to reform professional practice, let

us examine what competent professional practice is and how competence is to be acquired.

Competence in Professional Practice

Whatever *competence* means today, we can be sure its meaning will have changed by tomorrow. The foundation for future professional competence seems to be the capacity to learn how to learn (Schein, 1972). This requires developing one's own continuing theory of practice under real-time conditions. It means that the professional must learn to develop microtheories of action that, when organized into a pattern, represent an effective theory of practice. The professional must also be able to act according to his microtheories of action and reflect on his actions, relating them to the governing variables implicit in his behavior and determining the impact of his behavior on the behavioral world (on himself, the clients, the client system), on learning (especially on double-loop learning), and on effectiveness.

Models I and II show that there are certain criteria for an effective theory of practice. (1) The theory should not be self-sealing. It should permit detection of and response to its own inconsistencies, ineffectiveness, and ultimately to its degree of obsolescence. (2) The theory should make the interaction between client and professional conducive to mutual learning. (3) The theory should enable the professional to seek out, identify, and respond to new kinds of clients. (4) The theory should include a theory of reform of the profession that describes methods of transition from present to desired behavior. (5) The theory should be conducive to creating a professional community that undertakes explicit, public, cumulative learning. (6) The theory should make professional practice increasingly compatible with self-actualization, including engaging one's needs, values, and abilities in the job and setting realistic yet challenging levels of aspiration to promote growth.

These criteria strongly suggest that the kinds of theories of practice competent professionals should be able to develop are very much like model II—or, at least, have the consequences on the behavioral world and on learning that we have attributed to model

II. But what would it mean to develop model-II theories of professional practice? How is this compatible with the exercise of professional technique? And how would model-II techniques avoid, in Ellul's terms, the corrupting effects of technique?

Building One's Own Theory of Practice

Building one's own theory of practice includes diagnosis, testing, and accepting personal causality.

Diagnosis. Consider an architect who is about to design a university dormitory. He meets the administrative committee appointed to work with him. He senses the kind of people they are, their different expectations of him, the residual effects of their history with one another, and their internal conflicting perceptions of their own interests. These perceptions are important to the architect because they signal the issues he will meet as he goes about the design process. He also needs to know the student group that will be using the dormitory; they will have different perceptions from his own as well as a culture that is different from his own and from that of the administrative committee; he may need to study how the students feel about sharing space and equipment. The architect must also consider the community whose neighborhood abuts the dormitory. How is the community likely to respond to it? What features of it would be likely to bridge the rift that might grow up between students and neighborhood residents? Moreover, the architect will be engaging with contractors. He must understand their sense of the rules of the game and perhaps also of the workmen's probable response to the particular construction problems his design will create.

Even this incomplete list suggests that the architect's effective performance will depend on his ability to immerse himself in a network of behavioral worlds. The architect's ability to get inside these worlds and comprehend their cultures will affect his execution of the project. Like the anthropological visitor to a culture, the architect must encounter unstructured information presented to him in the form of human behavior, he must sense which pieces of information are central and which are peripheral, he must attempt to see the perspective of those he encounters. And he must somehow construct for himself their ways of looking at the world, at least insofar as their perspectives will affect his performance.

In varying degrees, and in different ways, each professional practitioner must encounter and interact with individuals, small groups, organization, institutions. In each case, the practitioner can choose how much he wants to respond to the cultures he is working with. He may opt for a stance of expertise, for example; he may want to learn only as much about the culture as he needs to impose his own concept of what needs doing. Significantly, one of the sources of discontent among students and young professionals is their inability to be more responsive in practice to the cultures of their clients. The practitioner cannot increase his responsiveness by reading or hearing or theorizing about other cultures. He must draw his own theory from unstructured information gained through his own interaction with others.

Testing. To avoid self-sealing theories of action, practitioners must learn to test their theories and assumptions. However, some assumptions may not be confirmable by direct observation ("My client has needs he is not willing to express"); then testing requires forming a hypothesis that links together the unobservable item, some directly observable sign of it, and an action from which the directly observable sign is thought to follow. Each situation of practice is an opportunity for testing some elements of theory of action. Acting is testing, and the practitioner is an experimenter.

Testing is not simple; there are two obstacles to testing in professional practice. The first obstacle is the difference between the practitioner's environment and a laboratory environment. In the laboratory, some variables can be controlled while others are varied. But in a practice environment, one does not know all the relevant variables, there are more variables than can be handled, it is not possible to keep some variables constant while others are manipulated, it is often impossible to measure outcomes without affecting the outcome, and the time required for the experiment and action based on the results of the experiment is often greater than the time required for significant change in the situation under study. These impediments to social experiment have been frequently noted (see von Wright, 1972),[1] and they all apply to efforts to carry out experiments in the framework of professional practice.

Another obstacle to testing in the setting of professional practice derives from the artificial nature of theories of action. Under our society's model-I theories-in-use, theories of action tend to be self-sealing. Our assumptions about the behavioral world lead us to act in ways that induce (or confirm) in others behavior that supports our assumptions. We cut ourselves off from sources of valid information that would disconfirm our assumptions, and efforts to test our theories—undertaken, as they are, under model I—yield only information that confirms our theories. Our theories-in-use become effective self-fulfilling prophecies (Schön, 1971).

If the terms *testing* and *experiment* mean anything in the practice setting, they mean something that is only analogous to what they mean under rigorous scientific conditions. However, there is a kind of intermediate rigor appropriate to testing in practice settings. Some of its features are as follows.

Inquire into the situation. Your experiences are taken as sources of data. Any unexpected or unconnected experiences are treated as phenomena to be explained. The situation is taken seriously as a source of knowledge.

Form a perspective on the data (*hypothesis* would suggest too close a resemblance to the laboratory situation). This perspective must represent a story about the data,[2] an argument concerning it, a conceptual structure about it, that has consequences for action according to your theory-in-use.

The perspectives must be faithful to your data—that is, they must account for the unexpected or unconnected aspects of your data without omitting an inconvenient datum. Moreover, you are bound to use those skills you have (for example, the "anthropological" skills) to generate data. The costs of further data-gathering should be weighed against the benefits of the data to be gathered.[3]

Maintain an apparently contradictory attitude toward your perspective on the data: you must be committed to it in order to act on it—since action is ineffective without commitment—but you must also be ready to accept a negative evaluation of the perspective as you gather new information. Your stance must include both commitment to the perspective and readiness to abandon it.

The perspective should yield sequences of action and consequence such that one finding or another can lead to a revision in the perspective—a revision that makes sense of the outcome observed. The confirmations or revisions are taken as valid for action in the situation as experienced. They are compatible with your commitment that other inquirers—or yourself at another point in time—could come to the situation with different assumptions, perceive a different constellation of data, go through a process comparable to your own, and emerge with a different confirmed perspective. When this occurs, it becomes a source of new data and must generate a new process of inquiry. Your theory-in-use must encompass such processes although there is no guarantee of convergence among conflicting perspectives.

The self-sealing nature of theories-in-use is altered by only one kind of action. If—using a self-sealing theory-in-use—we collude with others to withhold the information that would disconfirm our assumptions about each other, that collusion must be replaced by sharing directly observable data, by sharing interpretations of that data, and by sharing our testing of the attributions we make about others. There is no way of doing this for ourselves without also doing it for and with others. The characteristics of the shared behavioral world must be changed, and they will change only as we envisage a different theory-in-use and begin to act on it.

To illustrate, consider a department head, *A*, who has privately concluded that other department heads are planning to capture resources that his own department needs. He decides to respond by capturing these resources himself, before anyone else can. The other department heads, frightened by *A*'s action, respond in kind. *A* does not read their action as a response to him but as evidence of the behavior he sought to prevent; he feels his suspicion has been confirmed.

In order to test his assumption, *A* would have to acknowledge that he may be mistaken. He would have to notice the link between his and the other department heads' behavior. He would have to consider that they may be prepared, if he is, to change the nature of the competitive game they have all been playing. He would have to begin to act as if that possibility were true; that is, he and the other department heads would have to treat the allocation of scarce resources as a shared problem.

This kind of testing process does not conform to the criteria of laboratory-based experiments, but it is capable of achieving a kind of intermediate rigorousness that can be learned only by experiencing it. Just as one cannot learn effective laboratory procedures without undertaking experiments in the laboratory, so one cannot learn about the kind of testing possible in situations of practice without experiencing that testing process.

Personal causation. The practitioner must be willing to take responsibility for what he does. In actual situations of practice, the costs of failure are likely to be high. The practitioner performs under stress; he must meet deadlines; he is constrained by time and money; and he faces a finite risk of failure that depends on the complexity of the situation and how far it departs from normal routine. To perform in these situations while aware of these factors is to perform responsibly. The commitment to be responsible is a condition for competence; without it, theories of action cannot be put into effective practice.

The practitioner cannot generate theories of action without commitment to responsibility. Only data and theory-making that are taken seriously are useful.[4] Furthermore, one cannot generate a perspective on the data, which is essential to the formation of a theory-in-use, unless one focuses on his own values for the situation and takes them seriously. Values are the instruments through which we select from more information than we can handle (the typical condition of our first encounters with real situations) the simplified, constructed situations in which we can act. But it is not enough to have values for the situation and to have them form a point of view; one must also be committed to that point of view so it becomes a basis for action. Otherwise, one depends on the values of others or one is simply unable to function in the situation at all.

Taking one's own values seriously requires a strong commitment to self. This enables a practitioner to perform according to his own scruples in the face of others' disapproval, which often accompanies departures from the conventions of a profession; taking one's own values seriously is therefore essential to innovation in practice. Similarly, commitment to self is essential if one is to be willing to admit perceived failure. The institutions in which professionals function do not condone failure, but failure is a predictable consequence when the practitioner first begins complex, untested behavior. It is a cliché of experimental method that a negative result is as good as a positive one; but in practice, a negative result is much worse than a positive one because it means a disappointment of expectations. Unless negative results are valued, however, there can be no experiment and no learning from experience.

The espoused values and principles of today's professionals may conflict with clients' demands. Over the last ten to twenty years, practitioners have been asked to participate in the reform of institutions—they have been asked not only to learn the prevailing values but to change them.

This means that most situations of practice are situations of conflict between demands from the institutions the profession serves (health-care systems, courts, cities) and demands from the profession for change in those institutions. For example: demands from paying clients (who are often agencies charged with developing plans for others) conflict with demands for greater planning participation from users, consumers, and constituents who are affected by the plans; demands for loyalty to the institution employing the professional conflict with demands for commitment to the emerging concept of the profession;[5] demands for performance within the defined limits of institutions conflict with demands for reform of those features of professional institutions that reinforce self-sealing theories and behavior of practitioners. Such conflicts are endemic to professional practice; their resolution demands personal commitment.

It is not clear how we learn to make commitments, especially commitments that are essential for other kinds of learning. At least, we must be aware of the contexts in which such commitments must be made and perhaps also the consequences of failing to make them.

Model II and Aspects of Professional Practice

We have argued that, if professions are to respond to the issues we have described, theories of professional practice must have model-II consequences for the behavioral world and for learning.

But what aspects of professional theories-in-use do we mean? Clearly not the surgeon's theory of incision or the engineer's theory of structural stress. To answer this, we must first differentiate areas to which theories of professional practice apply. It is useful to differentiate technical theories from interpersonal theories. Technical theories state which techniques the practitioner will use in the substantive tasks of his practice. Interpersonal theories state how the professional will interact with clients and others in the course of his practice.

Interpenetration of technical and interpersonal theories. Model II applies to both interpersonal theories and technical theories. Interpenetration of the two theories occurs in varying degrees among the different professions. For example, in teaching, counseling, and psychotherapy, interpenetration is so great that every technical theory is also an interpersonal theory. However, architecture, surgery, law, and engineering appear to have zones of activity in which techniques can be practiced without human interaction; the architect can compute structural stresses and strains, the lawyer can examine regulations of the Securities and Exchange Commission, the surgeon can operate, and the engineer can study an airplane's flight characteristics without interacting with the client. Other zones of activity in these practices do require interaction with others. For example, architects have to bargain with building-code inspectors and contractors, lawyers have to interview their clients, surgeons may need to assess the client's frame of mind regarding the operation, and engineers may have to determine what designs are most attractive to clients.

The less the professional needs interaction with the client in order to carry out the professional task, the more autonomous the profession may be said to be. The more the professional needs interaction with the client in order to perform the professional task, the more interdependent the profession may be said to be.

Interpenetration of technical and interpersonal theories in theory building. The relative autonomy or interdependence of a profession may vary during its diagnostic, testing, and implementation phases, as Figure 5 implies. The internist may depend heavily on his interpersonal theories-in-use in diagnosing and testing the client's illness. However, the implementation (giving insulin for

	Diagnostic	*Testing*	*Implementation*
Technical			
Interpersonal			

FIGURE 5

diabetes) can be both relatively free of interpersonal dimensions as well as highly dependent on interpersonal dimensions (getting the client to exercise certain parts of the body or to stop the intake of certain foods). Similarly, the tax lawyer may require interpersonal skills in diagnosing and testing his client's tax problems but may not need him to be present when he argues his case. On the other hand, the criminal lawyer may need to rely heavily on the interpersonal dimension during all three phases. The city planner may require both technical and interpersonal skills during the diagnostic phase, may focus more on technical skills as he draws up plans, and may again use both technical and interpersonal skills during the implementation stage.

The relatively autonomous professions may require little of the client during the diagnostic and testing phases but involve him during the implementation phase. Each profession may have a certain ratio of autonomy to interdependence that varies according to the phase of professional/client activity.

For example, operations-research teams tend to conceive of themselves as relatively autonomous from their clients. In one study, they were observed to spend most of their time away from clients, developing models requested by the clients. Yet when the models were presented, even though they met the clients' requirements, they were resisted for reasons that had little to do with the techniques involved. The response seemed irrational to the professionals. What sense does it make for executives to resist the very models they have requested? The professionals usually (but unintentionally) surfaced their frustration and anger. The executives sensed this, and, with their greater organizational power, reprimanded the professionals. This angered the professionals even more, but, having sensed the executives' hostility, they struggled to suppress their tensions. The mounting tensions that were unexpressed soon began to undermine the operations researchers' technical professional competence. This, in turn, compounded the professionals' problems.

A study of the executives suggested that they perceived the successful models as potentially dangerous to their survival and to the effective use of their leadership styles. They believed that the models could reduce their ability to politick, increase others' control over them, and make them more vulnerable to evaluations from others. Indeed, the executives actually welcomed the distance between themselves and the professionals during the diagnostic and solution-generating phases because it made it easier for them to resist the products (Argyris, 1971).

The operations researchers' reactions to the managerial resistance were not effective in dealing with their own or other's emotions. Indeed, one might hypothesize that they had been attracted to the profession of operations research so they could avoid dealing with their own and others' feelings, especially regarding power, hostility, and rejection. Thus, although the techniques of operations research require little insight into emotional and interpersonal issues, getting clients to accept operations-research models may require great insight and skill in these interpersonal areas. Two leading scholar-practitioners have recently stated that client acceptance and effective implementation were critical problems for operations researchers (Grayson, 1973; Wagner, 1971). Indeed, one may argue that, in the long run, the difficulties generated between operations researchers and executives may create credibility gaps. These gaps may not only make acceptance more difficult but also influence the commitment to giving the professionals the raw data they need. Recall that in the marketing case cited in Chapter Three, the executives' main problems were not related to the product but to the apparently increasing credibility gap and mistrust between salesmen and customers. The gap seemed to get worse even though the organization tried hard to reduce it, the salesmen were rotated, and the product was the best of its kind.

Interpenetration of interpersonal theories of professional and client. Professionals who see themselves as autonomous nevertheless have interactions with clients in which the interpersonal theories of professional and client play a role. The interplay of these interpersonal theories may reduce the effectiveness of the professional's technical theory of practice, as it did in the preceding example of the operations-research team; the clients had interpersonal theories that determined their behavior toward the professionals. The city planner described in Chapter Three was faced with clients who mistrusted him and whose interpersonal theory-in-use required them to attack the professional. The city planner reacted by becoming even more defensive and hiding his true feelings. The clients apparently sensed that he suppressed his feelings, which convinced them that the city planner was not to be trusted. They reacted by making demands on the city planner that greatly reduced the probability that his cherished plans would be accepted.

Some professionals regard the interpersonal issues as irrelevant; this may mask an interpersonal theory-in-use that is ineffective or incongruent with the professional's espoused theory. For example, a field study of pediatricians and their patients showed that, although 76 percent of the mothers expressed overall satisfaction with an office visit, there was still significant dissatisfaction: nearly one-fifth (149) of the 800 mothers felt that they had not received a clear statement about what was wrong with their baby; almost half still wondered what had caused the illness after the visit was over; 42 percent carried out the doctor's advice, 38 percent complied only in part, and 11 percent not at all (9 percent were not scorable); and the severest and most common complaint of the dissatisfied mothers was that the physician had shown too little interest in their great concern about their child. The key variable was how clearly mother and doctor understood each other, not the length of visit; the technical language was a problem but by no means the most serious one (Korsch and Negrete, 1972).

Although some mothers may have distorted reality, the important point is that the doctors rarely created conditions in which the mothers could test their fears so the doctors could ascertain their actual impact. Korsch and Negrete conclude that effectiveness along these dimensions would not necessarily require more time of already overworked physicians.

Conceivably the mothers were aware that their personal feelings and the doctor's professional effectiveness were not related. Out of fear or out of concern for the doctor, they may have accepted the distance as legitimate. However, they dealt with the distance issue by developing internal tensions, dissatisfactions, and ignoring parts of the doctor's advice. Like the executives, they maintained the distance during the diagnostic and solution-generating phases; unlike the executives, they maintained the distance afterward as well.

In another case study, Kasper (1952) shows that patients are capable of altering the data they give the physician depending on their perception of the physician's specialty. They, too, keep their distance and withhold the fact that they are bending their descriptions to fit the physician's specialty. For example, several patients described a problem to both an internist (I) and a psychiatrist (P). Notice the variation: "Pain over heart brought on by exercise" (to I) versus "Pain over heart when nervous" (to P); "Stomach pain and bloating" (to I) versus "Vague fears keep stomach in knots" (to P); "Headaches, occasionally relieved by alcohol" (to I) versus "Alcohol is a big problem—occasional headaches" (to P); "Backache won't let me work" (to I) versus "Dislike business, have had headaches since I opened my store" (to P).

To complicate the matter, most professionals tend to hold espoused theories that differ from their theories-in-use. The espoused theories of the operations researchers do not require the executives to be frustrated, for that frustration to create further defensiveness, or for their models to make the executives feel less competent or powerful. Similarly, the physicians' espoused technical theories say little about how to interact with different patients or how to discourage distorted answers.

Nor does professional education tend to alert the student to become more aware of the client's espoused theory and theory-in-use for dealing with professionals. For example, some clients may believe that "Lawyers can't be trusted; all they want to do is make money," or, "Those lawyers have this stuff so fixed up that once you get involved with them, no one wins except the lawyers." Or, clients may believe that doctors are overworked because they are busy becoming big businessmen; that they are under much pressure, and when one goes into a doctor's office one should know exactly what to say; and that if one doesn't like the doctor's manner, he should suppress that feeling. So, professional effectiveness depends also on awareness of any incongruence between the client's espoused theories and theories-in-use. Figure 6 illustrates this distinction.

		Diagnostic	*Testing*	*Implementation*
Technical	Espoused theories			
	Theories-in-use			
Interpersonal	Espoused theories			
	Theories-in-use			

FIGURE 6

We can now see a closer relationship between building one's own theory of practice and the interpersonal zones of practice to which model II is relevant.

Each dimension of theory-building has an interpersonal component. In the diagnostic process, the practitioner interacts with his clients, seeking valid information on which to base his interpretations. In the testing process, the practitioner risks being trapped by self-sealing assumptions unless he can imagine an alternative view and gain valid information from others as he begins to behave according to that view. As the practitioner confronts the conflicts now inherent in the professional role, his ability to resolve them depends on his interactions with his several kinds of clients, with members of his own organization, and with others in his profession.

In all of these interactions, the practitioner's effectiveness depends on the effectiveness of his own interpersonal theory—which, if we are correct, will be effective to the extent that it conforms to model II.

Paradox of Model II as Technique

We have seen that technical and interpersonal theories of professional practice interpenetrate and that the practitioner's effectiveness depends on his ability to apply model II to the interpersonal

zones of practice. But since the current dilemmas of professional education and practice are traceable to the rise of technique and the
model-I worlds created by technique, one may ask whether model II
is it not also a technique that is susceptible to the criticisms levelled
against other forms of technique. Ellul argues, after all, that one
cannot fight technique with technique (1965).

Let us consider the criticisms of technique that might apply
to model II. They form three main categories: technique is power,
and power corrupts; techniques function as if they had lives of their
own, tending toward the broadest possible applications regardless
of the intent of the developers of technique (what can be done, will
be done); and technique requires institutional settings in which it
can be practiced, and therefore, institutions tend to take on the
characteristics required by technique, which are distorting and de-
humanizing for human beings.

We suggest that these criticisms of technique are not consequences of technique itself but of behavioral worlds in which
technical power is used unilaterally and is neither confrontable, testable, nor influenceable. In short, the criticisms of the impact of technique are accurate if that technique has model-I properties and
exists in model-I institutions that reinforce it.

Although model II is a technique, its governing variables
(valid information, free choice, internal commitment) are anti-
thetical to the governing variables attributed to technique by its
critics.

In behavioral worlds congruent with model II, techniques
would be used under conditions of bilateral rather than unilateral
power, conditions for psychological success rather than psychological
failure would predominate, evaluations and allocations of rewards
and penalties would be conducted under conditions of confirmation
or disconfirmation rather than through the unilateral acts of persons
in power, and the sense of self-acceptance would be highly valued
rather than the sense of the material worth of one's productivity.

Those who see technique as evil in itself tend to propose one
of three directions of reform. Some of them hope to eliminate technique and, by doing so, prevent its determination of the conditions
of human life. This remedy is sometimes advocated for societies as a

whole and sometimes is taken by an individual; in the latter form, it leads occasionally to young people heading toward rustic communes equipped with electric guitars and high-fi gear. Proponents of this remedy seldom, if ever, propose abolishing all technique (most seem to value modern medical techniques, for example) but seem to advocate the selective elimination of techniques. The feasibility of this response on an individual basis depends on whether active rather than passive choice is the norm in a behavioral world. Free choice has the best chance to thrive in model-II behavioral worlds, where individuals are encouraged to choose, design, and manage the factors that shape their lives.

Others would substitute faith in essential human values instead of technique. Palmer (1973) urges that professionals rededicate themselves to the original values of their profession—health, justice, truth. Rededication to humane values is commendable, but this remedy is incomplete. How is such dedication to be acquired or lived out? Such proposals are disconnected from a theory of effective practice.

Others, finally, would limit the power of the manipulators of technique by creating countervailing power centers made up of the victims of technique. In the United States, Ralph Nader's name is the one most frequently associated with this response. He has sought to build a movement around advocacy of the rights of the less powerful, whose lives are affected by the applications of technique. Such a movement is well matched to the evils it wishes to confront because it is itself organized according to model I. In the short term, it may be both necessary and effective, but in the long term it may manifest conditions of model-I behavioral worlds.

A more fundamental response is to help professionals (insofar as they are considered the principal carriers and manipulators of technique) to learn and internalize the governing variables and strategies of model II. This will make the manipulation of technique confrontable, enhance free choice in the solution of techniques, and link the pursuit of humane values to effective practice. This will not be easily accomplished, however. It requires a new design for the professions and for professional education.

Summary

Professional competence requires development of one's own continuing theory of practice, which must consist of both a technical and interpersonal theory if it is to be effective. There are no truly autonomous professions; indeed, the interpersonal zones of practice are probably much larger than is often supposed.

Theory-building for professional practice requires practitioners to have the special competences related to diagnosis, to the generation and testing of solutions, and to the experience of personal causality in implementing solutions. In each of these phases of theory-building, technical and interpersonal theories interpenetrate in different ways and degrees depending on the profession. The competent professional should be able to behave according to model II in the interpersonal zones of practice. His inability to do so constrains his development and use of effective technical theories of professional practice. His mastery of the technique of model II would enable him to confront and alter the model-I worlds associated with professional technique.

Chapter 10

Redesigning
Professional Education

Chapter Ten draws guidelines for the redesign of professional education from the preceding discussions. Two major elements of professional competence emerge from the issues now being raised in the professions and from the changing task environments of professional practice. They are the ability to build a developing theory of practice and the ability to apply model II to the interpersonal zones of practice. We have so far outlined the dimensions of competence needed to build theories of practice, and we have described some of the different configurations of technical and interpersonal theories manifested by the various professions. These various configurations pose somewhat different problems for the redesign of professional education, and we will begin with a discussion of the differences. In another respect, however, the problems of redesign are similar in all professions: they require the integration of various forms of practice into professional education. We will discuss this integration next, relating it to our previous analysis.

Professional Theories

If different professions have different configurations of technical and interpersonal theory, they may pose different problems of professional education. We will discuss three illustrative configurations: one in which incongruities exist between espoused theories and theories-in-use; one in which espoused technical theory and technical theories-in-use are obsolete or nonexistent; and one in which there are few espoused theories but many effective theories-in-use.

Incongruities between espoused theories and theories-in-use. Let us begin by considering the field of education. For example, there are conflicting theories about teaching mathematics. About two decades ago, a concerted effort to upgrade the content of mathematics taught in the primary and secondary schools focused on teaching the more basic aspects of mathematics. A camp of distinguished scholars objected to this design on the grounds that a generation of students would be unable to use mathematics effectively for simple but frequent everyday addition, subtraction, and division.

Another example of controversy in education concerns the open, flexible classrooms that usually include team teaching. The espoused technical theory contains inconsistent propositions about the proper number of students in the classroom, the degree of flexibility that the teachers should show, and how free the child is to ignore the suggested curriculum.

The literature shows that, in both of these examples, espoused theories and theories-in-use tend to be incongruous. For example, Sarason (1972) showed that teachers learned about the new mathematics curricula in ineffective, understaffed workshops. Many teachers quickly learned not to raise questions, especially not objections. Because they had never satisfactorily learned the new math themselves, their technical theories-in-use tended in their classrooms to become highly incongruous with the espoused theories.

The espoused concept of team teaching is that teachers should be an interdependent, co-equal, cohesive team. Unfortunately, such interdependence rarely occurs because, in many cases, the senior teacher takes over, other teachers are unable to confront this, and they react by overtly complying with the senior teacher but teaching as they wish. If they are unable to have such freedom, they become disillusioned.

Examples of inconsistencies at the interpersonal level in education include, first, the idea that every child is to be treated as a unique individual, yet teachers are given such large classes and such rigid time constraints that the individuality of the child is subordinated to maintaining the system. Second, teachers are taught to have faith in the child's capacity for organic development—according to which most children can accomplish much more than they do in classrooms. However, teachers find that even the understandably necessary classroom arrangements for learning tend to create a setting in which organic development rarely occurs. Moreover, the espoused theory is not very helpful because of the great individual differences in children's motivation to develop. The technical espoused theory neither specifies these differences nor specifies a valid and usable technique that the teacher can use to assess the capacities and motivations of each student.

The new mathematics and the new science curriculums, as elegant as they may appear, have not been as well accepted in the field as their creators had hoped. The biggest problems stem from what we would call the technical and interpersonal theories-in-use for introducing a new curriculum to teachers. Originally, most of the schemes for changing the curriculum assumed that a clear, rational picture, effectively presented, to individual teachers would result in the programs' acceptance. Ignored were the feelings, attitudes, values that had developed around the old curriculum, the group norms that protected them, and the bureaucratic arrangements that had evolved over the years to protect individual feelings and values as well as the group norms.

In law, there is a technical espoused theory regarding the payment of corporate and personal taxes that is so complex that few laymen understand it. Students are taught about tax law through exploration of countless cases, each of which is chosen because it illustrates key issues. This gives the student the impression that the lawyer's key competence is being able to retrieve the appropriate tax laws and regulations that fit the client's problems. Once lawyers get out into the field, they find that the theory-in-use is quite different. The key competence becomes knowing the relevant aspects of bargaining to determine how the case should be resolved.

Other technical espoused theories in law state that counsel must represent his client's interests faithfully and completely. Yet, it is common knowledge that many lawyers find themselves colluding with their legal adversaries in order to reach a settlement that guarantees a certain level of earnings for the law firms; such resolutions are then described as being in the clients' interests.

In an appropriately redesigned professional curriculum, courses would describe these inconsistencies and incongruities and perhaps begin to deal with them. This would require a faculty able to understand the importance of teaching both espoused theories and theories-in-use. Indeed, the faculty may also describe to students their own theories of practice that they have developed over the years to cope with these problems.

Exploring these issues should have several positive consequences. First, the students would realize from the outset the extent of the gap between their academic training and practice. Second, while at school, they would begin to think about and test with each other their own theories of practice. Third, students could then press for the additional courses they need to make their budding theory of practice more effective. For example, the law student may study processes of bargaining, of intergroup dynamics, and of client interviewing. Teachers may study the dynamics of interpersonal conflict and the competences necessary to confront power figures and students constructively.

Faculty might be encouraged to conduct research or to guide others to do so in order to reduce the gap between espoused theory and theory-in-use. This would make the kind of learning necessary to minimize self-sealing processes and maximize double-loop learning more likely in the academic setting.

Obsolete or nonexistent consensual technical theory. City planners do not agree on what constitutes competent practice. Earlier paradigms of city planning, with their focus on land-use, zoning, and the distribution of physical facilities, gave way in the early 1960s to broader concepts of social and economic planning.

Today the planner has become more of a generalist: he may have to develop skills in citizen participation and involvement; he has to develop skills in dealing with intergroup relations; he is faced with understanding complex economic and social problems as well as the inevitable political problems that accompany institutional change.

One result has been to invite the relevant social sciences into the city-planning curriculum. Microeconomics, community politics, organizational theory, decision-making, financial analysis are but a few of the subjects borrowed from other fields. This thrust has its problems. Although scholars from other disciplines may have valuable concepts for important specific planning needs, it is difficult to get them a fair hearing in the professional school. Since students are already anxious about relevance of their education, they may become even more anxious when they are exposed to difficult new concepts that have little apparent connection to the problems they believe they will face. They may react negatively to theory that does not immediately apply to reality and may therefore partly or totally reject the new inputs as not relevant to their profession.

Such reactions may disappoint the new senior scholars, who then withdraw to their established disciplines. The professional school may next try to attract younger scholars from these disciplines, but the senior people will be careful to steer the stronger young faculty away from these settings because what students and the professional-school faculty want is not new or experimental ideas but translations of already known basic concepts into the profession's terms.

Educating students under the conditions that we are suggesting requires competent teachers at the forefront of their field-- teachers who are secure enough to recognize and not be threatened by the lack of consensus about competent practice. The faculty should be skillful in helping students learn from their own experiences as they build new technical theories. Moreover, students need to learn how to translate concepts created in other fields, while at the same time using their own professional field as a starting point for generating new knowledge.

Brooks (1967) points out another dilemma in professional education. Discipline-oriented faculty may espouse values and needs that are not always compatible with the values and needs of the professional who plans to go into service. For example, in the field of educational administration, there is a recognized need to focus on the redesign of educational settings. Schools have attracted scholars who are interested in such design. These scholars tend to see the existing schools as designed incorrectly and managed inefficiently. Their designs call for a new set of values and skills; their concepts of management advocate a new view of effective leadership. Students studying educational administration may be enthusiastic about the new ideas, but the closer they come to graduation, the more they realize that they may be hired only if they know how to manage traditional schools in traditional ways. They may then suppress many of their beliefs, temporarily calling them romantic, and try to please the older faculty, who represent established practice, hoping to increase their chances of finding an appropriate job.

Few espoused theories but effective theories-in-use. The brilliant internist cannot specify the processes of clinical judgment that lead him to make a valid diagnosis of a difficult-to-identify illness, yet he can model the behavior repeatedly for the students. The creative architect is unable to provide an espoused theory of design, yet he can design new and creative structures. The school administrator cannot specify an espoused theory about how he senses when particular schools are in difficulty but, on the basis of visits and informal discussion, shrewdly diagnoses what is wrong in the climate of the school. These are examples of professionals who have few espoused theories but effective theories-in-use.

Mystique is central to such professionals, since the practitioner does not try to make his technical theory explicit.

The polarization of practice and theory may be most extreme under these conditions. The effective practitioner does not understand why he is effective but has directly observable evidence that he is. Such practitioners are identified as "wizards," "brilliant," and "intuitive"; they consequently receive many lucrative opportunities to practice their skills. The resulting busy practice and the lack of interest in or fear of self-consciousness about one's effectiveness may lead to further separation of theory and practice.

The successful practitioner who comes to be revered by his fellow professionals tends also to develop a psychological set that places great reliance on the mystical aspects of his competence. Under these conditions, the professional may find it difficult to admit that, although he knows he is successful, he does not know how to tell others how to behave equally effectively.

Such a practitioner may tend to become a part- or full-time teacher who cannot solve the problem of how to help students learn from someone who cannot be explicit about his theory-in-use. Moreover, if he has become dependent on his mystique, he may also fear behaving in ways that could destroy the intuitive skills and the capacity for tacit knowledge.

Such practitioners often resist being observed and studied by others who might infer their theory-in-use and eventually develop technical espoused theories. They curiously tend to be willing to talk about the problems in their field but not about the causes of their effectiveness. For example, they may be willing to describe the difficulties and challenges that face them as successful executives. However, when asked what leads to their effectiveness, the response tends to range from "I don't know, I just felt it was correct," to the apparently humble, "You'll have to ask others that question" (Argyris, 1961).

Each of these three conditions requires a different response. When there are incongruities between espoused theories and theories-in-use, faculty will have to surface inconsistencies, incongruities, and conflicts in and among espoused technical and interpersonal theories and theories-in-use. With obsolete or nonexistent consensual technical theory, it will be especially important to encourage the exploration of the underlying value conflicts that exist where professional activities are in transition. When there are few espoused theories but effective theories-in-use, the faculty must especially try to surface implicit issues, publicly test hypotheses, identify self-sealing processes, and value double-loop learning about the theories in their respective disciplines.

Although each of these requirements is especially important for each respective condition, many professions may experience all three conditions in different aspects of their field. In a given professional school, all three requirements may need to be emphasized.

This requires faculty members who do not create classrooms that generate energy for inquiry from competition, who do not let win/lose dynamics dominate, and who do not exert primary control of the learning environment and the tasks. Instead, faculty members are needed who can articulate their own views and still be confrontable and influenceable and who can help design learning environments without unilaterally controlling them. In these environments, conditions of psychological success predominate; students define goals and paths to goals, setting realistic but challenging levels of aspiration; evaluation, rewards, and penalties occur through processes of confirmation and disconfirmation; and students are loyal to the generation of valid information rather than to a particular professor's viewpoint.

Teaching Interpersonal Theories

Few changes will be made in schools and in practice unless faculties, students, and practitioners also become more aware of their espoused interpersonal theories and their interpersonal theories-in-use; until more of them are able to behave in accordance with model II; and until they integrate this kind of learning with the learning of technical theories and theories-in-use.

Insofar as clinical experience is aimed at helping students to develop interpersonal theories-in-use along the lines of model II, it should be designed so that it: produces behavior in directly observable categories; enables inferences to be publicly examined; requires hypotheses to be tested publicly and reduces self-sealing activities; focuses on double-loop learning; requires the learner to express his theory-in-use in such a way that he feels responsible for it and does not attribute his behavior to the structure of the simulation but to his personal causation; requires the individual to identify the governing variables of his behavior; and requires the individual to explore the immediate and long-term consequences of his behavior on the client (individual or group), the consequences for the relationship between himself and the client (degree of openness and trust), and the consequences for the client's and the professional's probability of double-loop learning.

In describing these model-II requirements, it is important to repeat that model II is not the opposite of model I. We do not recommend learning environments in which teachers abdicate their responsibilities and in which students can define their goals without also being confrontable and influenceable. We do not recommend learning environments where no evaluations and rewards or penalties occur.

Model II is not a kid-glove variation of model I in which everybody tries to be polite and civilized, yet where the faculty still exercises unilateral control; where win/lose dynamics still prevail; and where the rewards are provided in subtle ways—for example, in confidential letters of recommendation directly to prospective employers.

Nor is model II to be interpreted as a variation of model I. In many alternative schools, the teacher and students oscillate between controlling each other. For example, the students may encourage the teachers to design the educational program and then unilaterally evaluate it to see if they accept it or not. Teachers may impose a particular discipline in their class only to find that students insist that the teacher change it or students will strike or take other power-oriented actions.

Designing model-II learning environments is a very complex task, about which we know pitifully little. Moreover, it is so easy to fall into the trap of designing learning environments that are opposite to or oscillating within a model-I world.

Because the knowledge and skills required are complex, we recommend that seminars aimed at teaching model II be separate from the courses that focus primarily on the technical theories (although someday education in technical and interpersonal theories may be integrated more organically). But courses dealing with model II represent a new dimension of the curriculum. Will there be time for them? In examining various professional schools, we have found that the more a profession depends on client interaction, the more time may be available. For example, schools of divinity, education, business, city planning, and law do have flexibility to add these courses during the advanced years and in some cases during the first year. On the other hand, medical schools may not. This is an area of research that needs to be explored in each profession and each school.

Another mechanism for offering courses on interpersonal espoused theories and theories-in-use is to concentrate all such courses in one department that is to be used by all professional schools in the university. We make this recommendation cautiously because it risks separating the interpersonal and technical aspects of education still more. However, we believe that ultimately students will learn more if they are exposed to competent teachers located outside of their professional school than if they are exposed to less competent teachers who are part of the professional school. Experience with the latter in schools of education, divinity, law, and city planning shows that these programs become all the more isolated if the core faculty feel that such faculty members offer second-rate teaching.

   Some realities have to be faced. First, faculties in professional schools will not change overnight to give the teaching of interpersonal theories the genuine and central position it deserves. Consequently, the best faculty may not be attracted to it. Even if good faculty are available, a school may need only one or two people in the area. This is a small base on which to develop a bridgehead in a hostile setting or to generate the intellectual stimulation needed to go beyond translating existing concepts into a specific profession's terms and to create new concepts that develop the field. Moreover, many students will not opt for significant amounts of education in these areas unless they are necessary for professional accreditation. Even in a large professional school, many students would not choose this kind of education. Finally, there is the problem of cost. The education we have described is still in the primitive stages of design. As such, we recommend that it be done in small seminars with the faculty heavily involved in researching the activities. Such education is expensive.

   The best situation would seem to be for a university to create a learning setting that all professional schools could use. This could call for a large enough faculty to permit several senior and junior members to be appointed. A milieu of academic inquiry could then be developed, and senior positions could be made available for younger people.

Integration of Practice into Professional Education

   Each of the two main elements of professional competence—the capacity to build one's own technical theory of practice and the

capacity to apply model II to the interpersonal zones of practice—
can be acquired only by engaging in practice and reflecting on the
meaning of that experience. We will use the term *clinical* for this
hybrid process.

It has become a cliché to say that professionals must "relate
knowledge to effective action," or "integrate theory and practice";
however, it is not agreed that the professional school should effect
this integration.

There are three perspectives on the relationships among
basic theory, theory of practice, and skills that lead to sharp disagreement on which tasks are appropriate to the school and which
to the office.

One school of thought regards theory of practice as deriving
from basic theory and as testable without recourse to practice—for
example, through progressively more elaborate simulation of real-
world situations. Progress toward a more adequate technical theory
of urban planning, for example, would depend on development of
better basic theory about the growth and transformation of cities,
about institutional behavior, or about policies for the redistribution
of human resources. The professional school, then, should develop
more adequate technical theory of practice by grounding technical
theory in better basic theory. Or, in the extreme version, the professional school should develop better basic theory (that will apply
to professional practice), leaving the derivation of more effective
theories of practice to the practioners. This school of thought holds
that teaching about practice is a diversion from the essential academic tasks; the school should develop and convey basic theory relevant to professional practice, and the office should provide opportunity to acquire professional skills.

A second school of thought comes to the same conclusion by
a different route. Some professionals and educators advance the no-
tion that effective practice involves intuitive knowledge that is not
amenable to explicit formulation, even in principle. This is the position of the adherent of professional mystique—a position that is
found in all professions. This kind of professional knows that he
knows something, knows that students do not know it, knows that
he cannot tell others what he knows, but knows that they should
come to know it. How then do they come to know it? In mysterious

ways, perhaps by a kind of osmosis through proximity to a master, as
in apprenticeship. The student may find himself caught up in what
Laing calls a knot.

> There is something I don't know
>   that I am supposed to know.
> I don't know *what* it is I don't know,
>   and yet am supposed to know,
> And I feel I look stupid
>   if I seem both not to know it
>   and not know *what* it is I don't know.
> Therefore, I pretend I know it.
>   This is nerve-wracking
>   since I don't know what I must pretend to know.
> Therefore I pretend to know everything.
>
> I feel you know what I am supposed to know
>   but you can't tell me what it is
>   because you don't know that I don't know what it is.
>
> You may know what I don't know, but not
>   that I don't know it,
> and I can't tell you. So you will have to
>   tell me everything [1970, p. 56].

The adherent of professional mystique also believes that the intuitive knowledge central to professional skills must be acquired in
practice.

These two points of view may be merged: the professional
school is responsible for developing basic theory that leads to the
best technique, and practice is responsible for teaching, in some
mysterious way, how to apply theory and technique effectively.

The third school of thought says that the professional school
should teach the student to think like a professional—for example,
to think like a lawyer, a city planner, or a physician. It is understood that learning to think like a professional is different from learning the basic theory pertinent to the profession and also different
from the skills of concrete professional practice. Somehow, this manner of thinking is believed to be teachable. It is the task of the

school to teach it and of the office to allow the student to apply it to the problems of professional practice.

Each of these three positions seems to us to be flawed. Basic theory is not clearly related to professional practice. Specific bodies of information tend very quickly to become obsolete (for example, the city planner's information about federal housing programs or the architect's information about particular construction methods). Without a firm grasp of technical theory of practice, one must take on faith the relevance of a particular basic theory to professional competence. For example, should planners learn prevailing theory of social stratification in urban settings? Should managers learn prevailing theory of human motivation?

The relevance of basic theory to practical competence can be determined only through the intermediary of theory of practice, because basic theory comes to bear on action only through the light it throws on the assumptions underlying theory of practice. But we cannot infer applied theory from basic theory alone. Engineering theory cannot be generated only from physics, for example, as most schools of engineering have discovered since the days when engineering was considered applied physics, but the principles and methods of physics may be used to criticize assumptions underlying theories of engineering practice; similarly, chemical engineers need to know thermodynamics because certain assumptions in their theories of practice are very likely to be principles of thermodynamic theory.

In short, given a theory of practice, we may support or criticize its assumptions by referring to basic theory, yet in the absence of a theory of practice, we can be reasonably sure of the pertinence of a particular basic theory to professional competence only if we can be reasonably sure that some of the assumptions in a theory of practice are basic assumptions of that particular kind. This presumption is more feasible for some professions than for others.

With respect to the second point of view, what use is basic theory and its implications if it cannot be converted to effective practice? And, while the acquisition of professional skills may appear to be mysterious, on what grounds is it held to be mysterious in principle? If the views of skills presented in Part One are accepted —namely, that skills are programs for action of very great informational complexity—then there is at least a dimension of the acquisition of skills that need not be mysterious. Moreover, the professional mystique has been linked traditionally to elitist views of the professional's role and of the structure of the profession: one reason to try to dispel the professional mystique (given our ability in principle to dispel it, at least in part) is that is has served a questionable social purpose.

With respect to the third point of view, we have argued (in Chapter Eight) that learning to think like a professional now requires learning to build one's own theory of practice, which in turn, requires engaging in situations of practice. Practice must play a central role in the process by which students learn to think like practitioners.

However, the school cannot claim the entire function of helping students to acquire professional competence—at least not without restructuring the concepts of school and office so that the traditional boundaries between them virtually disappear. The variety, duration, and realism of work experiences required to provide opportunity for developing the full range of professional competences are simply incompatible with the boundaries and structure of school experience as it is currently defined. The structure of the school year, the demands on student time made by course work, the boundaries among discipline-oriented departments, the demands of term papers and theses, the ladders of academic security and prestige all limit the intensity and duration of involvement in practice that would enable the student to acquire a full range of professional competence.

Both simulation and field practice have advantages and disadvantages; each must meet distinct criteria if it is to be used to help build the two kinds of competence.

Simulation is valuable because it can be slowed down, diagnosed, and repeated; it offers practice under the control of the student and with the easy intervention of the faculty; it is psychologically safe for the student; and it protects the clients from being misused in the name of education.

The disadvantage of simulation is that it is a game whose correspondence to reality in the crucial respects is always questionable. This disadvantage may be minimized by design and timing.

Simulation is probably not as effective as field experience when the student has practiced most of the skills and is ready to try them out in a noncontrived setting. On the other hand, a simulation may be useful for the experienced practioner who wishes to examine why certain actions are not usually effective or wishes to learn new concepts and skills.

Field experience—experience in actual rather than simulated practice—has become a popular subject in professional education circles. In schools of law where case methods and moot courts have long been used, the last five years have seen a spate of new efforts at student involvement in real-world practice. To some extent, the initiative for these experiments has come from students themselves, and the field work has taken the form of projects of legal advocacy for the disadvantaged. These are roughly similar, in motivation and content, to the involvement of architectural and planning students in various forms of advocacy. Such efforts have been more or less informal and peripheral.

There have also been more radical efforts to make field work central to professional education, as at the SUNY Buffalo School of Environmental Design. Even in professional schools long familiar with practical experience in professional education—the business schools, known for their use of case method, and the medical schools, from whom the term *clinical* has been borrowed—there is an effort to rethink and to experiment.

All of these activities have given rise to a series of operational questions concerning administrative requirements, credit, supervision, relation to academic course work, selection of students, definition of student responsibility, and degree of faculty involvement. There are, in addition, more serious questions that reflect the mismatch between field experience and the culture of the academy.

The formal structure required by field activity does not match the structure of semesters, courses, and departments. Faculty tend to resist the intrusion of field work into the curriculum, or, at any rate, tend to carry on the academic program parallel to field work as though the latter did not exist.

The motives of students and faculty for engaging in field activity are diverse, and they are variously satisfied and dissatisfied with their involvement. For some, engagement in the field provides an insight into the nature of work in the real world and therefore serves to confirm or modify the students' career aspirations. For some, field work allows a sense of involvement in service to the disadvantaged; depending on their experiences, students and faculty are variously satisfied and frustrated by the degree to which they have been able to be of help.

Educationally, the meaning of field work has been unclear. Many students learn about their own incompetence, that work in the field is harder than they thought, and that they fail. In reaction, they may attack course work with a new energy, or they may express frustration that course work is less responsive to what field work has taught them they need to know. Often, when students feel they have learned something important, they are unable to state what they have learned.

In our opinion, the field experience should not be designed simply to give students experience in the real world. Important as it is to obtain such an experience, it is not enough. The school is obligated to offer more to the student; otherwise, the student finds himself paying tuition fees to learn something for which he does not need a faculty's help and that he could be paid to learn if he took a job and began to work.

Moreover, experience in the real world tends to increase the probability that model-I, self-sealing, interpersonal techniques will be learned. Under pressure, the student may begin to consider model I as the road to success and alternatives to it as at best a dream— someday he may learn alternatives, after he has succeeded financially or when he obtains the personnel he wants or if he finds an enlightened client who is interested in plannnig a city comprehensively.

The objective of the field experience, like the objective of all clinical experience, is to learn to become more reflective under real-time conditions so that effective ad hoc theories of action can be created and tested.

Insofar as clinical experience is intended to help the student learn to build his own theory of practice, the real or simulated situations of practice ought to have different characteristics depending on the functions to be filled, as the following list shows.

Functions

Gap-filling, translation, internalization. The task is to help the student relate preprogrammed, applied theories to concrete situations of practice, which means (1) learning to fill the information gap between theory and practice, (2) learning to translate verbal learning to settings in which information is conveyed through interaction with others, and (3) learning to internalize complex programs so that they can be carried out smoothly and effectively.

The ease with which the student can recall and apply stored theories of action frees him to carry out theory-building when this is required.

Theory-building: diagnosis.

Practice situation

Because these functions use existing applied theory, the prerequisite for being in the situation of practice is that the student know the theory. The theory, moreover, limits the situations: they must be the concrete situations to which the theory corresponds. Practice may take the form of a series of small exposures, each of which provides an opportunity for the application, testing, translation, or internalization of a segment of theory (the medical student's exposure to patients on rounds is prototypical). Ideally, these small segments of practice are also repeatable to permit the student to live through versions of them again and again.

Teaching or supervision connected with these experiences would take the form of modeling the tasks to be undertaken, structuring the sequence of tasks, and criticizing responses.

There are antecedent skills—observation, listening, entering new settings. The practice experience consists of immersion in a particular organization, institution, system, or culture with the task of description and diagnosis. Risks and pressures are low. Duration should be no longer than required for immersion in the culture.

The experience should be repeatable in different organizations, institutions, and settings so as to

Functions   *Practice situation*

yield understanding of the different perspectives of the world held by different cultures.

Supervision consists of debriefing the student; questioning him about dimensions of the system he may not have noticed; modeling the kinds of listening, observing, and interviewing that is essential to his role as anthropological visitor; encouraging him to express what puzzles him in the phenomena observed; encouraging him to build an explanatory theory to account for puzzling phenomena.

Theory-building: testing.

Preconditions are familiarity with models of valid inference and techniques for testing hypotheses. There must be an involvement of enough duration, range, and freedom of action to permit development and testing of a theory of action.

The scope of involvement may vary enormously, depending on the scope of the theory to be tested and the scope of the test. It may vary from one-to-one intervention to long-term efforts at institutional reform, so long as it permits theory-building, conceiving of the intervention designed to test the theory, carrying out the intervention, noting and interpreting the outcome.

Supervision consists in helping to structure these steps, helping the student to think them through, and helping him to identify the

Functions	*Practice situation*
	kinds of criteria that are appropriate to each step (and identifying how the criteria are different from those applicable to laboratory experiments).
Theory-building: personal causality.	Preconditions are enough competence to enable the student to respond to the task environment and student competence that approximately equals the demands of the task environment. The situation of practice should be one in which the structure, duration, setting, and conditions of the situation are set by the client's situation.
	Similarly, the student should be selected for the task by the client and negotiate his contract for performance with the client. The task will be characterized by high risk, pressure, deadlines, accountability.
	Supervision consists of helping the student to identify and confront the commitments demanded of him and to notice what is happening to him, including the occasions that demand building a theory of action, confronting hostile judgments, admitting failures. Supervision would encourage the student to see the situation as one in which his own values and point of view are relevant and to encourage him therefore to try to understand them clearly.

There may be considerable overlap in the functions a single situation of practice may serve. Several of the functions in the preceding list may be served either by simulated or by field experience. However, the last function—the learning associated with commitment and personal causality—is best achieved through field experience because of its real problems, real clients, high-risk situations, deadlines, and demands for performance and accountability. On the other hand, it is difficult to slow field experience down, to make it repeatable in crucial respects, and to make it accessible to supervision.

However the situations of practice may be designed, practice must be made central to professional education rather than peripheral to it. The several diverse functions of professional education, including those served through student involvement in clinical experience, must be integrated.

The peripheral position usually occupied by clinical experience in professional schools is indicated by clinical faculty tending to be part-time, young, without tenure, of lower academic status, and to have high mortality.

The first requirement for effective clinical education is to have a full-time supervising faculty member and to include some senior members of the school. These faculty members should be open to exploring their technical and interpersonal theories-in-use. Ideally, they should see their scholarly research mission as developing new applied and basic theory, deriving new clinical experiences from that theory, and testing them to ascertain their effectiveness.

There is a way that one can bring the part-time, successful practitioner into this model, in a way that would be profitable to the practioner, to the students, and to the school. The strategy would be to find practitioners who want to become more skilled at being reflective about their actions and to increase their competence in creating their own theories of effective practice. Let us say that several school superintendents wish to become more aware of their work-related theories-in-use. A seminar of the type described in Part Two could be designed with as many as six superintendents and six students. The practitioners and the students could then become resources for each other. When the group moved into the field, the students could become observers of the superintendents' behavior. They could meet with the superintendents—and, during the early stages, with the faculty—to analyze the effectiveness of their actions and to design alternative ways of behaving.

With progress, the students may be assigned by the superintendents to actual tasks with real clients. The superintendents could now observe their respective students to see how effectively they behave in noncontrived situations. But why would a busy superintendent be willing to take the time to observe a student in action? There are at least three possible reasons: (1) The superintendent will sharpen his observational and diagnostic skills, which he can use to observe his own behavior and in helping colleagues for whom he might act as observer. Moreover, the student and the faculty member will help the school superintendent to examine how effectively he helps others. (2) To the extent that faculty are present in these sessions, the school superintendent would be receiving consulting help at a significantly lower cost than would otherwise be available. (3) Finally, the superintendent will probably feel some degree of responsibility to the student who has been acting as observer and consultant to him.

These reasons imply a contract between the school and the practitioner. The latter must be assured that competent faculty members will be as concerned about his learning as they presumably are about the students' learning. This means that faculty members must have time to observe the superintendent in the field. Such observations would serve as a basis for helping the superintendent and for checking the validity of the students' observational skills.

Moreover, the faculty member needs to be present when the student is commenting on the superintendent's behavior and vice versa. As Part Two suggested, the skills to provide model-II learning conditions are very difficult to learn, and few students or practitioners have them. Consequently, skilled faculty members must be available.

If such faculty help is made available, then the school can more easily make demands of its own regarding the quality of learning experiences the superintendent may be able to design for the student.

Again, internal commitment of faculty members will not tend to be high unless they are centrally interested in studying these learning processes, whether simulated or in the field.

Clinical experience must be integrated into the curriculum not only so the quality of the clinical experience is high but also for the sake of the rest of the curriculum. In Chapter Nine, we discussed the difference between espoused theory and theory-in-use insofar as it pertains to technical theory; we described why it is important to identify the incongruities between espoused theory and theory-in-use. It is in the clinical experience that these incongruities are most likely to surface because it is here that espoused theory is most likely to be confronted with practice. If these incongruities are confronted in a separate course or clinical component, the professional school misses a crucial opportunity. These incongruities are best identified by the instructors in the substantive, technical fields because they know best the intellectual history and development of their fields. Moreover, one way of helping the faculty to free itself from the intellectual rut that model-I technique tends to create and perpetuate is to ask them to focus on the incongruities between what they are teaching and what is practiced.

Practice is best illuminated by connecting it with theory, and faculty members are most competent in theory-building related to their subjects. Leaving the theory of practice to be formulated by the busy practitioner, who often tends to abhor explicit theory-building, causes practice to be taught at best as informed speculation and at worst in the form of war stories.

Finally, dealing with the incongruity between espoused technical theories and theories-in-use only in peripheral clinical courses allows clinical courses to become isolated from the mainstream of intellectual activity of the school. The faculty, having now psychologically and administratively separated the clinical program from the core, becomes willing to lower academic, teaching, and research standards for students and faculty in the clinical component.

For example, clinical practice in schools of education usually means immersing the student in the field to observe a practitioner in action or to perform some task that the practitioner requires of the student. If the former, the student may take copious and complete notes and yet never have a chance to discuss them with the busy practitioner. If the latter, the student soon becomes so busy that again he no longer has time to be reflective about his activities. He has become as harried as his practitioner model—an accomplishment that may earn him plaudits from his model for being able to get his hands dirty, for working hard, for getting certain jobs done, but not for thinking reflectively about his behavior and developing his theory-in-use. Such lower intellectual standards often go unquestioned by the clinical faculty, many of whom are practitioners who have withdrawn from practice to replenish themselves or lick their wounds and are not themselves equipped to reflect explicitly about technical and personal espoused theories and theories-in-use.

The core academic faculty may see these results and feel confirmed that their decision to separate the clinical program from the core intellectual program was a wise one. They may see neither the self-fulfilling prophecy they have created nor the intellectual excitement of bringing their conceptual skills to bear on the development of theories of practice. The practical tends to have been separated from the theoretical not because it is easy but because it is so difficult to understand.

Recently, very bright graduates of professional schools have tried to make their education more relevant. Their faculty supervisors, partly out of fear and partly out of bewilderment, permitted them to work with the poor, the disadvantaged, the troubled. We know of very few cases in which these students did not eventually become frustrated and withdraw. The few who remained began to see the intellectual challenges inherent in making professional education more relevant to professional practice. Some of these students have returned to continue their graduate work and to become faculty members in their respective professional schools. They have built an important bridgehead—they are helping to educate their elders about the incongruities and conflicts that exist in their professions. These individuals need to be helped to fulfill their mission and to conduct the research that will lead to courses in which espoused technical theories are confronted with theories-in-use so that students may be helped to develop their own hybrid theories of practice.

These courses will require faculty who are competent in surfacing conflicts and incongruities in their fields; whose sense of self-esteem and intellectual integrity are high enough so they can admit the differences between what they teach and effective practice; who are strong enough to invite confrontation of their teaching and to make themselves vulnerable to inquiry into the incongruities in their teaching and practice; and who, finally, will confront themselves with the conflict of values implicit in these incongruities.

Notes

Chapter One

[1] Just as there are things we can say about a theory simply because it is a theory, so there are criteria that apply to good theories regardless of their subject matter. Criteria at this level of generality apply to theories of persons and institutions as well as to stars, tides, and atoms.

Anything that claims to be a theory must have *generality*—it must apply to more than one instance; although it may refer to individuals, it must do so in ways that allow similar attributions to be made to other individuals of the same kind. Theories are about kinds of phenomena rather than unique, individual phenomena.

A good theory must be *relevant* to its subject matter; if it claims to be about x, statements about x must be inferrable from it.

It should be *consistent*. Simply stated, it should not contradict itself. It must not state in one place that all horses are white and in another that they are not. Nor must it make statements that imply the contradiction of other statements in the theory.

A theory should be *complete*. It should contain the full set of propositions required to explain what it sets out to explain. If y is to be inferred from x, there should be no hidden or unstated component of x that is necessary to explain y. But the requirement for completeness is one that can never be strictly met. The set of assumptions on which our theories of the world depend are multiple—perhaps nonnumerable—and are at any given time only partly available to us.

Frequently the generation of a new theory starts with the discovery of previously unstated assumptions on which the old theory rested. It would be more accurate, then, to say that good theories should aim at completeness.

Theories should be *testable*. It should be possible to envisage conditions under which the theories would be found to be mistaken. If one cannot do this, it is unclear that a theory is about the world at all. Its testability is a sign of its meaning. In order for a theory to be testable, one must be able to infer from its predictions, which can be found to hold or not to hold.

Theories contain propositions of different orders of *centrality*. The more central the proposition, the more other propositions depend on it; the more peripheral the proposition, the less would change if it were to change. Axioms in geometry are more central than particular theorems, and some theorems are more central than others. In a good theory, the relative centrality of propositions is clear. One is able to assess the soundness of the foundations on which other propositions rest and to understand what is at stake when change in a given proposition is under consideration.

Theories labor under two related imperatives: to take account of the full *complexity* and concreteness of what is there and to do so in the *simplest* way possible. Given its subject matter, the theory should be maximally comprehensive and concrete; it should account for the full range of phenomena with which it is concerned at a level of concreteness that leaves a minimum gap between the theory and its application to reality, and it should do so with the fewest concepts and the simplest relations of concepts. The last requirement—not to multiply entities beyond necessity—is usually associated with the Bishop of Occam.

[*] We believe the point made here is substantially the same as that made by von Wright (1972), who speaks of a schema of practical inference in a sense that is very close to our sense of schema of applied theory. He says: "*X* now intends to make it true that *E*. He thinks that, unless he does *A* now, he will not achieve this. Therefore *X* does *A* now, unless he is prevented or else cannot accomplish his action" (p. 49).

He comments on the particular explanatory function of the schema of practical inference: "The author contends that, as a schema of explanation, the practical inference pattern holds a position in the human and social sciences similar to that of the deductive-nomological pattern (the 'covering law model') in the natural sciences. Since the patterns are of different logical types, there is thus also a difference in kind between explanation in the natural sciences and in the sciences of man" (p. 39).

Von Wright also distinguishes the retrospective and prospective uses of the schema of practical inference. Retrospective: "We start from the conclusion and so to speak reconstruct a set of premises to match it. . . . We *explain* his action by placing it in the 'teleological perspective' of his aiming at some tendency and his epistemic attitude to the requirements of the situation, i.e., his judging that the action is a practical necessity under this end" (p. 49–50). Prospective: "We set out from the premises and 'extract' from them a conclusion. In the first-person case the argument ends in a declaration . . . of intention to do a certain thing. . . . In the third-person case, the perspective argument produces a prediction. Since so and so is the agent's aim and he evidently considers the doing of A necessary for its attainment, he will (probably) do A" (p. 50).

Von Wright thus formulates a schema of practical inference like our schema of applied theory and perceives that the schema that is normative for action (a declaration of intention or commitment) for the agent is also explanatory and/or predictive when attributed to the agent. Moreover, he points out that his schema is a schema of explanation in the sciences of man comparable in importance to covering laws in the natural sciences. In our language, the study of applied theories of action is a major part of the study of deliberate human behavior.

[3] Espoused theory of action and theory-in-use constitute a distinction analogous to the distinction between espoused logic and logic-in-use proposed by Abraham Kaplan in *The Conduct of Inquiry* (1964).

[4] The view presented here is greatly simplified. Characteristically, a theory of action for a situation or practice takes the form of a complex "tree," each branch of which takes the form of the schema of applied theory. In situation S, if you intend C, under assumptions $a_1 \ldots a_n$, do A. If the outcome of A is C_1, consider options A_1, A_2, and A_3; if the outcome is C_2, consider option A_4. . . .

William Schwartz, A. Gory, and others (unpublished paper, 1973) have undertaken to formulate such explicit applied theories representing, in their view, competent medical practice for particular situations of diagnosis, testing and treatment in medicine. It is, of course, debatable whether competent practice may be reduced to such formulations, even in principle. And it is debatable what the particular form and content of applied theories of practice turn out to be. For example, is it only one applied theory that spells out what competent practice means for a certain kind of situation of practice, or is there a range of possibilities? In the formulation of a particular applied theory, how many options for action and their consequences must be spelled out in order to reflect faithfully what is espoused in the profession as a theory of competent practice for that situation? Questions such as these point to a field of inquiry to which we will refer again in Part Three.

It is also important to describe what might be meant by basic theory of professional practice and to distinguish it from what we have called applied theory of practice. We will call *basic theory* an explanatory and/or predictive theory of phenomena pertinent to applied theory of the practice. Pertinence is determined through the intermediary of the assumptions made in the applied theory of the practice. Thus, in medicine, biochemical theory; in management, theory of human motivation; in urban planning, theory of the location of enterprises. All may be pertinent basic theories because they bear on the truth or falsity of assumptions critical to applied theories of the practices of those professions. Applied theory may be considered an application of basic theory in the sense that its enactment represents an instance of the principles formulated in a basic theory. When a physician acts according to a theory of action recommending the use of an antibiotic for the treatment of infection, his actions and its consequences represent an instance of the basic theory of the effects of antibiotics on processes involved in infection. The theory of action derives its justification from that fact, which must figure as an assumption in the schema of that theory of action. But applied theory need not originate in basic theory; that is, in terms of the order of appearance, applied theory may not be deduced from basic theory. On the contrary, applied theory (however arrived at) may come first, and basic theory may be formulated in order to explain the effectiveness of a particular theory of action. In this sense, the relationship between applied and basic theory of professional practice is analogous to the relationship between technology and physical science.

The framework for describing theories of action that we present in this section has much in common with that adopted by Angyal in his *Foundations for a Science of Personality* (1941). Angyal tried to understand deliberate human behavior from within, as we have been doing, by postulating a structure of attitudes and axioms of behavior that could be connected and tested by observation of behavior. "If we trace the connection between attitudes, starting out with the actual behavior sample, we arrive successively at attitudes of a broader and broader range. If one carries out such an analysis on a large number of behavioral samples of the same person, one arrives at a rather limited number of very general attitudes. These few attitudes seem unquestionable, axiomatic for that given person. Such a group of *axioms of behavior* is highly characteristic of a given person and forms the basis of an active philosophy of life. Every person's attitudes can be traced back to more general attitudes leading finally to certain axioms of behavior and in this sense one could say that every person has an active philosophy of life. . . . The personal axioms of behavior, however, need .neither to be adequately formulated intellectually nor to form a self-consistent system. . . . A person may know nothing of such axioms but he *behaves* according to them. They may be intellectually formulated and in such a case we may speak of maxims of personal behavior" (pp. 144–145).

Angyal's axioms of behavior seem to correspond to our principles and his active philosophy of life to our model of theory-in-use. His distinction between axioms and maxims parallels our distinction between theory-in-use and espoused theory.

[5] Polanyi (1967) defines tacit knowing as knowledge involving two terms such that we " 'know' the first term only by relying on our awareness of it for attending to the second" (pp. 9–10).

Polanyi takes the example of an experiment in which the subject learned to avoid a certain sequence of words for which he was punished by electric shock although he could not formulate the sequence to which he was responding. Polanyi says, "I would say . . . that we are attending *from* these elementary movements (muscular acts) *to* the achievement of their joint purpose, and *hence* we are unable to specify those elementary acts" (p. 10).

Later, in another context, he says, "Tacit knowing of a coherent entity relies on our awareness of the particulars of the entity for attending to it; and . . . if we switch our attention to the particulars, this function of the particulars is cancelled and we lose sight of the entities to which we had attended" (p. 34).

This is as close as Polanyi comes to a definition of tacit knowing, but his definition does not do justice to the full range of his examples. It focuses on a characteristic essential to the tacitness of some and peripheral to the tacitness of others.

According to Polanyi's definition, we know x tacitly because, if we were to know it explicitly—paying attention to its particulars—we would lose our awareness of the coherence (the Gestalt property) of the entity to which we are attending.

This may, indeed, be true of the relationship between our awareness of the particulars of an entity and our awareness of the Gestalt of the entity as a whole. What this account overlooks, however, is the difference between this sort of tacit knowing in which we could specify the particulars of x simply by shifting our attention to them, and the sort of tacit knowing in which we could not do so. The former might be the case of our awareness of a familiar face or our awareness of the movements involved in a physical skill. But in the case of our tacit knowing of a problem whose solution we do not yet have or the intimation of a discovery we have not yet made, we are not able to specify the particulars of what we tacitly know. It is not that we would lose our awareness of the Gestalt of x if we were to specify it but that we have not yet learned to specify the particulars of x and to formulate their relationships to one another. In fact, our tacit knowing of x is a stage on the way to our explicit knowing of x. As Polanyi says in another context, the former guides our inquiry toward the latter.

Polanyi does not, then, explain what it means to be tacitly aware of relationships of particulars that we are not yet able to specify. He does not explain the kind of knowledge involved in our performance of operations that we cannot explain or in intimations that we have not yet rendered explicit.

Others have also criticized Polanyi's account of tacit knowing, but have done so on a different basis. Weimer (1973) takes Polanyi to task for a different reason: "I believe that Polanyi has lost sight of the primary problem that Plato proposed the doctrine of recollection to solve. . . . I think that Plato had the seeming anomaly . . . of the productivity of behavior very clearly in mind in the *Meno*. His message is thus primarily that we know and do more than our prior experiences have given us practice with, and only incidentally that we can do things which we cannot express verbally. . . . [Polanyi's version] cannot account for knowing in the absence of a learning history. . ." (p. 31).

Thus, the issue of tacit knowledge becomes bound up with the new rationalism of Chomsky and his followers. It is alleged that we know tacitly not only that which we cannot specify but that which is in the nature of innate knowledge—knowledge that is a condition rather than a consequence of learning experience.

* Those who now defined tacit knowledge of linguistic universals and principles of grammar—see Graves, Katz, Nishiyama, Soames, Stecker, and Tovey (1973)—also have in mind Chomsky's positing of innate knowledge of rules of language. These authors need the concept of tacit knowledge in order to account for innate knowledge that speakers of the language are unable to express.

We do not posit innate knowledge of the principles of theories-in-use. Our use of the concept of tacit knowledge is designed to make it more feasible to approach the problem of existence, inference, and learning outlined above.

† The concept introduced here is essentially that of the homeostasis used in theories of bodily functioning—for example, by Cannon in *The Wisdom of the Body* (1939). To say that the behavior of anything is homeostatic is to say that it seeks to maintain the variables that govern it within acceptable limits. Homeostasis requires (1) certain variables whose values range over scales of intensity, (2) sensors capable of detecting the variation of these values, (3) feedback loops that connect the values of these variables to action, (4) actions capable of affecting, positively or negatively, the values of the variables, (5) some means of setting acceptable limits to the ranging of the variables, and (6) some means of designing actions so as to keep variables within the limits of acceptability.

Homeostatic systems range from the simplicity of a steam engine and its governor to the complex physiology of the system that controls body temperature in warm-blooded animals and the man-made systems for maintaining industrial process control.

⁸ The variables-of-interest have not only the foreground-background relations specified here but also the kinds of relationships Abraham Maslow described in his scale of needs—that is, some are able to come to the foreground only when others have been brought within range. But those same variables take priority over others if, for some reason, they fall out of their acceptable range.

⁹ All of the above is theory in its own right, of course. Its truth

does not depend on one's consciousness of what has been described but on the accuracy of the theory as a description of actual constancy-seeking behavior on the part of human beings.

We don't know whether anyone has ever tried to build a comprehensive theory of values and valuing around the idea of the field of constancy. Certainly, Harry Stack Sullivan uses these concepts in his approach to the self system and its maintenance.

[10] In a marvelously fertile book, Simon (1969) introduces a very special sense of the artificial. "The thesis is that certain phenomena are 'artificial' in a very special sense: they are as they are only because of a system's being molded, by goals or purposes, to the environment in which it lives. . . . Artificial phenomena have an air of 'contingency' in their malleability by environment" (p. ix).

It is this contingency of artifacts—made by men according to their purposes—that raises for Simon the interesting question about sciences of the artificial: "The genuine problem is to show how empirical propositions can be made at all about systems that, given different circumstances, might be quite other than they are" (p. x).

Organizations are artifacts in Simon's sense, but so are economic systems, human rational behavior, thinking, problem-solving, and learning; the sciences of these systems are all sciences of the artificial. Engineering, medicine, business, architecture, and painting are also concerned "not with the necessary but the contingent—not with how things are but with how they might be—in short, with design. The possibility of creating a science or sciences of design is exactly as great as the possibility of creating any science of the artificial" (p. xi).

This characteristic of being designed, and representing therefore a process of adaptation according to some purpose, is central to the concept of the artificial. For Simon, the artifact is "centered on the interface between inner and outer environments; it is concerned with attaining goals by adapting the former to the latter" (p. 57).

inner environment > artifact < outer environment

The design of the artifact represents the attempt to mold the natural laws of the inner environment to the requirements of the task environment. A paradigm is the computer. The inner environment, which consists of the materials and components of the machine, is adapted to the task environment, which sets the functions (for example, computations) it must carry out. It is Simon's dual premise that the inner environment sets constraints on the design of the artifact—that is, on its adaptation to the task environment. But, subject to these constraints, the system designed takes on the shape of the task environment (p. 11). The apparent complexity of an artificial system may then be understood in terms of relatively simple operative constraints of an inner environment as that system adapts to a complex outer environment. It is in this way that he looks at human behavior.

Simon very much shares the perspective of our inquiry in that he regards all deliberate or rational behavior as designed—that is, as an artifact. "Everyone designs who devises courses of action aimed at changing existing situations into preferred ones. The intellectual activity that produces material artifacts is no different fundamentally from the one that devises a new sales plan for a company or a social welfare policy for a state. Design so construed is the core of all professional training: it is the principal work that distinguishes the professions from the sciences" (p. 55). Hence the critical role of sciences of the artificial in the design of professional education.

Simon regards human rationality (human thinking, problem-solving, learning) as a process of design in this sense. He also regards it as itself an artifact—that is, as the subject of a science of the artificial in its own right. His book is taken up with an attempt to set forth the elements of design from both points of view.

There is one crucial respect in which our concept of the artificial differs from Simon's. Simon uses the concept of man's behavior and his behavioral world (for example, his organizations) as artifacts. Hence, he regards the problem of devising courses of action as a problem of designing behavioral artifacts that adapt inner environments to the requirements of outer task environments. What he does not do, however—at least in his 1969 work—is to consider the outer task environment as itself the artifact of human behavior.

In our sense, action (conceived as an artifact) also has the property of creating the behavioral world that is the task environment for action. The design problem involved in the development of theories of action is not only that of adapting one's inner environment to the requirements of the outer task environment, but that of doing so in such a way as to create a preferred task environment will set the requirements for future adaptations.

To put the matter differently, in Simon's paradigm of imperative logic (p. 61), he sees the problem of optimizing as one of finding means through which constraints (characteristics of the inner environment) may be adapted to fixed parameters (characteristics of the outer environment). (The parallel to our schema for applied theory—with its actions, consequences, and assumptions—is noteworthy.) In our terms, the problem of optimizing is always a double problem that involves (1) finding means to adapt the constraints of the inner environment to the fixed parameters of the outer environment and (2) given second-order requirements for the outer environment, finding means of acting so as to meet those second-order requirements as well. Every problem of the design of action is a problem in both senses.

It may well be that what is true of action as artifact is also true of the entire world of artifacts—that is, of technology. One of the recurrent dilemmas in technological design is the tendency of particular technologies to influence their task environment in such a way as to alter the very requirements the technologies were designed to meet. A most familiar example is the tendency of new transportation systems to cause shifts in the origin-destination pattern that set the targets for the original system. Hence, the interest in self-modifying or self-adapting technological systems.

[11] We will examine the implications of this fact for the meanings of good theory of action and of testability in Chapter Two. At this point, however, we will explore further the mutually determining relationship between theory-in-use and the behavioral world.

Bateson, in his remarkable book *Naven* (1958), describes one of the principal forms of interaction through which theory-in-use and the behavioral world create one another. His concern is with a certain kind of cumulative behavior he calls *schizmogenesis*. In complementary schizmogenesis, one person's behavior creates complementary behavior on the part of others. Dominant behavior on the part of the male head of the household creates complementary submissive behavior on the part of other members of the household, and their submissive behavior will lead to more dominant behavior on the part of the head of the household. The process will develop progressively (more dominant, more submissive) unless it is constrained by other factors. In symmetrical schizmogenesis, the behavior of one person creates symmetrical rather than complementary behavior on the part of others. Competition is the prototype of symmetrical schizmogenesis. Systems of complementary and symmetrical schizmogenesis are systems in which x's behavior creates progressively more complementary or symmetrical behavior in y, and y's behavior does the same for x.

Following Bateson, we may add that x's theory-in-use toward y may lead y to behave as x's theory would lead x to believe y would behave. And y's theory-in-use toward x may lead x to do the same; x's theory-in-use may in this way create y's confirming behavior, and y's theory-in-use may create x's confirming behavior. Their theories-in-use may in this way become self-sealing.

Laing (1966) has introduced a more elaborate picture of these kinds of relationships, pointing out the fuller range of interactions involved. There are not only x and y and their respective behaviors, there is x, x's view of himself ($x \longrightarrow x$), the way x sees y ($x \longrightarrow y$). Similarly, there is y, y's view of himself ($y \longrightarrow y$), y's view of x ($y \longrightarrow x$). There is x's view of the situation he is in with y ($x \longrightarrow s$), and y's view of that situation ($y \longrightarrow s$). There is x's view of his action, a ($x \longrightarrow a$) and y's view of that action ($y \longrightarrow a$). There is, moreover, x's view of y's view of x ($x \longrightarrow [y \longrightarrow x]$) and so on.

In any given situation, x's behavior will depend on x's view of himself, of y, of y's view of x, and of the situation, s, in which they both exist; all of these things will determine x's action, a. But a may also help to determine all of these things. Moreover, as Laing is at pains to point out, x's views of x, or of y or of y's view of x may be very different than y's view of these things. Interactions between them may need to be understood in terms of mutually interacting fantasies of self, other, action, and situation. One's own action has not only the meaning one intends it to have, under one's theory-in-use, but the meaning it is given by the other under his theory-in-use. And one's action's effects on the behavioral world must be a function of those mutual (complementary, symmetrical) interpretations.

Any student of interpersonal, organizational, or international relations will recognize that these complexities of interaction are anything but academic.

Chapter Two

[1] We might have chosen to speak of two inconsistent values. But remembering our earlier discussion of the field of constancy, there is a much larger set of variables for which under a given theory-in-use one strives toward keeping values within a desired range. It is among larger subsets of these that relations of consistency or inconsistency hold.

[2] Not all governing variables need behave this way. For some, perhaps, there may be no question of degrees of achievement. One either achieves them or does not; they are binary. Perhaps justice or truth-telling can be taken to be such variables. When two such vari-

ables in a given behavioral context interfere with one another, they exhibit internal inconsistency. Given the behavioral context, the injunctions to achieve these two values are in relation to one another very much like a logical contradiction.

[3] In nonlaboratory situations, the concept of experiment is not rigorously applicable; it is not usually possible, for example, to institute strict controls. But a similar sense of experiment is applicable. We will return to this matter in Part Three.

[4] We will argue in Part Two that the testability of theories-in-use is essential to their effectiveness over the long run because effectiveness over the long run depends on double-loop learning. There is no learning without testability.

If there is no requirement for double-loop learning, the argument falls. But we will argue further that circumstances of progressive change—the loss of the stable state—make testability and double-loop learning an essential feature of theories-in-use. Otherwise, the protagonist cannot discover ahead of time the changes in conditions that will influence his effectiveness; and, when such changes have occurred, he will not be able to discover in a differentiated way the aspects of his theory that have failed him.

[5] The concept of dilemmas and their role in precipitating change in values is not a new one. For example, Rokeach (1968) offers the following view: "The greatest pay-off should come about by bringing into an inconsistent relation the most central elements of the system. . . . Attention is thus drawn especially to . . . an inconsistent relation between two or more terminal values . . . since these terminal values are the most centrally located structures; having many connections with other parts of the system, we would expect inconsistencies which implicate such values to be emotionally upsetting . . . to dissipate slowly, to be long-remembered, to . . . *lead to systematic changes in the rest of the value system,* to lead to systematic changes in connected attitudes, and finally, to culminate in behavior change" (pp. 21–22).

Chapter Seven

[1] It is interesting to note that the issue of intimidation has not arisen in two seminars held recently with presidents of organizations and graduate professional students. Each group reported that they expected to have instructors of high competence whom they could con-

front. These experiences reinforce recent research being conducted by one of us that intellectual competence may be more threatening to students who have had extensive T-group or encounter-group experiences (which was true for the students in the case cited).

    [2] The description of the learning processes that we have just explored is primitive and, at best, only suggestive. It is our hope that enough has been presented to cause others to join the research that is needed urgently.
    One of the thrusts of our research is to discover new processes that may speed up learning. For example, since this book went to press, new tasks have been developed that accelerate the diagnosis of individuals' espoused theory and theory-in-use. One such task is for the individuals to analyze their cases in terms of maps of models I and II. This task can be done by each person working alone. We have found that if, before the other members of the group read their cases, individuals diagnose the extent to which they behave according to model I, they are able to come to the group much less defensive and much more ready to move toward action recommendations to exploring model-II behavior. The degree of dependency on and the competition with the other members and with the instructor also appears to diminish greatly. The member may feel an inner sense of strength and hope that, by himself, he can recognize the blindness that in previous groups others had to point out to him. Experiencing their capacity to rediscover aspects of themselves with the use of cognitive maps not only increases participants' readiness to experiment with new behavior but it apparently increases their sense of confidence in their ability to continue learning after they have left the seminars.
    This brings us to another phase of research. One of us is exploring learning experiences that individuals can use to continue to learn in their everyday work under real-time conditions. One of the great difficulties is to help our participants continue their learning in a world where other than learning tasks are salient and where many people do not understand anything about models I and II, do not seek to understand anything about them, and, if they were to understand, might consider such learning undesirable, pointing to many organizational and cultural arrangements in support of their views.
    One group of participants is composed of presidents of moderate-sized corporations. These men were selected for several reasons in addition to their genuine interest in learning to increase their effectiveness. If the learning is effective, these men have the power to open up op-

portunities for others in their organization to learn; they can also encourage the exploration of new organizational structures and processes that will be needed if model-II behavior is to survive and spread.

On the other hand, the group of participants represents a category of individuals who are extremely busy, horribly overworked, and whose adherence to model I tends to be so tenacious that one may describe them as model I^2. Thus, the group represents a difficult sample to work with, although if the learning takes hold, this increases the opportunities for the learning not only to be offered to others but for the exploration of systemic changes and redesigns that will be necessary.

Progress to date is very encouraging. The men are highly committed to continue their learning beyond the seminars so that they can use model-II behavior in their work settings and maintain such behavior under conditions ranging from low to moderate stress. The type of learning experiences that the men have gone through has minimized the conversion phenomenon typical of other experiential learning and has helped the men to develop a realistic level of aspiration about how long it will take them to become more effective. The realistic level of aspiration feeds back to maintain high commitment in spite of difficulties and to minimize either the condemnation of their subordinates (for not being helpful) or their pushing their subordinates into effectiveness seminars. They say, for example, that one of their critical problems in application is to learn how presidents can ask for help, how to use their vice-presidents as resources for learning and simultaneously advocate positions in which they believe, and how to accomplish this with subordinates who may be leery if not distrustful of the president's desire to change his behavior. As one president put it, "The going is slow and difficult, but it's also fun."

When a president's learning advanced most, conditions altered to the point that some vice-presidents began to ask to be exposed to the learning environments and some began to think creatively about the redesign of organizational structures, problem-solving processes, management information systems, and reward and penalty processes.

Also, all the presidents have eagerly tried to apply their learning to their home life, only to find that some of the greatest resistance comes from the people they love most but with whom they have dealt, for too long a time, with model-I behavior. Characteristically, they feel neither anger nor discouragement. They appear to understand the disbelief and perhaps even distrust of their family members. To date, such responses have led the executives to work harder at altering their theories-in-use and developing more effective behavior.

Chapter Eight

[1] It is interesting to compare this sketch to a more serious effort to trace the history of a particular profession and of education for that profession. Woodward's (1972) elegant and provocative monograph casts a historian's glance at the current unrest in legal education, ". . . a mood of uneasy restlessness among many students and faculty members. . . . What should we teach? How? To what end? With all our new knowledge, we are, as André Breton has observed, 'lost in a forest of signposts' " (p. 331).

Woodward begins with a concept of the religious origins of the law: "In earlier times, the law was almost as mystical and certainly as ritualistic as the Church itself. . . . the practice of the law was itself a sacrament. . . . As late as 1833, Joseph Story pointed out in his inaugural lecture as Dane Professor at Harvard that . . . 'Christianity is a part of the common law, from which it seeks the sanction of its rights' " (pp. 334–335).

According to Woodward, the secularization of the law involves three propensities, "the growth of rationalism, the development of a scientific outlook, and the invention of new technology (p. 333).

Rationalism ". . . brought law to earth, but alone it was not enough to bring law to its present state of secularization. This rationalistic outlook had to be conjoined with an equally rationalistic method of analysis before law could be transformed into 'legal science' " (p. 336).

The "mass of undigested material that made up the law . . . was made over into a science at roughly the same time that the physical sciences were coming into being and at approximately the same pace that 'scientific method' itself was developing" (p. 337).

Woodward sees the science of law as having passed through four stages. "First, the might morass had to be put into some semblance of order (1750–1800); secondly, a sizeable body of factual and theoretical data about the law itself had to be gathered (1800–1870); thirdly, the principles underlying this data had to be deduced and the science of law reconstructed on truly scientific foundations (1870–1930); and finally—to speak of the stage at which we have now arrived—the science of law had to be integrated into a still-evolving and only dimly perceived 'science of sciences' " (p. 336). Woodward regards Langdell's well-known development of case method as, first, an inductive approach to the scientific formulation of the principles of law—"the cases being the data from which the true legal principles could be derived" (p. 344)—and only secondarily as a teaching method.

Modern legal technology, Woodward thinks, developed in America out of an effort "simply to make the law—the science of law—more useful" (p. 347). Under the banner of legal realism, lawyers began to believe that "The real problems of law were to contrive a language technique, a judging technique, and a statistical technique whereby, in short, the science of law could be put to practical use solving solvable problems" (pp. 347–348). As a result, "Legal education has been transformed in the twentieth century from an inductive science based on case method into an applied science based on practical considerations" (p. 362).

Woodward's historian's perspective makes the law seem to have emerged from its mystical origins toward a secularization in which rationalism led in the nineteenth century to a scientific outlook that was transformed in the twentieth century, into legal technology. Other legal historians may disagree about the ordering and elaboration of Woodward's stages of development. Historians of other professions undoubtedly discover different stages in the patterns of professional evolution, date them differently, and interpret differently their significance for the current professional predicament. From our point of view here, we wish to stress those respects in which Woodward's account appears to confirm the sketch of the history of the professions presented earlier. (1) The origins of the profession were religious; in its early form, the paradigm of the profession was heavily imbued with religious values and ideals. The practitioner derived his authority from the sacred ideology of the profession. (2) The profession evolved through a secularization that separated the profession from its religious context and moved toward rational and systematic formulation of the body of professional knowledge. The practitioner's authority derived now from his expert grasp of professional knowledge. (3) By the twentieth century, technique had come to dominate the professional paradigm, and the ideological components of the paradigm had begun to fade in relation to technique. Ellul (1965) defines technique in a way that is useful here: "The twofold intervention of reason and consciousness in the technical world, which produces the technical phenomenon, can be described as the quest of the one best means in every field. And this 'one best means' is, in fact, the technical means. It is the aggregate of these means that produces technical civilization. . . . In every field men seek to find the most efficient method. . . . It is really a question of finding the best means in the absolute sense, on the basis of numerical calculation" (p. 21).

Chapter Nine

[1] See the writing of philosophers and logicians on confirmation theory, and the literature of what is variously called normative, modal, or deontic logic in, for example, von Wright (1972).

[2] See Rein and Weiss (1970).

[3] William Schwartz and his collaborators have attempted an explicit program for undertaking such a calculus in the course of medical diagnosis and treatment.

[4] There is a dilemma here whose resolution is essential to performance that is more than competent. Playfulness and commitment are both essential if performance under stress is to consist of more than return to the last thing done well. Creative performance under stress means bringing playfulness and responsibility together.

[5] It is a dilemma for the contemporary professional how he may keep alive his allegiance to professional values when he spends his working life in organizations whose values and requirements often conflict with professional ones. Engineers, for example, function largely in bureaucracies—subject to all of the constraints and demands of bureaucracies—and very little in one-to-one relations with clients. The high mobility of planners, cited earlier in this chapter, may be seen as a way of maintaining professional identity across cycles of residence in organizations.

References

ANGYAL, A. *Foundations for a Science of Personality.* New York: Commonwealth Fund, 1941.

ARGYRIS, C. "Puzzle and Perplexity in Executive Development." *Personnel Journal,* 1961, *39,* 463–466.

ARGYRIS, C. *Interpersonal Competence and Organizational Effectiveness.* Homewood, Ill.: Irwin, 1962.

ARGYRIS, C. *Integrating the Individual and the Organization.* New York: Wiley, 1964.

ARGYRIS, C. *Organization and Innovation.* Homewood, Ill.: Irwin, 1965.

ARGYRIS, C. "Conditions for Competence Acquisition and Therapy." *Journal of Applied Behavioral Science,* 1968a, *4,* 147–177.

ARGYRIS, C. "Some Unintended Consequences of Rigorous Research." *Psychological Bulletin,* 1968b, *70,* 185–197.

ARGYRIS, C. "The Incompleteness of Social-Psychological Theory." *American Psychologist,* 1969, *24,* 893–908.

ARGYRIS, C. *Intervention Theory and Method.* Reading, Mass.: Addison-Wesley, 1970.

ARGYRIS, C. *Management and Organizational Development.* New York: McGraw-Hill, 1971a.

ARGYRIS, C. "Management Information Systems: The Challenge to Rationality and Emotionality." *Management Science,* 1971b, *17* (6), 275–292.

ASHBY, W. R. *Design for a Brain.* New York: Wiley, 1952.

215

BARKER, R., DEMBO, T., AND LEWIN, K. "Frustration and Regression." *University of Iowa Studies in Child Welfare,* 1941, *18*(1).

BATESON, G. *Naven.* (2nd ed.) Stanford, Ca.: Stanford University Press, 1958.

BROOKS, H. "Dilemmas in Engineering Education." *IEEE Spectrum,* 1967, *4,* 89–91.

CANNON, W. *The Wisdom of the Body* (rev. ed.) New York: Norton, 1939.

Carnegie Commission on Higher Education. *Higher Education and the Nation's Health.* New York: McGraw-Hill, 1970.

COPE, O., AND ZACHARIAS, J. *Medical Education Reconsidered.* Philadelphia: Lippincott, 1966.

ELLUL, J. *The Technological Society.* New York: Knopf, 1965.

FRIEDMAN, J. *Retracking America.* New York: Doubleday, 1973.

GEIGER, J. "*The New Doctor.*" In R. Gross and P. Osterman (Eds.), *The New Professionals.* New York: Simon and Schuster, 1972.

GOFFMAN, E. *The Presentation of Self in Everyday Life.* New York: Doubleday, 1959.

GORDON, R. A., AND HOWELL, J. E. *Higher Education for Business.* New York: Columbia University Press, 1959.

GOTTESFIELD, H. *The Critical Issues of Community Mental Health.* New York: Behavioral Publications, 1972.

GRAVES, C., KATZ, J., NISHIYAMA, Y., SOAMES, S., STECKER, R., AND TOVEY, P. "Tacit Knowledge." *Journal of Philosophy,* 1973, *70* (11), 318–331.

GRAYSON, C. J., JR. "Management Science and Business Practice." *Harvard Business Review,* 1973, *51,* 41–48.

GROSS, R., AND OSTERMAN, P. (Eds.) *The New Professionals.* New York: Simon and Schuster, 1972.

HAINER, R. "Rationalism, Pragmatism, Existentialism." In M. W. Shelly and E. Glatt (Eds.), *The Research Society.* New York: Gordon and Breach, 1968.

HAVENS, L. *Approaches to the Mind.* Boston: Little, Brown, 1973.

KAPLAN, A. *The Conduct of Inquiry.* New York: Intext, 1964.

KASPER, A. M. "The Psyche Doctor, the Soma Doctor, and the Psychosomatic Patient." *Bulletin of the Menninger Clinic,* 1952, *16,* 80.

KELMAN, H. C. "Compliance, Identification, and Internalization: Three Processes of Attitude Change." *Journal of Conflict Resolution,* 1958, *2,* 51–60.

KORSCH, B. M., AND NEGRETE, V. F. "Doctor-Patient Communication." *Scientific American*, 1972, 227, 66–74.

LAING, R. D. *Knots*. New York: Pantheon, 1970.

LAING, R. D., PHILLIPSON, H., AND LEE, A. R. *Interpersonal Perception*. New York: Harper and Row, 1966.

MAYHEW, L. B. *Graduate and Professional Education*. New York: McGraw-Hill, 1970.

MAYHEW, L. B. *Changing Practices in Education for the Professions*. Atlanta: Southern Regional Education Board, 1971.

PALMER, P. "Professions in the Seventies." *Church Society for College Work*, March 1973.

PERRUCCI, R., AND GERSTLE, J. E. *Profession Without Community: Engineers in American Society*. New York: Random House, 1969.

POLANYI, M. *The Tacit Dimension*. Garden City, N.Y.: Doubleday, 1967.

REIN, M., AND WEISS, R. "The Evaluation of Broad-Aim Programs: Experimental Design, Its Difficulties, and an Alternative." *Administrative Science Quarterly*, 1970, 15(1), 97–109.

ROKEACH, M. "A Theory of Organization and Change Within Value-Attitude Systems." *Journal of Social Sciences*, 1968, 24(1), 21–22.

SARASON, S. B. "The School Culture and Processes of Change." In S. B. Sarason and F. Kaplan (Eds.) *The Psycho-Educational Clinic*. New Haven, Conn.: Yale University, 1972.

SCHEIN, E. H. *Professional Education: Some New Directions*. New York: McGraw-Hill, 1972.

SCHEIN, E. H., AND BENNIS, W. G. *Personal and Organizational Change Through Group Methods*. New York: Wiley, 1965.

SCHON, D. *Beyond the Stable State*. New York: Random House, 1971.

SCOTT, R. *The Making of Blind Men*. New York: Russell Sage Foundation, 1969.

SIMON, H. A. *The Sciences of the Artificial*. Cambridge: Massachusetts Institute of Technology Press, 1969.

WAGNER, H. M. "The ABCs of OR." *Operations Research*, 1971 19, 1259–1281.

VON WRIGHT, G. H. "On So-Called Practical Inference." *Acta Sociologica*, 1972, 15(1), 39–54.

WEIMER, W. B. "Psycholinguistics and Plato's Paradoxes of the *Meno*." *American Psychologist*, 1973, 28(1), 15–33.

WHITE, R. "Motivation Reconsidered: The Concept of Competence." *Psychological Review*, 1956, *66*, 297–334.

WOODWARD, C. "The Limits of Legal Realism: An Historical Perspective." In H. L. Packer and T. Ehrlich (Eds.), *New Directions in Legal Education*. New York: McGraw-Hill and Carnegie Foundation for the Advancement of Teaching, 1972.

Index

Values: in behavioral world, 28-29;
defined, 162; dilemmas of, 31-32

Variables: consistency among, 20-23,
207; constancy of, 15-17, 203-204;
foreground and background, 16,
203; incompatibility among, 21-22,
207-208; internal inconsistency
among, 21-22, 197, 207-208. *See
also* Governing variables

VEBLEN, T., 151

VON WRIGHT, G. H., 10, 159, 198-199,
213

W

WAGNER, H. M., 166
WEIMER, W. B., 202
WEISS, R., 213
WHITE, R., 85, 100
Win/lose situation, 45-47
Winning as governing variable, 66-67,
68, 79-80
WOODWARD, G., 211-212

Z

ZACHARIAS, J., xxix